THE WORKING-CLASS TORIES

The Working-Class Tories

AUTHORITY, DEFERENCE AND
STABLE DEMOCRACY

ERIC A. NORDLINGER

1967
UNIVERSITY OF CALIFORNIA PRESS
BERKELEY AND LOS ANGELES

FOR MY FATHER AND MOTHER

ACKNOWLEDGEMENTS

THIS survey study could not have been done without the co-operation of two persons in England. Humphrey Taylor, who was then with National Opinion Polls, Ltd., allowed me access to a set of their past surveys so that I could construct a national sample of manual workers. His daily queries of 'Are you happy?' were always answered in the affirmative during the three weeks that I sat in his office. Dr Timothy Joyce of the British Market Research Bureau was most kind, and 'uncommercial', in agreeing to have his firm carry out the great bulk of the field work. He also made a number of valuable suggestions for revising the interview schedule for use in the English working-class milieu.

Whatever the merits of this study, they would have been sorely reduced without the advice and criticism of some half dozen people. Since this book was originally written as a doctoral dissertation, I am particularly grateful to three of my former teachers at Princeton University. Sidney Verba offered suggestions throughout every stage of the questionnaire's development, and then gave the first draft a much needed critical reading. While analysing the data, Richard Hamilton was most generous in assisting me until I was able to stand on my own feet in front of the IBM machine, and as a practising sociologist, he was especially helpful in getting me to clarify my thoughts about Chapters 7 and 8. Although my dissertation supervisor was officially on a leave of absence while I was writing this thesis, Harry Eckstein gave me a good deal of his time in reading the draft chapters and discussing them with me. My intellectual debt to him is particularly evident in the first and last chapters. But even these are only pale indications of what I owe to him.

I should also like to thank Samuel H. Beer, Seymour Martin Lipset, and Richard Rose for their suggestions and needed proddings in forcing me to be more specific about some of my meanings.

For financial assistance I am grateful to the Council on Human Relations at Princeton University, and its chairman, Marvin Bressler. The Office for Survey Research and Statistical Studies provided me with both the facilities for analysing the data and secretarial assistance in carrying out the agonizing coding, punching and verifying operations. For the typing of the manuscript I am indebted to Brandeis University, and for her endurance, to Linda Giardina.

Most importantly, of course, there is Carol, whose charm, understanding and assistance, made the writing of this book almost a pleasure.

London, 22 July 1966   E.A.N.

CONTENTS

The nature of our intelligence is such that it is stimulated far less by the will to know than by the will to understand, and, from this, it results that the only sciences which it admits to be authentic are those which succeed in establishing explanatory relationships between phenomena.

MARC BLOCH

This may be true, Cratylus, but is also very likely to be untrue; and therefore I would not have you be too easily persuaded of it.

SOCRATES

CHAPTER I

English Political Culture
HIERARCHY, SOCIAL STATUS AND DEFERENCE
—

THIS STUDY focuses upon those English manual workers who vote for the Conservative Party. They constitute slightly more than one-third of the manual workers in a country whose population is two-thirds working class. And in voting for the Conservative Party they provide the party with nearly half of its electoral strength.[1] In order to elucidate the characteristic types of political behaviour and attitudes held by this section of the population, comparisons will be made both between working-class Conservatives and Labour supporters (the latter constituting somewhat more than one half of the working-class population), and between two types of Conservative supporters: deferentials and pragmatists. Although it is these comparisons which form the main body of this book, the study will by no means be confined to such an analysis alone. Analysis of the political behaviour and attitudes of the manual workers who vote Conservative and Labour allows us to raise a whole range of larger questions. For example, to what extent do these workers stand within the mainstream of the traditional English political culture? What is the relationship between the class structure and the workers' attitudes toward governmental authority? How does the socialization process help shape the workers' attitudes towards political authority? How do the workers' political attitudes affect the contours and operation of the political system? Given the stability, representativeness, and effectiveness of British democracy, is it possible to delineate the conditions under which *any* democratic system will be stable, representative, and decisionally effective on the basis of this study's conclusions?

[1] See, for example, Mark Abrams, 'Social Class and British Politics', *Public Opinion Quarterly*, Autumn 1961, p. 343. Also see the Gallup Poll data in Richard Rose, ed., *Studies in British Politics: 1966*, pp. 122–128. For comparisons with other working-class voting patterns, see Mattei Dogan, 'Le vote ouvrier en Europe occidentale', *Revue Française de Sociologie*, 1960, esp. pp. 30–31.

It is the purpose of this introductory chapter to provide the necessary reference points if these and other broad questions are to be answered, and to offer an analysis of the political and social context within which working-class politics take place.

I. HIERARCHICAL AUTHORITY RELATIONS

All political systems are hierarchical and every society has at least one political elite. However, there are wide variations in both the form that these authority relations take and the elements which support them. These differences centre about the extent to which a hierarchical strain permeates a political system and its society, the ideas which legitimize these hierarchical authority relations, the interconnections between the political, economic and social elites, the backgrounds of the men who reach the topmost pinnacles of authority and the paths by which they arrive and maintain themselves there. In these respects England greatly differs from other societies; and it is in the support given to these characteristic hierarchical patterns that the English working class varies markedly from its foreign counterparts.

In a singularly important sense England is a democratic anomaly; the country's gradual political development has allowed traditional attitudes towards authority to become fused with more recent democratic values to form a governmental tradition in which leaders are expected to lead. Due to this fusion the modal authority pattern brings together democratic and hierarchical elements, and in comparison with all other western democracies, the emphasis falls on the latter. However, the actions of both leaders and led are circumscribed by a vast body of unwritten conventions and norms. These norms (expectations of behaviour) at one and the same time place limitations upon the elite's independence of the non-elite, and legitimize the authority relations which allow the elite the independence to act in the name of the non-elite without prior consultation or even approval. The characteristic aspect of British history in this respect is that attacks were not made against governmental authority *per se*, but only against the mismanagement and normative transgressions of those holding positions of authority. And this pattern may in turn be traced back, at least in part, to the establishment of a centralized authority (as opposed to warring feudal principalities) at the time of the Norman Conquest, which was then permanently secured by the beginning of the thirteenth century. Whereas the Continent experienced centuries of conflict in the process of establishing a central government, in England its existence and authority were quickly and permanently legitimized.

The contemporary relationship between the Government and the governed was perhaps best described by L. S. Amery, himself a former Conservative Cabinet Minister: 'Our Constitution has throughout conformed to that principle of balance between initiative and control which Burke laid down. It has never been one in which the active and originating element has been the voter, selecting a delegate to express his views . . . and to select an administration conforming to his views. The starting point and mainspring of action has always been the Government.'[1] The Government tries to remain attuned to the voters' desires, but it does not automatically follow that the Government will act in accordance with them. For as Amery goes on to write, a British Government is an 'independent body', responsible for 'leading and directing Parliament and the nation in accordance with its own judgement and convictions'.[2] Amery's values and existential beliefs are perhaps most felicitously expressed in a single sentence: 'Our system is one of democracy, but of democracy by consent and not by delegation, of government of the people, for the people, with, but not by, the people.'[3]

Here is indeed an accurate appraisal of the British governmental tradition. The 'balance' of which Amery speaks pinpoints the Government's preponderant weight in the control of policy, while the electorate is left with the secondary power of saying 'yes' or 'no' to these policies *after* they have been effected—what Amery has described as the voters' 'essentially passive' role.[4] And the phrase, 'democracy by consent

---

[1] *Thoughts on the Constitution*: 1947, p. 15.

[2] Ibid., p. 31. Harry Eckstein takes this point one step further when he writes that the British conception of authority 'attributes to leadership a far larger scope of legitimate independent action than any other democratic country—"independent" action meaning action taken on the leaders' own initiative rather than as an expression of popular or parliamentary will.' See his 'The British Political System,' in Samuel H. Beer and Adam B. Ulam, eds., *Patterns of Government*: 1965, p. 75.

[3] Ibid., pp. 21–22. In fact, according to British constitutional thought, sovereignty resides with the Crown rather than with the people.

[4] In fact, the main purpose of a General Election is not to express the electorate's views, but to produce a government—one with a working majority in Parliament. See R. T. McKenzie, 'Some Problems of Democratic Government in Britain', in Henry W. Ehrmann, ed., *Democracy in a Changing Society*: 1964, p. 55.

and not by delegation' highlights that feature of the English political culture which is the underpinning for the Government's decisive role —the non-elite's readiness to accept rather than to question or direct governmental authority.[1]

It is no accident that a staunch Tory such as Amery came to describe the British 'Constitution' in such terms, for there is a clear-cut divergence between the Conservative and Labour Parties' orientations towards governmental authority. 'Order requires Hierarchy'—this, according to Samuel Beer, is the 'essential proposition' of the Tory philosophy of government.[2] The Tory tradition underlines hierarchy, leadership, independent governmental authority, and rule by an elite educated to rule. In a closely reasoned article entitled 'The Toryness of English Conservatism', Harvey Glickman has stressed the importance of the Tory belief that it is 'authoritative leadership' which is thought to produce the ordered community and good society. 'This conception of authority,' he writes, 'also has profound constitutional implications, since it means that the essence of Toryism is fundamentally anti-democratic—it distrusts the capacity and the will of the people to govern themselves.'[3] But this ought not to be taken to mean that Toryism is authoritarian. For as already suggested, the hierarchical structure of governmental authority is hemmed in by numerous and effective constitutional conventions and norms to prevent it from becoming arbitrary government. The ultimate basis of Tory government is agreement and constitutionalism rather than compulsion. It is only after these conventions have been respected and competing interests balanced off against each other that the Tory conception of authoritative leadership may be realized.[4] In contrast, the Labour Party's ideology is egalitarian. Out of the Labour Party's Chartist and Radical roots, and its early attacks against the hierarchical structure of society, there emerged an egalitarian ideology pointing to the people as the fountainhead of governmental authority, the government being assigned to the primary job of representing and

---

[1] For contrasts with the French political system, see pp. 234–250 below.

[2] *British Politics in the Collective Age*: 1965, p. 92. Quintin Hogg has written that 'Constitutional authority remains the first article of a Conservative creed' in his presentation of *The Conservative Case*: 1959, p. 53.

[3] Harvey Glickman, 'The Toryness of English Conservatism', *Journal of British Studies*, November, 1961, pp. 131–132. It might have been more appropriate to substitute 'hierarchical' for 'anti-democratic' in this quotation.

[4] Ibid., p. 134.

executing the will of the electorate. The difference between the two parties in this connection is sharply illustrated by a motion introduced by the Parliamentary Labour Party in 1955, unsuccessfully urging the removal of the phrase 'unbecoming to the character of an officer and a gentleman' from the Armed Services' regulations. In the debate the Labour side argued that the words symbolized an aristocratic conception of leadership, setting officers apart as a 'different order of human being', and contradicting 'the present-day conception of individual relations'.[1]

This is not the place to discuss the differing views of governmental authority and political leadership held by the two parties.[2] The point to be made here is simply this: notwithstanding these differences, it is basically the Tory conception of the relationship between the Government and the electorate which is widely diffused throughout the population. Or stated differently, even in a democratic age, the pre-democratic Tory tradition has easily made a larger contribution to the English political culture than has the Socialist tradition.

This argument will find more than ample confirmation when the Tory and Labour manual workers' attitudes are compared. Here it can be noted that within the population as a whole, there appears to be only a small difference between the Conservative and Labour voters' attitudes, both groups manifesting a willingness to subordinate themselves to political leadership. In a national survey the respondents were asked to select the four most important characteristics (from a list of fifteen) of a 'good party leader'. The results show that the population is primarily concerned with having a 'strong leader', with 59 per cent of the Conservatives and 53 per cent of Labour supporters selecting this attribute. Furthermore, the quality of a good party leader which was selected nearly as often as the first, 49 per cent and 43 per cent of the Tory and Labour voters respectively, choosing it, is 'strong enough to make unwelcome decisions'. When it is seen that these two related characteristics are not only thought to be the most important ones for a party leader by half the people interviewed, but are also ranked above such qualities as 'really honest and sincere' (37 per cent),

[1] Philip Abrams, 'Democracy, Technology, and the Retired British Officer', in Samuel P. Huntington, ed., *Changing Patterns of Military Politics*: 1962, pp. 154–155.

[2] For an excellent discussion of the Conservative and Socialist traditions, and their influence upon the behaviour of the elite of these two parties, see Beer, op. cit., esp. pp. 69–105.

'best man in the party for the job' (25 per cent), and 'some qualities of greatness' (12 per cent),[1] the Conservative *and* Labour supporters' desire for strong and self-explicit leadership is sharply underlined.

The authority relations between the Prime Minister on the one hand, and the Cabinet and his backbench supporters on the other, are markedly similar in their hierarchical form to those between the Government and the voters. The Prime Minister is ultimately dependent upon the presence of his parliamentary supporters in the proper division lobbies, their support at parliamentary meetings, and especially the allegiance of the key ministerial figures. These groups are consequently able to define the political boundaries beyond which they refuse to follow the Prime Minister's lead, and in some instances they are also able to modify the Prime Minister's initiatives by expressing their displeasure through the proper intermediaries.[2] But within this broad sphere it is the Prime Minster, usually in conjunction with his leading front bench advisers, who remains in command.

Although the Cabinet is charged with the formulation of major policies, the legislative programme, and the setting of taxes and expenditures, these responsibilities are now infrequently exercised by the Cabinet *qua* Cabinet. Already at the turn of the twentieth century, Sidney Low could write that 'the Prime Minister does not often take all his colleagues into his confidence; or even consult them, except at the more formal Cabinet Councils. There is no reason why he should; for the majority of them are not of sufficient personal or official weight to affect his decisions'.[3] Since then, the burgeoning demands of policy formation placed upon the Cabinet by the welfare state and the related need for detailed and specialized knowledge, have led to a further decrease in the Cabinet's role, with the civil service and individual ministers enjoying a concomitant expansion of their power. Furthermore, as the roles of Prime Minister and Party Leader have become inextricably fused, the Prime Minister tends more and more to rely upon the advice of people in the party organization in deciding matters which must be formally approved by the Cabinet. And as these two roles have merged, combined with the new-found importance of mass

[1] Mark Abrams and Richard Rose, *Must Labour Lose?*: 1960, p. 25.
[2] Richard Rose emphasized the 'reciprocal flow of influence between the Leader and followers', in his 'Complexities of Party Leadership', *Parliamentary Affairs*, Summer, 1963.
[3] *The Governance of England*: 1915 edition, pp. 163–164.

media electioneering techniques, 'the personification of the Party in the image of the leader gives the Prime Minister . . . an almost impregnable position *vis-à-vis* his lieutenants and backbenchers. For each Party the investment in the leader is so large that only the most reckless would dare to challenge him'[1]—at least while he is enjoying a high rating in the opinion polls. Nor must it be forgotten that within certain limits, the majority of Cabinet Ministers and their respective positions in the Cabinet hierarchy, and the Prime Minister's party advisers, are all creatures of his own choosing.[2]

The prerogative of British leaders to act with the minimum of consultation is illustrated by Eden's decision to invade Egypt. After a careful sifting of the evidence, the only writer who has yet analysed the Suez decision in a dispassionate fashion, came to the conclusion that Parliament was in no way given the opportunity to state its prior approval or disapproval; whether Eden consulted a handful of advisers, as both his left- and right-wing critics assert, or whether the Cabinet discussed the issue in hypothetical terms two weeks before the invasion was launched, remains something of an open question.[3] On the basis of the Suez decision, Attlee's decision to manufacture the atomic bomb, taken without Cabinet discussion or an announcement in the Commons, and his own parliamentary experience, R. H. S. Crossman concluded that 'a British Premier is now entitled on really momentous decisions to act first, and then to face his Cabinet with the choice between collective obedience or the political wilderness'.[4] And it cannot be overemphasized that, notwithstanding the criticisms levelled at Eden for his decision, not a single body of opinion accused him of acting in an unconstitutional fashion.

If the standard interpretation of the internal structure of the Conservative and Labour Parties is accepted, it is abundantly evident that their authority relations are congruent with the modal pattern being described. It is McKenzie's thesis that the Leaders of the two parties

---

[1] Mark Abrams, 'Party Politics After the End of Ideology', Erik Allardt and Yrfo Littunen, eds., *Cleavages, Ideologies and Party Systems*: Transactions of the Wertermarck Society, Vol. X, 1964, p. 63. Although Abrams correctly stresses the significance of mass propaganda techniques as they bear upon the Leader's position, he neglects the limitations placed upon his power.

[2] 'So long as he does not ignore those commanding personages whom the public and the party know, [the Prime Minister] can do very much what he likes with the remainder of his staff.' Low, op. cit., p. 159.

[3] Leon D. Epstein, *British Politics in the Suez Crisis*: 1964, pp. 68–74, 93.

[4] 'Introduction' to Walter Bagehot, *The English Constitution*: 1963, p. 55.

are invested with an 'enormous' amount of independent authority, though always subject to certain limitations: the need to listen to, and sometimes to conciliate, the Annual Conferences which serve as the parties' democratic founts, the party supporters in Parliament to whom the Leaders are responsible, and the party leadership upon whom the Leaders are dependent for public and private sustenance.[1] However, this writer for one, cannot agree with the assertion that the power structure of the two parties are almost identical. Over and above other methodological and substantive lacunae, McKenzie does not take into account that it is the Conservative Party—dating back to the reign of Charles II and thereby standing in the mainstream of the English political tradition—which is more deeply imbued with hierarchical values and beliefs than is the Labour Party, originating in protest against just these values. Indeed, in his concluding chapter, McKenzie notes 'the traditional Conservative concepts of leadership and discipline' and the 'subtle considerations of social deference' as they have dampened any enthusiasm for rebellion among the members of the extra-parliamentary organization.[2] However, this argument only appears in the final chapter and refers to the members of the National Union alone; these factors are not analysed in relation to the authority of the Leader *vis-à-vis* the parliamentary party.

The Tory Leader's independence of his supporters is clearly manifested and symbolized in his relation to the Annual Conference. It is only after the Conference is officially over that the Leader addresses the delegates at the mass rally—a rally convened for the sole purpose of allowing the constituency representatives to cheer their Leader, without affording them an opportunity for criticism.[3] More important is the slightly mystical process by which Tory Leaders have until recently 'emerged', as it underlines the party's hierarchical attitudes.[4] Whereas the Labour Party Leader is elected by the parliamentary party, the Conservative Leader previously emerged through a process of consultations among a small group of party leaders, of which a handful were assigned the job of 'sounding' opinion among Tory

---

[1] R. T. McKenzie, *British Political Parties*: 1963.

[2] Ibid., p. 638.

[3] However, at the 1965 Conference held at Brighton, Heath remained on the platform throughout most of the conference.

[4] It should be noted that this change in the rules of the game did not emanate from a change in Tory attitudes, but from the public embarrassment caused by the undignified struggle for the leadership after Macmillan's resignation.

peers, MP's, and leaders of the National Union. On the basis of these consultations and soundings, one of the party leaders—on the last three occasions it has been Churchill, Salisbury and Macmillan respectively—'advises' the Queen who to call to the Palace. Only after the new Leader took over the reins of power was a party meeting convened for his unanimous confirmation. The party's wishes were thus first filtered by the leaders responsible for taking soundings, then weighed up according to a rough system which assigns heavier weights to the opinions of certain leaders than others, followed by a final assessment made by the one or two men whom the Queen asks for 'advice', in which considerations other than those of party opinion are taken into account.[1] Equally illuminating as it sheds light on the hierarchical structure of the Conservative Party is Macmillan's (presumably single-handed) purge of one-third of the Cabinet in 1962 —what McKenzie has called 'the most drastic reorganization of [a] Government ever undertaken within . . . modern times'.[2]

Pressure groups are quasi-political institutions. They serve as structures linking the social and economic spheres with the political system. As such, their authority patterns are particularly relevant here. It is significant that in attempting to specify more concretely the organization of authority within the British Medical Association, Eckstein chose to use the two major parties, but the Conservative Party in particular, as analogies. 'If the annual conferences of the political parties correspond most closely to the Annual Representative Meeting of the Association, then the closest analogy to the position of the Council is perhaps that of the parliamentary parties, especially the parliamentary Conservative Party. Just as the parliamentary parties dominate the constituency organizations, so the Council towers over the Annual Representative Meeting. Just as the Leader of the Conservative Party is the locus of most of its power, so the Chairman of the Council looms as the most powerful political figure in the BMA. He is elected by the Council "for such time as it determines", but in practice, as long

[1] Bagehot's description of the electoral process in a 'deferential nation' is therefore also applicable to the modern Conservative Party. In such nations 'certain persons are by common consent agreed to be wiser than others, and their opinion, is by consent, to rank for much more than its numerical value. We may in these happy nations weigh votes as well as count them, though in less favoured countries we can only count them.' *The English Constitution*: 1961 edition, p. 141.
[2] Op. cit., p. 594.

as he wants to hold office'.[1] This same pattern is also found to exist in a trade union (the National Union of Teachers),[2] and an employers' organization (The Federation of British Industries),[3] which has led Eckstein to argue that the BMA's authority structure is typical of British pressure groups.[4]

In attempting to delineate the common hierarchical authority patterns found in the political system, we have relied solely on descriptions of the actual relations between the various levels of the hierarchies. The argument can be further developed by briefly noting some of the outward manifestations of these hierarchical authority relations. Most obviously, there are the elaborate and dignified characteristics of those symbols, institutions and procedures of authority: the splendour of the monarchy and its symbolic position at the pinnacle of the political system, allowing the Queen to speak of 'My Army', 'My Ministers', and 'My people', the mixture of mystical, dignified and traditional elements attaching to the coronation, the aristocratic heritage of the House of Lords, the 'pomp and circumstance' of the Lord Mayor's parade, and the stylized procedures of the House of Commons. Ritual and symbolism extend even to the law—a mundane sphere in most countries—so that a barrister could write a scholarly volume entitled *The Pageantry of Law*.[5] There is also the style of political leadership which, with a few exceptions such as Attlee and Wilson, has preciously little of the 'common touch' about it. Political and governmental leaders make no attempt to pose as representatives of the 'common man', to which must be added the many honorific titles that accrue to political leaders and the formalized manner in which they address each other across the floor of the House. Lastly, there is the high social status enjoyed by the majority of the national leadership, with public-school backgrounds and upper-class accents and modes of behaviour making a further contribution to the hierarchical structure of authority.

---

[1] Harry Eckstein, *Pressure Group Politics*: 1960, p. 60. This last sentence would, of course, be modified when applied to the Conservative Leader.

[2] Asher Tropp, *The School Teachers*: 1957.

[3] S. E. Finer, 'The Federation of British Industries', *Political Studies*, February, 1956.

[4] Harry Eckstein, *A Theory of Stable Democracy*: 1961, pp. 13–14. Eckstein not only argues that the authority patterns of pressure groups are similar, but that these are congruent with the authority patterns found in the political system, the economy, and the society.

[5] James Derriman, *The Pageantry of Law*: 1955.

This is a subject which is more fully developed in the next section of this chapter.

II. CLASS, STATUS, AND HIERARCHICAL AUTHORITY RELATIONS

The various hierarchical arrangements of the political system not only resemble each other, they are also congruent with the social structure which encompasses them—the system of stratification and the inter-relations among the different strata. For the purposes of this analysis there are three crucial characteristics of the English social structure. In the first place, the lines of demarcation between and within the various classes (defined here according to occupational groupings) are relatively clearly drawn, and together, the occupational groupings form a pyramidal outline having a broad base and a narrow pinnacle; the number of people falling into the pyramid's upper reaches is a small fraction of the number constituting its lower rungs.

Secondly, there is a close correspondence between occupational stratification and the distribution of social status (i.e. prestige, honour and respect). The higher up one resides in the occupational pyramid the greater the amount of status one enjoys. The Honours List is a manifestation of this confluence between class and status. Whereas an Army general who has served in singularly inauspicious capacities will be made a Knight Commander of the Order of the Bath, a post office worker who risked his life attempting to prevent a robbery will be awarded a simple MBE.[1] Evidence for this general argument is also found in the results of a survey study carried out to determine the extent to which there is a correspondence between occupation and status. Two sociologists grouped thirty different occupations into seven categories, ranking them on the basis of the amount of experience, knowledge, skill and responsibility required. These occupations were presented to more than 1,000 respondents who were asked to rank them according to the social status attaching to each occupation.

---

[1] To quote Anthony Wedgwood Benn, 'The Honours' System, as it now exists, serves to buttress the class structure in Britain, dividing people into social categories on the basis that there are superior and inferior human beings. Even decorations for gallantry are awarded according to rank. Army officers get the Military Cross, but for the same act of courage NCO's and privates get the Military Medal, and it's the same in other Services as well.' The *Observer*, January 3, 1964.

It was then found that only three occupations out of the thirty were assigned a status ranking which was not commensurate with their class position. Two relevant conclusions emanated from this study: there is a high degree of correspondence between occupational and status positions, and that this confluence is widespread throughout the population.[1] However, it must be admitted that things are changing. To the extent that individuals of low-status birth and education are moving into the middle positions of the occupational pyramid as managers and skilled technicians, it is necessary to recognize the existence of what Stacey has called a 'non-traditional status system' alongside the predominant 'traditional' hierarchy.[2]

The third feature of the stratification system is both the most relevant one here and the most characteristic of English society; namely, the close correspondence between occupation and status rank on the one hand, and the assumption of parallel positions of authority on the other. Those people with the greatest amount of authority also tend to be members of the highest occupation strata, enjoying a large measure of social status. This applies not only to authority relations within the political system—a subject to be discussed in the next section. In the sphere of social relations one has only to notice the authoritative tones and expressions of command used by many upper and upper middle-class people when addressing members of lesser status than themselves.[3] Even within the portals of Pall Mall clubs it is not unknown for peers to forget themselves in ordering about middle-class members. And one writer who did a study of the organizational structures on British and American ships, found that while the ships of both nationalities had the same occupational and authority structures, the social status of the petty officers on the American ships is de-emphasized compared

---

[1] C. A. Moser and J. R. Hall, 'The Social Grading of Occupations', in D. V. Glass (ed.), *Social Mobility in Britain*: 1954, pp. 30–35. Cf. Michael Young and Peter Willmott, 'Social Grading by Manual Workers', *British Journal of Sociology*, 1956, pp. 337–345. The overlap between class and status positions is by no means peculiar to England. It is also found in the United States, Russia, Germany, Japan and New Zealand. See Alex Inkeles and Peter H. Rossi, 'National Comparisons of Occupational Prestige', *American Journal of Sociology*, January 1956, esp. Table 2, p. 332.

[2] Margaret Stacey, *Tradition and Change*: 1960, pp. 144–165.

[3] This is not to imply that such tones are widely resented, for the 'word "Sir" is much used in England, and the man of obviously upper-class appearance can usually get more than his fair share of deference from commissionaires, ticket collectors, policemen, and the like'. George Orwell, *The English People*: 1947, p. 29, cited in Seymour Martin Lipset, *The First New Nation*: 1963, p. 18.

to the importance placed upon status differences on the British ships.[1]

The English tradition of the amateur[2]—the de-emphasis placed upon, and the mild social stigma attaching to, the specialist and the expert—can be interpreted as both a manifestation and a support for the crystallization of class, status and authority. The belief that the best leader and the best administrator is the man who is a generalist, unencumbered by the expert's narrow outlook, opens up the top positions of authority to just those individuals who do not have any specialized training—the upper and upper-middle classes.[3] At the same time, individuals of low status whose only opportunity for social and economic mobility lies in the acquisition of some type of *expertise*, have little chance of reaching the middle and upper levels of authority. A grammar school education and a degree from a provincial university are certainly adequate for achieving a middle-class position, as a metallurgist for example. But that same specialized education with its low-status stigma sometimes becomes a determining hindrance in the acquisition of high managerial authority.[4] If this were not the case there would no longer be a congruity between the three hierarchies; in this instance, the metallurgist who has become a company director would enjoy high class and authority positions, but a low status position. However, the so-called scientific revolution is beginning to have its effects; it is becoming difficult to exercise the highest authority without some acquaintance with the latest technology. In 1959, for example, with the reminder that 'Science is becoming yearly more important to the Army', the Secretary of State for War announced that technical officers would be *eligible* for the very highest offices.[5] But by 1965, 'what has actually been done remains rudimentary . . . and Army "technicians" entering Sandhurst from Welbeck are

---

[1] Stephen A. Richardson, 'Organizational Contrasts on British and American Ships', *Administrative Science Quarterly*, September 1956, esp. pp. 204–206.

[2] For an insightful discussion of amateurism in the civil service, see Thomas Balogh, 'The Apotheosis of the Dilettante', in Hugh Thomas, ed., *The Establishment*: 1959, pp. 83–129.

[3] For the operation of this tendency as it helps pattern the social composition of the civil service, see H. E. Dale, *The Higher Civil Service*: 1943, and R. K. Kelsall, *The Higher Civil Servants in Britain*: 1955.

[4] In the United States, it is not unusual for a prestigous company like American Telephone and Telegraph to start executives (just recruited from Yale and Princeton) on their careers as linemen and polemen with the same pay as other manual workers. Sidney J. Kaplan, 'Up From the Ranks on a Fast Escalator', *American Sociological Review*, February 1959.

[5] Cited in P. Abrams, in Huntington, op. cit., p. 160.

reported to be treated as something less than equals by their more conventionally "military" fellow cadets.'[1]

Examination of the educational system not only lends further support to the argument to the extent that it exhibits a clear-cut crystallization of occupational, status, and authority rankings according to an hierarchical pattern. The analysis is also intended to show how one of the society's most important institutions supports and even heightens these patterns. The educational system is itself infused with hierarchical characteristics regarding the exercise of authority, thereby socializing succeeding generations in conformity to this principle, while early selection and early segregation procedures insure a correspondence between an individual's adult occupation, status, and authority positions.

The selection process which segregates the population into the three basic educational strata is carried out as early as possible. In order to be able to attend a public school at age thirteen, it is necessary to have previously attended a preparatory school since the former's entrance requirements (e.g. a writing knowledge of Latin) can only be acquired in these private schools. In the state sector, notwithstanding a recent reaction against the eleven-plus examination, a minority of pupils are still channelled into the grammar schools by age twelve, the majority attending the non-academically oriented secondary modern and technical schools.[2] As adults, the public school products will almost invariably be found in the upper or upper-middle classes, the grammar school graduates will form the solid middle class, with a few rising to upper-middle class heights, while the secondary modern and technical school students shall constitute the next generation's lower-middle and working classes. That is to say, the adult occupational positions of the vast majority are for the most part already established when they are twelve years old because of the educational system's early selection procedure.

Over and above early selection, there is also early segregation of the three educational streams. This is most obviously true of the boys who attend public school. Living apart from the rest of society there

---

[1] Philip Abrams, 'The Late Profession of Arms: Ambiguous Goals and Deteriorating Means in Britain', *European Journal of Sociology*, number 2, 1965, p. 249.

[2] Until recently, the comprehensive schools have educated a relatively insignificant proportion of the population, and here too there is early selection and little interchange between the different streams.

is little opportunity for contact with their non-public school peers.[1] But it is also true of the state sector. When the time comes to enter secondary school there is a painful disintegration of neighbourhood friendship groups as the type of school the students attend replaces the neighbourhood as the new social focal point. Grammar school students tend to associate with each other, leaving the secondary modern and technical school students to their own devices.[2] Nor is this simply a matter of intellectual apartheid.[3] For the gulf separating the grammar school boy from his intellectual inferiors is further accentuated by the social status associated with the two types of schools. A distinctively middle-class air pervades the grammar schools in the expectation that these students will take their places as solid members of this social class. Emphasis is placed upon punctuality, neatness, respect for authority, and learning for the sake of learning, while outside the classroom, the privilege of wearing a school uniform accorded the grammar school students takes on the form of a middle-class status symbol. For the students in secondary modern and technical schools, education is generally seen as something to be endured for as short a time as possible, and at best, as a useful preparation for a clerical or manual occupation.

The combination of early selection and early segregation supports the stratification system in a threefold manner. In the first place, the scramble for higher occupational and social status positions does not occur except on an *intra*-class basis. In a society such as the United States where the most strenuous competition begins after twenty-one, the stratification system tends to be in continuous flux; individuals follow whatever 'deviant' or unexplored paths are convenient in the search for occupational mobility and increased social status. In England, on the other hand, this competition has already been settled by

---

[1] Even when the boys are at home there is a geographical separation between themselves and students in the state sector. In a study of the locations of Eton students' homes, it turns out that these are almost entirely found in rural England, especially the Thames counties, and in the exclusive areas of London. Only the minutest sprinkling live in provincial cities and towns. See Ron Hall. 'The Family Backgrounds of Etonians', in Rose, ed., op. cit., pp. 54–63.

[2] For a sympathetic discussion of the strains arising within the neighbourhood and the family when a working-class boy attends a grammar school, see Brian Jackson and Dennis Marsden, *Education and the Working Class*: 1962.

[3] This sharp intellectual division is manifested in the common saying that a non-grammar school boy has 'failed', even though only a minority win grammar school places.

early adolescence at a time when the people affected are too young to question the selection criteria. Moreover, segregation according to future occupational positions leads the adolescents to expect a close correspondence between occupational and social status positions, and intensively socializes them in the social mores of their occupational ranks, making it exceptionally difficult for adult social aspirants to learn the social styles of higher occupational strata. This is certainly not meant to imply that occupational and social mobility do not occur. But that inter-class mobility does not affect the bases of the stratification system because it is usually accomplished by age thirteen. The upward and downward mobility which is found in all but the most traditional societies therefore occurs within a stable stratification system.

Secondly, early selection and early segregation make it unlikely that the students in the secondary modern and technical schools will develop unrealistic expectations about their adult occupational and status positions; for the students are already well aware of their future positions by the time they reach fifteen. The inferior or subordinate place of these two types of schools relative to the grammar and public schools has been abundantly impressed upon the students throughout their secondary schooling, while their education and training is designed to socialize them for their subordinate positions in the stratification hierarchies.[1] There is consequently little disappointment and even less surprise in finding oneself at the lower rungs of these hierarchies,[2] obviating the possibility of adult frustrations and questionings of the stratification system.[3] And thirdly, if the socialization

---

[1] Samuel Everett, *Growing Up in English Secondary Schools*: 1959, pp. 14, *passim*. In America, it would seem that the socialization process is not designed to provide lower-class individuals with conservative expectations for the future: the culture emphasizes equal opportunity for all, to which must be added the non-segregated nature of the educational mainstream. The result is that nearly two-thirds of the workers believe that 'there's plenty of opportunity, and anyone who works hard can go as far as he wants'. See V. O. Key, *Public Opinion and American Democracy*: 1961, p. 130. But cf. Herbert Hyman, 'The Value Systems of Different Classes', in R. Bendix and S. M. Lipset, eds., *Class Status and Power*: 1953, pp. 426–442.

[2] This point is made in an excellent analysis of the British and American educational systems and their inter-connections with their respective mobility patterns in Ralph H. Turner, 'Sponsored and Contest Mobility in the School System', *American Sociological Review*, December 1960.

[3] For a discussion of the various ways that workers may adapt to their low positions, see Robert K. Merton, *Social Theory and Social Structure*: 1964, esp. pp. 139–157.

process were not effective in developing these realistic expectations, it would be extremely difficult for the people residing at the lower rungs of the pyramid to demand entry into a higher occupational strata since they have not received the training which would permit adult mobility.

These characteristics of English education not only support the hierarchical stratification system; as socializing agents the schools perform an equally important function in preparing the different social strata for their respective roles in the hierarchical political system. Certainly the 3 per cent of the population who attend public school are most deeply exposed to the dictates of hierarchy. Notwithstanding the fact that it is often done unconsciously, at least at the best schools, and that at present it takes on a somewhat diluted form compared to the past, the boys are still imbued with the virtues of the Christian gentlemen in the expectation that these qualities will be needed in the future exercise of authority over the 97 per cent of the population who did not go to public school.[1] To the extent that some of the public schools prepared the boys for the more demanding leadership responsibilities of the Colonial Service, the boys were even more intensively imbued with the idea of a governing class as both necessary and desirable for the peoples being governed.[2] In the classroom and in the chapel[3] the boys are taught the ethical sanctifications of authority, although this is largely done through the medium of example and intuition rather than through the process of detailed instruction or rational argument. In order to be able to exercise authority properly as an adult, it is thought that one must first learn the discipline of having to accept authority. As house fags, the boys are made to experience the act of submission, but submission to an authority which is thought to be morally and intellectually superior. Even the boys' classroom instruction is thought of as a disciplinary training. In the words of one public school master, 'Work is regarded not as something which boys should enjoy doing (as in a "progressive" school),

---

[1] See Rupert Wilkinson, *The Prefects: British Leadership and the Public School Tradition*: 1964.

[2] For a discussion of the public schools as preparatory institutions for the Colonial Service, see Ralph Furse, *Aucuparius*: 1962; Robert Heussler, *Yesterday's Rulers: The Making of the British Colonial Service*: 1963, esp. Chapter IV; also *Wilkinson*, op. cit., Chapter 9.

[3] For an analysis of the public schools as 'chapel-centred' institutions, see Ian Weinberg, *The English Public Schools*: 1967.

nor as something which will be of practical value (as in a secondary modern school), nor yet as something which must be done to insure passes in examinations and hence success in getting good jobs (as, perhaps, in most grammar schools), but as a form of *discipline*. Certain things are expected of a boy without any obvious reasons being given.'[1] It is only towards the end of their school careers that some of the boys (the prefects) are given the opportunity to exercise authority for the benefit of the school, the house, and the younger boys.[2]

Given the important role the 'meritocrats' will be playing in the future, it is important to note that they too are being socialized in an elitist fashion.[3] According to Richard Rose, 'The character training in the grammar schools is one that accustoms pupils to hierarchical authority', complemented by 'the implicit assumption that all in this selective category will assume the responsibilities of leadership *vis-à-vis* those in secondary modern schools.'[4] One illustration of this attitude of superiority towards their intellectual inferiors is found in the examination essays of some 100 grammar school pupils. When asked whether or not the bulk of the population is 'a near-moronic mass', the majority agreed. And as one boy went on to say, 'fortunately, thinking people usually occupy high positions in our country and government'.[5] Generalizing about the educational system as a whole, Rose concludes that 'Implicitly, (it) transmits and emphasizes cultural norms concerning inequality. Inequality is presented as natural, and often as desirable . . . English governments have repeatedly upheld the cultural belief that the great majority of the population is fit only for the most rudimentary sort of education . . . There are still more people in England who have left school at the age of 14 than there are persons who have attended universities.'[6]

---

[1] John Wilson, *Public Schools and Private Practice*: 1963, pp. 75–76, italics in the original.

[2] One Oxford don reports that 'many of these (public school) boys go around looking for people to lead; they actually say at the university interviews that they feel that they have been trained to lead'. John Vaizey, 'The Public Schools', in Hugh Thomas, op. cit., pp. 28–29.

[3] According to one sociologist, 'The most important fact to understand about grammar school education is that it copies, in so far as conditions permit, the attitudes and practices of English public schools'. Everett, op. cit., p. 13.

[4] Richard Rose, *Politics in England*: 1964, American edition, p. 69.

[5] Brian Jackson, 'The Moronic Mass', *New Statesman*, November 3, 1961, cited in ibid., p. 67.

[6] Ibid., pp. 65–66.

And there can be little question about the success of the educational system in preparing individuals for their political roles. There is no need for 'citizenship' courses to inculcate the proper attitudes towards governmental authority through manifest means. The homogenously hierarchical dimensions of the socialization process are perfectly adequate for shaping the requisite adult attitudes of the various strata. The success of the educational system in this regard is evidenced by a whole range of behaviour patterns, perhaps culminating in the absence of legally defined 'offices' circumscribing the authority of the governing class. There is no need for a written constitution or a reliance upon legal formulae when both the people who exercise the authority of the unwritten constitution and those who are subject to its dictates, maintain a hardy respect for its essence; and in the case of the former, the constitution's precepts have been internalized to such an extent that dishonourable transgressions are almost unheard of. One could go so far as to say that the remarkably efficient socialization processes have played an important part in sustaining the traditional features of English society based upon usage rather than codification.

While the educational system plays a crucial part in supporting the society's stratification and authority patterns, these patterns are structured in such a way that in and of themselves they tend to be stable and mutually supportive. There is not only a congruence between the authority patterns in all of the major political institutions, which is of itself a stabilizing factor. The social fabric within which these institutions are embedded are also hierarchically stratified, thereby preventing any structural or psychological strains from arising.[1] And the crystallization of occupational, status and authority positions around hierarchical patterns means that each stratification system is mutually supportive of the other two and their hierarchical forms.[2]

Since any given individual tends to hold equivalent class, status and authority positions, there is a mutual reinforcement as high rank in

[1] For an analysis of the psychological strain caused by an incongruity of authority patterns, see Eckstein, *A Theory of Stable Democracy*, op. cit., pp. 23–28.

[2] This formulation should not be taken to mean that there is a single 'power elite' or a unified power structure. To say that individuals enjoy corresponding positions in the occupational, status and authority pyramids refers to the internal structure of particular institutions (e.g., a political party, the civil service, or a pressure group). The argument does not refer to the inter-relationships between these institutions.

one sphere sustains a high rank in the other two. In a sense, individuals present a solid front to the world, for there are few openings (i.e. low rank in one sphere) through which the individual's position in society can be easily challenged. Or to state the argument in reverse fashion—if there were a discrepancy between, say, class position on the one hand, and status and authority positions on the other—there would in all probability be a disruption of the stratification system as those strata assigned to positions of status and authority which are not commensurate with their high-class position, would either attempt to attain these values through 'deviant' channels, or question the entire stratification system. We can therefore agree with Dahrendorf when he writes that 'it could be argued that a certain correspondence between people's share in authority and in social rewards in general (i.e. their class and status positions) is a functional imperative of relatively stable societies'.[1] Moreover, in those organizations where the different classes come into contact with each other—political parties, voluntary associations, business firms, the civil service and the military—hierarchical authority relations are reinforced because those in authority are able to buttress their positions with the outward trappings of their class and status ranks. The necessarily hierarchical structure of a business firm, for example, can only be further sharpened when the employer is (literally) wrapped up in the garments of middle-class authority and speaks with a public school accent when giving orders to his employees. In fact, it was just this argument that was used by the Armed Services to defend the preponderant recruitment of public school products into the officer corps. Their high status was said to be important in enhancing their authority as officers. In the words of a former Air Chief Marshal: 'So long as officers came from homes about which there was an atmosphere of the unknown—"out of our class, chum!"—so long did they have that little something that inspired not only the respect, but the awe of the men. As soon as they came from the same class, however good they may have been at their job—they lacked this quality.'[2]

This preceding argument refers to the effect of 'crystallization' upon those individuals who find themselves at the middle and lower levels of the status and authority pyramids. At the same time, 'crys-

[1] Ralf Dahrendorf, *Class and Class Conflict in Industrial Society*: 1959, p. 140. Note the special usage which Dahrendorf assigns to the concept of class.
[2] Cited in P. Abrams, in Huntington, op. cit., p. 156.

tallization' patterns also influence the attitudes and behaviour of those men at the upper reaches of these pyramids. Their hierarchically ordered relations with those below them would seem to be further accentuated by their own conception of the high class and status positions that they enjoy. Admittedly, this is an especially difficult hypothesis to document, for the transference of social self-identification to one's role in a hierarchical institution is probably done unconsciously. Both points—that high status accentuates the conception of one's role as an authority figure, and that this transference occurs unconsciously —are found in Simon Raven's essay about a section of the Army officer corps.[1] Raven expected to find 'that the officers' claim to authority and command would be based on a professional sense of professional status attained as a result of professional qualifications and professional training', yet the reality turned out to be completely different. The officers Raven describes 'regarded themselves as so much set apart as to belong to a totally different class of human being—a class naturally designed to impose its will on all inferior classes.' And it is their status as officers, gentlemen and public school products that unconsciously leads them to assume the 'absolute right to exercise unquestioned personal authority'. They are continually inculcated with the idea that officers and gentlemen ought to have a certain morality that is essential for the exercise of authority. There is then an easy transition from the imperative that ' "officers must have these qualities" to the general "officers always do have these qualities" '.[2] Although suggested in a highly tentative fashion, it may be that the public schools have a similar influence: the values of the Christian gentleman are continually set in front of the boys; whether they have attained these values or not, the boys come to believe that they have done so; and this combination of moral and social superiority then serves to heighten their conception of themselves as authority figures. At a minimum, high status does tend to eradicate questionings of one's own 'right' and ability to exercise authority. It provides the confidence and reassurance that encourages a more distinctively hierarchical relationship with one's subordinates.[3]

It is this 'crystallization' of high class, status and authority positions,

---

[1] 'Perish by the Sword', in Hugh Thomas, op. cit.

[2] Ibid., pp. 67, 75–76.

[3] See Roger Holmes, 'Freud, Piaget and Democratic Leadership', *British Journal of Sociology*, June 1965, esp. pp. 125, 137.

the support it renders to the social stratification system, and its accentuation of hierarchical authority relations, which serve as the setting within which socially deferential behaviour takes place.

III. SOCIAL DEFERENCE

In the first section of this chapter it was shown that the authority exercised by political leaders rarely comes up against any cultural impediments; in the previous section the argument was suggested that positions of authority in English society are closely bound up with high occupational and status positions, each reinforcing the others. In both sections practically all our generalizations have been nearly as applicable to the Labour as to the Conservative halves of the country, though not necessarily to the high-ranking members of the two parties. However, in delineating one interconnection between these two themes—the support given to hierarchical patterns by socially deferential behaviour—a parting of the ways takes place. This section focuses upon social deference within the Conservative Party not only because this is primarily, though not exclusively, a Tory phenomenon; it is also necessary to offer an interpretation of the contemporary Conservative Party which will serve as a reference point in our analysis of the political behaviour and attitudes of its working-class supporters.

'It has been thought strange,' wrote Bagehot, 'but there *are* nations in which the numerous unwiser part wishes to be ruled by the less numerous wiser part. The numerical majority—whether by custom or by choice, is immaterial—is ready, is eager to delegate its power of choosing its rulers to a certain select minority. It abdicates in favour of its elite, and consents to obey whoever that elite may confide in.'[1] According to Bagehot this deference was offered both on the basis of a belief that men of rank and wealth who were superior 'in these indisputable respects were superior also in the more tangible qualities of sense and knowledge', and the majority's desire 'to have one of their "betters" to represent them; if he was rich, they respected him much; and if he was a lord, they liked him the better'.[2] It is this *social* deference—this preference for leaders with high social rank and conformity to their hierarchical expectations, justified by the assumption

[1] Op. cit., p. 235.
[2] Ibid., pp. 263–264.

that there is a close correspondence between social rank and leadership ability—which is a marked characteristic of English political culture.

To some extent Bagehot, the Whig elitist, was correct when he prophesied that universal suffrage would sweep away the deferential orientation before it: 'In communities where the masses are ignorant but respectful, if you once permit the ignorant class to begin to rule, you may bid farewell to deference forever. Their demagogues will inculcate, their newspapers will recount that the rule of the existing dynasty (the people) is better than the rule of the fallen dynasty (the aristocracy). A people very rarely hears two sides of a subject in which it is much interested; the popular organs take up the side which is acceptable, and none but the popular organs reach the people. A people *never* hears censure of itself. No one will tell it that the educated minority which is dethroned governed better or more wisely than it governs.'[1] Attitudes of social deference are certainly manifested less frequently today than in the nineteenth century. Yet the deferential outlook which was to have vanished as the majority came to rule remains very much in evidence—and this despite a pervasive industrialization and urbanization, two processes which are hardly conducive to socially deferential behaviour. But here Bagehot can be used to correct himself. In another part of *The English Constitution* he recognized the important role played by habit in governing behaviour: 'The active voluntary part of a man is very small . . . It is the dull traditional habit of mankind that guides most men's actions, and is the steady frame in which each new artist must set the picture that he paints.'[2] The steady deferential frame is then the influential setting which continues to affect men's actions long after the new picture of majority rule has been painted.[3]

[1] Ibid., p. 240.

[2] Ibid., p. 8, Bagehot's references to 'habit' as 'guides to most men's actions' and habit as a 'steady frame' indicate that in a rudimentary, but fundamental sense, he was adhering to what is currently known as the political culture approach. See below, Chapter 2, for a discussion of this approach.

[3] Cf. A. L. Lowell's remark that 'the sentiment of deference, or snobbishness, becomes, if anything, stronger as the social scale descends. The working man, when not provoked by an acute grievance to vote for a trade union candidate, prefers a man with a title, and thus the latest extensions of the franchise have rather strengthened than weakened the hold of the governing class upon public life'. *The Government of England*: 1924, Vol. II, p. 513, cited in Beer, op. cit., p. 254.

The high regard in which the Conservative half of the country tends to hold men of social eminence does not only serve as a crucial support for the party's hierarchical structure, legitimizing the leadership's authority with the belief that ability attaches to high social rank. This social deference has also provided the party with a socially homogeneous elite. 'In some ways the leadership ranks of the Conservative Party', writes Guttsman, 'are probably as socially monolithic as that of any political party in the world. Seen through the eyes of its leadership cadre, it is the Conservative Party rather than the Labour Party which has the character of a class party.'[1] It is these two themes that are explored in this section.

Socially deferential behaviour was already much in evidence at the founding of the party's extra-parliamentary organization in the nineteenth century. Although the National Union originated as local Associations of Conservative Working Men, thereby giving the workers a legitimate claim for the enjoyment of a number of leadership positions, only one working-class member protested against the upper-class domination of the National Union at the time of its formation. In fact, as McKenzie reports, a number of working-class members who were nominated for election to the Council were 'overcome by the honour which was being offered them'. One of them replied to his nomination with these words: the National Union would not 'wish to have second-rate names on the committee (sic). His own was there and he was sorry to hear it read out. He objected to it very strongly. The committee was not the place for a working man, but should be composed of the best men they could possibly obtain.'[2] Partly through this identification of the 'best men' with members of the social elite on the part of working-class and middle-class members of the constituency organizations, the leadership of the National Union has maintained its class character down to the present. Of the forty-five people who have held the positions of President of the National Union (primarily an honorific post) and Chairman of the

---

[1] W. L. Guttsman, *The British Political Elite*: 1963, pp. 279–280.

[2] Op. cit., p. 153. Cf. the nineteenth-century middle-class example of social deference quoted by Hippolyte Taine. 'It is not our aim to overthrow the aristocracy: we are ready to have the government and high offices in their hands. For we believe, we men of the middle class, that the conduct of national business calls for special men, men born and bred to the work for generations, and who enjoy an independent and commanding situation.' *Notes on England*: 1957 edition, p. 155.

Executive Committee, sixteen are members of the aristocracy by descent, while the remaining twenty-nine come from solidly middle-class backgrounds.[1] The workers' predilection for leaders with high status is also found within the local constituency organizations. In the town of 'Squirebridge', for example, there are sixteen officials of Conservative organizations, of whom twelve belong to the higher and four to the middle occupational strata. There is not one officer from the lower occupational group even though 40 per cent of the members belong to this group.[2] And in his study of the Conservative Association in Reading, Jean Blondel concluded that the 'old Reading families still have most of the power and continue . . . [to hold] key positions in the executive. Something undoubtedly remains of the old idea that certain Conservatives have a sort of family right to shape the Association's destiny, while new members, as it were, should be content with having been admitted as members.'[3]

Whereas the Tory middle classes in the latter half of the nineteenth century attempted to 'integrate' the working-class Tories into the party in order to prevent them from turning into Liberals or Radicals, in the middle of the twentieth century their efforts are aimed at convincing the working class that the Conservative Party is not a class party, that it is a national party concerned with all classes. Toward this end the party has created the Conservative Trade Unionists' Organization, having also made some attempts to have the constituency parties adopt trade unionist candidates for Parliament. But as in the earlier period, attitudes of social superiority continue to intrude themselves. Although everyone would agree that it would be advantageous to have a greater number of trade unionist MP's on the Conservative benches, the constituency parties' selection committees have consistently backed down when presented with the chance of choosing one.[4] To cite one particularly striking instance, in 1963 the National

---

[1] Guttsman, op. cit., p. 295.

[2] Thomas Bottomore, 'Social Stratification in Voluntary Organizations', in Glass, ed., op. cit., p. 362. If the organizations' largely honorary vice-presidents were included there would be even a sharper distinction between the status of officers and members.

[3] 'The Conservative Association and the Labour Party in Reading', *Political Studies*, June 1958, p. 108. But cf. the situation in Newcastle-under-Lyme as described by Frank Bealey, *et al.*, *Constituency Politics*: 1965, pp. 387–388, *passim*. It is primarily in the south-west and Scotland that the Tory associations remain the exclusive preserve of the 'established' families.

[4] See A. Ranney, *Pathways to Parliament*: 1965, esp. pp. 33–34.

Chairman of the Conservative Trade Unionists was turned down for a 32-year-old member of the Bow Group in his own home constituency.[1] The upshot of the constituency parties' negative attitude towards trade unionist candidates was that Ray Mawby found himself to be the only manual worker in the parliamentary party.[2] Although middle-class attitudes of social superiority prevent the trade unionists from playing a significant part in their party, this has not stood in the way of their being put to propagandistic advantage. In 1948, a Vice-Chairman of the National Union thought it necessary to warn the Annual Conference 'about trying to pull around, like performing bears on a chain, spectacular trade union candidates', in order to say, ' "Look whom we have adopted on behalf of the Conservative Party" . . . For if snobbery is a vice, inverted snobbery is just as bad a vice.'[3] By 1964 certain party members were beginning to question the wisdom of keeping trade unionists in a special hothouse of their own. In the words of one constituency agent: 'We'll never really get anywhere so long as we insist on treating them (the Tory trade unionists) as if they were Africans or something.'[4]

Nor has this combination of a middle-class social superiority and propagandistic exploitation gone unnoticed by the Tory trade unionists themselves. The manual workers are not only made aware of this situation in an impersonal manner when a party leader publicly chastises the annual conference on this score; it also impinges upon them in face-to-face personal terms. At the 1952 Party Conference, a member of the Conservative Council of Trade Unionists related how 'in some constituencies we are tolerated, in some constituencies we are helped a great deal; in others we are cold-shouldered and looked upon as a necessary evil'.[5] Although the Conservative embrace is sometimes genuine, frequently it is a particularly cold embrace. For as related by one Conservative Trade Unionist, the treatment he and others like him received from other Tories depends upon the particular setting in which the two classes come into contact with each other: 'He (the Conservative trade unionist) is a jolly good fellow when he gets up and

---

[1] The *Sunday Times*, March 8, 1964.
[2] But as reported by *The Economist* (May 14, 1966), 'the 1964 election saw a doubling of the number of Conservative trade unionists in the Commons', with Sir Ted Brown joining Mr Mawby.
[3] 69th *Annual Conference Report*, p. 120.
[4] The *Sunday Times*, March 8, 1964. Also see n. 3 pp. 198–99 below.
[5] 72nd *Annual Conference Report*, p. 64.

makes a speech, and when they meet him in the street they don't recognize him.'[1]

If the working-class members of the Conservative Party have continued to subscribe to a set of socially deferential attitudes despite the rebuffs many have received, the middle-class members maintain a similar set of attitudes but without having to meet any impediments in their expression. It is the holding of socially deferential attitudes on the part of the upper- and middle-class dominated constituency parties and within the parliamentary party itself, that has contributed to the particularly hierarchical structure of authority in the Conservative Party. At the same time it has resulted in a sharp correspondence between a person's social status and his position of authority within the party.

In an analysis of the constituency party resolutions submitted to the Conservative and Labour annual conferences from 1955 to 1960, it was found that about one-third of the Conservative parties did not submit any resolutions in the five-year period, while only a quarter of the parties forwarded an average of one resolution or more a year. In his interpretation of these figures Rose suggests that they 'may well be related to the deferential relationship which exists, socially as well as politically, between party leaders and members. Balfour is reported to have said that he would as soon take orders from his valet as from a Conservative Party annual conference. Perhaps some party members would equally regard it as wrong to depart from the obligations of their station in life.'[2] It ought to be said, however, that the small number of Conservative resolutions put forward by constituency parties might partially be explained by the middle-class members' political sophistication in not wanting to embarrass their leaders in public, especially when the leaders also constitute the Government as was the case in the period studied, or perhaps because of a lack of issue concerns on their part.

The most important prerogative adhering to the constituency parties is the selection of parliamentary candidates. The social deference of

---

[1] The *Guardian*, Manchester, March 15, 1964.

[2] 'The Political Ideas of English Party Activists', *American Political Science Review*, Vol. 2, 1962, p. 364. The Conservative figures are not strictly comparable to those of the Labour Party because Labour constituency parties are each limited to one resolution and one amendment annually. But notwithstanding this limitation, the Labour parties send a greater number of resolutions to their conferences than do the Conservative associations.

the invariably middle-class dominated selection committees is clearly manifested in their choice of candidates enjoying a higher social rank than themselves. The fact that usually more than two-thirds of the Tory candidates in recent elections had attended public school is a significant figure in itself considering that only 3 per cent of the population received such an education. To this must be added the high correspondence between public school attendance and electoral success. Of the eighty-nine Old Etonian candidates in the 1959 General Election 82 per cent were elected; the successful proportion of the total public school group was 70 per cent; while only 40 per cent of the non-public school candidates ended up in the House.[1] There would appear to be two explanations for this pattern. Among parliamentary hopefuls there is clearly a desire to be adopted by a safe constituency, ensuring that they will enter the House at the next General Election. Given the intense competition for such safe seats, these constituency parties have a great number of possible candidates with national reputations and high social status from which to choose. Presented with a choice between an Old Etonian and a grammar school product, the constituency parties' attitudes of social deference allows for little doubt as to which one will become the prospective candidate.[2] Secondly, it would seem warranted to assume that the social status of the members of constituency associations in the 'safe' Tory areas of rural and suburban England is higher on the average than it is for members in the marginal constituencies. And since these party activists are searching for men with higher status than themselves to send to Westminster, the prospective candidates in the safe constituencies have a higher status than their counterparts in the marginal areas.

The greater electoral success of candidates with high status not only serves to indicate the party activists' preference for such leaders; it also effects the pattern of authority within the parliamentary party. In the 1955–1959 Parliament, of the Tory MP's who went to one of the Clarendon public schools only 7 per cent held marginal seats,

---

[1] These figures were calculated from data presented in David Butler and Richard Rose, *The British General Election of* 1959: 1960, p. 128.

[2] 'In the selection of men for Parliament the basic character of Conservative Party leadership is generally perpetuated. Local selection committees, composed of the leaders of the local organization, men and women of worth and status and generally of advanced years, are inevitably and perhaps almost unconsciously prejudiced in favour of men who in their social background are like themselves or above them.' Guttsman, op. cit., pp. 288–289.

of the members who went to one of the other less exclusive public schools 15 per cent sat for marginal constituencies, while 21 per cent of the non-public school group held marginal seats.[1] Given the close association between influence within the parliamentary party, particularly in the party committees, and the length of time the members have sat in the House (i.e. the 'safeness' of their seats), it follows that for this reason alone the Tory MP's with higher status also have a larger amount of influence upon their colleagues and the party leadership.

Similarly, in the climb to the top of the parliamentary pyramid, those Tories with higher status seem to have a more secure footing than their colleagues at the next lower rungs of the status ladder. For notwithstanding the high social status of the parliamentary party as a whole, its leaders enjoy an even higher social rank. In Eden's Cabinet, for example, two-thirds of the members had been to one of the Clarendon schools, compared with only slightly more than one-third among the backbenchers. But even more significant is the fact that four members of Eden's Cabinet sat in the House of Lords, while of the remaining fourteen ministers with seats in the Commons, ten were directly related to aristocratic families.[2] Having married the daughter of a Duke, when he came to power Macmillan formed a Government in which thirty-five of its eighty-five members were related to him by marriage, while his nineteen-member Cabinet contained seven relatives.[3] Nor should it be overlooked that half of Sir Alec Douglas-Home's Cabinet was made up of Old Etonians like himself.[4]

To be sure, there are Conservative leaders whose status did not match their high positions of authority. But two of these exceptions indirectly support the generalization being put forward. In the case

---

[1] S. E. Finer, et al., Backbench Opinion in the House of Commons: 1955–1959: 1961, p. 84.

[2] Beer, op. cit., p. 382

[3] John Bull, January 4, 1958.

[4] A comparison of the 1951 Labour Government with the Conservative Government of 1960 brings to light the following contrasts: the Conservative Government contained fifteen aristocrats compared to three within the Labour Government; there was one man with a working-class background in the Conservative Government in contrast to the thirty in the Labour Government; seventeen Old Etonians found their way into the Tory Government compared to the five in the Labour Government. For additional contrasts, see Guttsman, op. cit., p. 336.

of Bonar Law, the divergence between his status and authority caused him some apprehension. 'The fact that [he] had no experience of government did not trouble him when he took the leadership. What he was afraid of was his wanting of birth. He was confident that he could lead without experience but afraid that the party might follow unwillingly because he had no blue blood in his veins.'[1] And when a man from a humble family did enter a Conservative cabinet, not only was he himself surprised at finding himself there, he 'recognized that within the larger community of the Commons . . . there was the smaller community bound together by strong if invisible ties of birth and background and public school to which I did not and could never belong'.[2]

Especially in view of the shroud of secrecy enveloping Tory high politics, it is difficult to gauge the degree and manner in which social factors play a part in the formation of Governments and the intra-party decisions of Conservative leaders. To what extent do the leaders' common public school backgrounds serve as a communications network resulting in the selection of public school products for positions of leadership? To what degree do public school graduates feel confident of each other and at ease in each other's presence, leading them to co-opt men with similar backgrounds into the party leadership? We can even speculate about the frequency with which possible parliamentary leaders are in part evaluated on the basis of their performances as a prefect or Captain of the school some twenty years earlier. The social differences between Tory leaders and followers in the party strongly suggest that factors such as these are operating, consciously or unconsciously, to ensure a close correspondence between status and authority in the party hierarchy. A striking instance of this confluence is found in Iain Macleod's disclosures about the way in which Sir Alec Douglas-Home (an Old Etonian) was chosen to succeed Macmillan (also an old Etonian). Among the men whom Macmillan gathered around himself in order to sound out opinion in the party

---

[1] Sir Charles Petrie, *Life and Letters of Sir Austen Chamberlain*: 1940, Vol II, p. 159. A related nineteenth-century example is Disraeli's felt need to buy a country house in order to solidify his position as leader, going to the extent of borrowing the money for the purchase.

[2] Charles Hill (Lord Hill of Luton), *Both Sides of the Hill*: 1964, pp. 11, 235. Also see the comments of Reginald Bevins who was born into a lower-class family and then rose to become Postmaster-General in the Macmillan Government. *The Greasy Pole*: 1965, pp. 102, 136, 141.

and advise him on the succession—the group that Macleod has called the 'magic circle'—eight of the nine were Old Etonians.[1]

IV. TORY GOALS AND MOTIVATIONS

The Conservative Party, and its upper-class leaders in particular, are the chief inheritors of the nation's political tradition. Genealogically descended from the King's party during the reign of Charles II, over the last three centuries the Tories have at once imbibed the English political ethos and contributed to its formation. The contemporary Conservative Party is itself structured in accordance with the political culture's two characteristic features—particularly sharp hierarchical authority relations and social deference. It is therefore hardly surprising that the Tories' conception of their role and place in society are heavily influenced by these cultural traits.

For the Tories the hierarchical principle is not only relevant to the party's internal functioning; it also influences their conception of the relationship between the party and society. The Conservative Party still is, as it was centuries ago, the party dedicated to carrying on the King's government. The exercise of governmental authority is the party's chief *raison d'être*. In the words of one unnamed writer, 'The Tories' guiding principle . . . is simply the assumption, unquestioned at any level of the party, that the Conservative Party ought to govern and will govern, even though there be no other principle to guide its course when in power or to dictate its pattern of revival when it goes through the rare, unnatural, but at the same time calcining, process of electoral defeat.'[2] The relevant point here is the unquestioning nature—the ingrained belief—of the Conservatives' assumption that they are the country's rightful and natural governors. This assumption is clearly evidenced in the fact that the Conservatives think it curious that they should lose a national election. After each electoral defeat in the twentieth century except for the last—in 1906, 1911, 1929, and 1945—the Tories conducted an inquiry into the reasons for these set-backs. The débâcle of the 1945 election temporarily shattered the calm assumption that the traditional ruling class had a monopoly on government, yet this was hardly sufficient to cause a questioning of the Tories' will-to-authority. In 1964, even after thirteen years in

---

[1] 'The Tory Leadership', The *Spectator*, January 17, 1964.
[2] 'The Adaptable Party', *Political Quarterly*, July–September 1961, p. 210.

office, internal party struggles, sordid political gossiping, a major public scandal, and an exceptionally arduous parliamentary session, the Conservatives still had an 'unquenched appetite for power.'[1]

The corollary of the Conservatives' will-to-authority is the eschewing of all but the broadest of principles—those of order, stability, and tradition. In the last three centuries other parties have arisen and fallen away as the principles they were committed to were either widely accepted or proven to be irrelevant to the country's needs. The Tories, on the other hand, by shunning permanent attachments to any single principle or policy have been able to survive and flourish. Lord Salisbury's remark cuts to the quick of Conservatism and implicitly points to the relationship between the Tory will-to-authority and its corollary: 'If I were asked to define Conservative policy, I should say that it was the upholding of confidence'—confidence in the abilities and good intentions of the governors largely irrespective of their policies. The most perspicacious of contemporary Tory journalists would wholeheartedly agree with Salisbury: 'The essence of Toryism,' according to Peregrine Worsthorne, 'is that good government depends far more on men than measures, and that its peculiar and unique contribution is in the high quality of leaders it can be relied upon to produce.'[2]

Nor are the Tory leaders loath to admit their lack of any strong attachment to particular principles and policies whether it be in their philosophical discussions or their day-to-day party management. In a chapter entitled 'The Philosophy of Conservatism', Quintin Hogg (formerly Viscount Hailsham) could write that the Tories 'see nothing immoral or even eccentric in "catching the Whigs bathing and walking away with their clothes." There is no copyright on truth and what is controversial politics at one moment may after experience and reflection easily become common ground.'[3] An equally illuminating insight into Conservative motivations is provided by Lord Blakenham, writing as party chairman in the foreword to the party's 1963 annual report. He nonchalantly assured the party members that the policy-

---

[1] James Margach, The *Sunday Times*, August 2, 1964. John P. Mackintosh has also noted that the Conservatives, 'no matter how they disagree, have always tended to feel that they ought to be the government and that it is better to have the worst Conservative in power than the best possible opponent'. *The British Cabinet*: 1962, p. 450.

[2] 'The Tories Must Have Clean Hands', *Sunday Telegraph*, June 9, 1963.

[3] *The Conservative Case*: 1959, p. 16.

making committees 'will strive, in the years ahead, to make whatever adjustments of policies may be needed so as to optimize their electoral attractiveness'.[1] The Conservatives then not only openly advertise, but are proud of the fact, that 'more than other parties in a democratic state, the Conservative Party—the party of expediency—is prone to imbibing an overdose of opportunism'.[2]

[1] Cited in the *Observer*, January 1, 1964.
[2] Glickman, op. cit., pp. 138–139.

CHAPTER 2

Methodological Considerations
POLITICAL CULTURE AND SURVEY ANALYSIS

I. THE POLITICAL CULTURE APPROACH

AN EXTENSIVE discussion of the political culture approach is beyond the scope of this study, especially since this has been admirably done elsewhere.[1] However, given the adoption of this approach here, a few methodological issues need to be clarified. Being both susceptible to differing interpretations and having recently been bandied about in a loose fashion as it has gained academic fashionability, it would be well to define the political culture concept and those related to it. At the same time it is necessary to set out the methodological difficulties associated with the political culture approach, with particular reference to the applicability of survey methods.

As conceived here, the political culture of a society, social class, regional group or any other stratum is simply the particular distribution of political orientations of the individuals comprising it. The key term in this definition is 'political orientations'. Following Parsons and Shils, these are viewed as the internalized aspects of political objects and relationships which *predispose* individuals to act in a specified manner over a period of time.[2] Orientations are then stable, internalized, dispositional traits, underlying and guiding individual behaviour. In order to be able to handle and operationalize the orientation concept most advantageously, a number of analytical distinctions need to be drawn.

[1] See Sidney Verba's essay 'Comparative Political Culture' in Lucian W. Pye and Sidney Verba, eds., *Political Culture and Political Development*: 1965, pp. 512–561. For the development and different uses of the concept of political culture, see Y. C. Kim 'The Concept of Political Culture in Comparative Politics', *Journal of Politics*, May 1964.

[2] Talcott Parsons and Edward Shils, eds., *Toward a General Theory of Action*: 1962, pp. 53ff. and 159ff.

46

Whereas the orientation and attitude concepts are commonly used interchangeably, here a rough distinction will be made between them. Though defined in the same way as orientations, attitudes will be taken to refer to their constituent parts, orientations being composed of an inter-related set of attitudes. The difference between the two concepts is analogous to the sometimes fuzzy dividing line between strategy and tactics or ends and means, but on the whole they are analytically separable. For example, one can speak of a 'democratic' or participant orientation toward politics which is made up of an inter-related set of attitudes referring to the proper role of governmental leaders, the rights of the individual citizen and a positive emotional attachment to the political system. The making of this distinction serves two purposes. It alerts us to the possibility that certain attitudes 'fit' together in a coherent fashion, and thereby raises questions regarding the psychological inter-relations among attitudes: How do specific attitudes lead to the acquisition of related ones? Must there be a 'cognitive balance' between attitudes referring to the same type of phenomena? Are isolated attitudes more susceptible to rapid change than is a structured set of attitudes? Secondly, the separation of orientations and attitudes allows for the use of the more generalized orientation concept as a stronger explanatory factor in the construction of hypotheses relating to the operation of political systems. For instance, if an attempt were made to specify the cultural conditions which are conducive for the establishment of a two-party system, it is unlikely that any single political attitude would be a sufficiently powerful explanatory variable, but it may well be that a more generalized orientation would be. Thus in the study's concluding chapter in which a theory of stable democracy is delineated, the explanatory centrepiece is a generalized orientation towards authority rather than a set of discrete attitudes towards authority.

Following Parsons and Shils again, attitudes can be broken down into their cognitive, affective and evaluative components.[1] Cognitions are beliefs about, knowledge of, or an awareness of the objects and relationships to which the individual is orienting his actions. The affective component refers to the emotional attachments, positive, negative or neutral, which the individual holds. Evaluations are the confluence of empirical beliefs and relevant normative standards in arriving at a

---

[1] Ibid., p. 59.

judgement about political phenomenon. Besides permitting a more detailed and reliable analysis of political attitudes, this threefold analytical division may suggest certain problems for exploration. For example, in attempting to assess the extent to which a population supports a democratic political system, it has been found useful to draw the distinction between their cognitions about the political system and their affective attachments to it. For example, in the case of Germany there is a great awareness of the democratic rules of the game and of political events, but this knowledge is not matched by a corresponding affective attachment to democratic norms and the symbols of the Bonn Republic.[1]

Attitudes were defined as behavioural predispositions towards political objects and relationships. They can therefore also be characterized according to the types of political objects and relationships thought to be significant for explaining the structure and process of political systems. It is at this point that the political culture approach is transformed from pre-theory to the beginnings of theory. As an approach to a theory all it does is to direct our attention to the very general statement that a country's political culture is important for explaining the contours of its political system, at the same time providing a few (and as yet underdeveloped) basic conceptual tools with which to explore that culture, while raising a number of potentially powerful questions for analysis (e.g. in what ways may culturally fragmented societies be politically integrated?). It is only after a particular approach with its distinctive central focus has been adopted that the real work begins, entailing the construction and testing of hypotheses and theories which purport to explain the emergence and variations of political phenomena. The first step in this direction is the selection of what are thought to be particularly important political objects and relationships, and the conceptualization of the attitudes which refer to them.

In the leading political culture study, Almond and Verba began with the broadest possible classification of objects and relationships: those attitudes which refer to the self as a political actor, and those which refer to the input and output structures of the political system.[2]

---

[1] The consequences that this dichotomy has for the German political system are delineated in Sidney Verba, 'Germany: The Remaking of Political Culture', in Pye and Verba, op. cit., esp. pp. 138–152.

[2] Gabriel A. Almond and Sidney Verba, *The Civic Culture*: 1963.

From this starting point they developed a threefold typology of paro-chial, subject and participant cultures. In the abruptest possible terms, a parochial culture is one in which there is no awareness whatsoever of the central political system, in a subject culture individuals relate only to the output activities of government (i.e. the execution and administration of governmental decisions), while in a participant culture the individuals are aware of both input and output processes and are predisposed towards influencing the making and admini-stration of governmental decisions. In their concluding chapter Almond and Verba outline the mixture of these three ideal-typical orientations that is most conducive for the stability of democratic systems. In the present study the central set of political objects and relationships chosen for analysis are those which refer to political authority. We shall be examining the workers' preferences for different types of governmental leaders, the extent to which the Government is legiti-mately permitted to act independently of the electorate, the basis upon which that independent authority is legitimized, the frequency with which the workers acquiesce in the expectations of party leaders, and the workers' beliefs and norms regarding the influence of the non-elite upon governmental decisions. This set of political objects and relationships is being emphasized not only because it is their attitudes towards authority which most distinctively characterize the political culture of the English manual workers. It is also thought that attitudes towards political authority are a powerful explanatory variable in accounting for the stability, effectiveness and representativeness of democratic systems—an argument that is developed in the con-cluding chapter.

Most political culture studies have focused upon attitudes as the explanatory variable, specifying their effects upon the political system.[1]

---

[1] Attitudes have also been used as the independent variable to account for patterns of behaviour. This procedure is not employed here because of the rela-tively small advantages that are usually to be gained—i.e. the short distance separating the two variables on an analytical plane means that not very much is being explained—and because of the logical difficulties involved. In attempting to explain behaviour by its underlying attitudes there is the danger that the result will be a descriptive behavioural statement set out in misleading cultural terminology. Secondly, there is the tautological problem of utilizing behaviour as an indicator of underlying attitudes and then 'explaining' the behaviour by these same attitudes. And thirdly, an explanation of behaviour in terms of attitudes is logically incomplete without a concomitant statement about the particular type of stimuli which lead to the activation of attitudes at the

However, political attitudes can also be utilized as the dependent variable. Two questions are then raised regarding their formation and inter-generational continuity, attempting to identify the conditions under which a society's political attitudes were first formed and the socialization processes by which they are maintained. For example, the normative expectation that two or more political parties ought to be in competition with each other and that the opposition party not be penalized when out of power, is widespread in all the western democracies. Especially considering its relevance for the underdeveloped countries, it would be most instructive to determine how this normative expectation originally developed and how it became institutionalized. Is its origin to be found in a near balance of power between the two competing parties so that it became impossible for the stronger to eliminate the weaker one by force? Another intriguing problem for dynamic historical analysis might be the transformation of Weimar's emotion-charged politics of the street (at least during 1923 and 1932) into Bonn's passive politics of the voting booth. Such an analysis might very well come to the conclusion that the Nazi regime served as the midwife to German democracy by providing a prolonged political trauma.

If past events and conditions call political attitudes into being, the political socialization process maintains them through succeeding generations.[1] It is the process by which each generation transmits its own political predispositions to succeeding ones. This is accomplished through both latent and manifest means. Attitudes are manifestly transferred when a conscious effort is being made to do so by the socializing agents (e.g. a teacher instilling democratic values in a history class). Latent socialization is accomplished unintentionally, so to speak. In the present study for instance, the workers' readiness to attempt to influence a governmental decision is traced back to their participant experiences in the making of parental decisions. It is thus possible to carry out an extensive analysis of a political system within the broad confines of the political culture approach: the first step being

---

behavioural level. These last two points are tangentially explored below. For a discussion of the logical implications and uses of 'dispositional explanations', see Carl G. Hempel, *Aspects of Scientific Explanation*: 1965, pp. 457–463, and Robert Brown, *Explanation in Social Science*: 1963, pp. 75–98.

[1] In fact, Ralph Linton once defined culture as 'social heredity', thereby conceiving of it in terms of the socialization process.

the specification of the system's most important or characteristic attributes, next suggesting cultural hypotheses which explain these particular attributes, then going on to analyse the political socialization process as it is instrumental in shaping and transferring the relevant political attitudes from one generation to the next, and finally going back into the country's history to locate those conditions and events responsible for the original development and institutionalization of these cultural traits.

II. ATTITUDES AND BEHAVIOUR

In defining the political culture concept the emphasis was placed not upon political behaviour, but upon the underlying orientations which guide that behaviour. This emphasis is at once its major strength and major difficulty. The difficulty arises from the problems encountered in attempting to isolate and identify orientations and attitudes. For if the approach is to be meaningful and distinctive—something other than the making of behavioural statements in cultural language— and if it is to escape a crucial methodological pitfall, orientations must be differentiated from the behavioural patterns they shape. In terms of the psychologists' Stimulus-Organism-Response (S-O-R) model, it is the O that must be viewed independently of the R.[1] To take a simplistic example, after watching one of the Conservative Party's elderly authority figures on television, a group of workers in a pub express their admiration. In this instance the S (the politician's speech) and the R (the expression of approval) are easy to isolate. The difficulty occurs in determining how the S was perceived and interpreted by the O which gives rise to the R; that is, specifying the substantive content of the O through which the S is 'filtered', thereby giving rise to the R. Presumably the workers' positive reactions to the party broadcast were shaped by attitudes of social deference, a high evaluation

---

[1] By relying upon this model one could arrive at a different formulation of attitudes and culture. Attitudes then become consistent conjunctions of a particular stimulus and response. For example, a participatory political attitude might be defined as the attempt to influence governmental decisions whenever the stimulus of unjustified governmental action arises. Such a formulation would get us around the difficulty of identifying the individual's predispositions independently of his behaviour, for we would be disregarding the O in the S-O-R model. But on the other hand, the explanatory power of the attitudinal concept would be impaired in a number of ways, and it would lead to the making of behavioural statements in cultural language.

of the particular politician, a favourable attitude towards the policies expressed in the speech, or an unquestioning affective attachment to the Tory Party. In determining which of these attitudes influenced the workers' positive reactions the procedure (ideally speaking) should disregard the political behaviour which is presumably the product of the attitudes; the evidence for the conclusion should not be 'contaminated' by the behaviour which is being explained. Unfortunately, it is impossible to develop such a procedure. Underlying orientations and attitudes must be inferred from one type of behaviour or another; it is impossible to get at the orientations directly. Whether we are observing the working-class men in the pub through a secret keyhole, directly asking them their reasons for their favourable reactions at the time, or getting an interviewer to come around to their houses a few days later to ask them the relevant questions under the guise of a 'scientific' study, the upshot is always the same: it is only from their actual behaviour that the individuals' attitudes can be inferred. In short, the inability to isolate attitudes means that there can be no guarantee that an individual's behaviour can be taken as a valid reflection of his underlying attitudes.[1]

Broadly speaking, there are two types of data from which attitudes may be inferred: in one instance the behaviour is observed in its 'natural' setting, in the other it is artificially induced. The first type of data was utilized in the introductory chapter in which a number of generalizations were made about English political culture based upon the behaviour of Englishmen as observed by various writers. There are no limitations upon the nature of the data falling into this first category so long as it refers to actual behaviour, thereby including voting statistics, the social backgrounds of party leaders at differing levels in the organizational hierarchy as these indicate the relations between party leaders and followers regarding advancement in the hierarchy, the writings of party leaders, the number of manual workers from Bristol who visited aristocratic houses between 1960 and 1964, the intensiveness with which pressure group leaders press their demands, etc. However, utilization of such diverse data is oftentimes precarious because of the wide gap separating the available behavioural data from the underlying attitudes which are thought to pattern that

---

[1] This point is found in Ernest Nagel's essay, 'Problems of Concept and Theory Formation in the Social Sciences', in Maurice Natanson, ed., *Philosophy of the Social Sciences*: 1963, pp. 204–206.

behaviour. For instance, even if reliable data were available showing annual increases in the number of manual workers paying admission to visit the aristocracy's historic houses between 1960 and 1964, these data could not readily be taken as evidence for the hyopthesis that attitudes of social deference are increasing within the working class. To draw this inference about the workers' attitudes, it would be minimally necessary to disconfirm certain alternative explanations (e.g. the number of workers owning motor cars has increased, allowing those workers with a deferential predisposition to visit the nobility's homes more frequently, even though the number of deferentials has not increased, or that the workers have developed a new desire to spend their holidays in the country rather than in the city, the aristocracy's parks and gardens providing an ideal country setting).

The validity attaching to generalizations about cultural patterns stemming from this type of behavioural data are markedly enhanced when two conditions are met. When a behavioural trait is observed over a long period of time, there is good reason to believe that it is a manifestation of an underlying attitude, one of the defining characteristics of an attitude being its persistence over time. A long-term endurance of a behaviour pattern indicates that it is being shaped by a stable set of underlying forces rather than external stimuli which are oftentimes undergoing change. Secondly, if a behaviour pattern is found to exist in more than one sphere of activity, it would suggest that the behaviour is not shaped by particular conditions or institutional influences. Rather it would appear to be the product of well-embedded attitudes which give rise to a particular type of behaviour largely irrespective of environmental circumstances. For instance, the characterization of the German population as legalistically oriented is not solely based upon their behaviour in governmental offices, for in this environment they may simply be conforming to the expectations of elite members in order to curry favour with them; this legalism even extends to their driving habits, as they slavishly obey the letter but not the spirit of the traffic laws. In short, the observed recurrence of a behaviour pattern over a period of time and under differing conditions indicates that this behaviour is being shaped by a stable, and therefore, powerful, set of underlying attitudes—attitudes which could then be deduced from the behaviour patterns.

The second type of data from which attitudes can be inferred, rather than constituting 'natural' behaviour, is artificially induced or manipulated. The most common tool employed here is obviously the survey study, allowing for the generation of behaviour (the respondents answering the interviewers' questions) which is then taken as a proximate indicator of the attitudes which are being tapped. There would appear to be three advantages in using survey methods for political culture studies.

Most importantly, the central problem of inferring attitudes from behaviour is markedly alleviated when the behaviour involved is a matter of selected respondents answering pre-tested questions put to them by trained interviewers. The interview situation is designed to place the informants in as nearly as neutral a frame of reference as possible, thereby maximizing the chances that their behaviour is an accurate reflection of their underlying attitudes; that the behavioural data is minimally 'contaminated' by aberrant or passing circumstances. Secondly, systematic sampling methods allow for reliable and precise measurement of the pervasiveness of the various cultural dimensions. National character studies which were the precursors of the political culture approach almost invariably relied upon crude generalizations about the presence or absence of attitudes within entire societies, coming up with statements of the kind: 'the people of country A are particularly prone to manifest attitudinal syndrome X'. There was little specification of what exactly is meant by 'particularly prone', and few attempts were made to distinguish the relative frequency with which various strata in the population manifested the particular attitudinal trait. With the coming of survey techniques it is now possible to state with what frequency a population subscribes to an attitudinal syndrome, to compare two or more societies in this regard, and also to delineate the cultural differences among population strata, whether it be among social classes or between political elites and non-elites. Thirdly, survey analysis is able to identify those attitudes which are so widely accepted that they remain unspoken except when directly tapped in an interview situation. It is very possibly just those attitudes whose unquestioned acceptance by the population makes any debate about them redundant and their behavioural expression unnecessary that form the crucial element in the cultural matrix which patterns the form and operation of the political system. This appears to be true of the English working class' unspoken attitudes towards political authority. The value of survey analysis is consequently enhanced in so far as it can effect the verbalization of just these latent, unquestioned and crucial attitudes.[1]

III. THE SAMPLING FRAMEWORK

In constructing a sample of manual workers who are Tory supporters and a control group of working-class Labour supporters, two possibilites presented themselves. The first possible procedure would have entailed the selection of some two dozen working-class constituencies, followed by a systematic sampling of their electoral rolls. Notwithstanding the attractive simplicity of such a sampling framework it turned out to be inappropriate for purposes of the present study. Such a sampling design would have necessitated the rejection of those respondents whose attributes did not conform to the study's purposes (e.g. middle-class people, politically neutral or apathetic workers). It would consequently have been necessary for the interviewers to reject a large number of respondents at the outset of the interviews. Such a procedure would have cast some doubt about the reliability of the resulting sample, not to mention the additional cost involved. Secondly, there would have been many more Labour than Conservative voters in the resulting sample—a balance which ought to be reversed given this study's focus. Thirdly, if the constituencies to be sampled were selected so as to contain a solidly working-class population, the sample would not have been a national one, with those workers living in areas that are not predominantly working-class not being represented. For these reasons, and others of a more detailed nature, this possible sampling method was rejected.

Since this study required a sample of manual workers living in urban areas with a preponderance of Tory voters among them, it was thought best to proceed by locating a large enough national sample or samples from which those respondents having the required attributes could be systematically selected. In this way a sample could be constructed which avoided the rejection of respondents on their front-steps because

[1] On the other hand, when respondents are induced to answer questions which they have never before thought about and which may have no significance for them, there is the danger that the analyst will attribute a real meaning to these responses—something that clearly is unwarranted. Yet, this danger cannot be completely circumvented until large strides are made in the development of questions which measure not only the direction but the intensity of the responses.

they do not have the requisite attributes in the desired proportions, and allows for generalizations about the urban working-class as a whole, the respondents having been originally selected on a national basis. The national surveys utilized for this purpose were those done by the National Opinion Polls, Ltd in their monthly political surveys in the spring and summer of 1963, each utilizing the same non-interlocking quota sampling frame and totalling approximately 1,800 respondents.

According to which criteria were the respondents from the six National Opinion Polls surveys selected in the construction of the present sample? The first criteria of selection employed was obviously that of social class, the study being limited to the English working class.[1] Without jumping into the ink-filled waters of debates about the meaning of social class, let it simply be said that working-class is here taken to mean manual workers.[2] This definition is thought to be most relevant for the objectives of the study.[3] Included under this operational definition are occupations ranging in skill and responsibility from that of foremen, skilled workers such as machinists, toolmakers, electricians and carpenters, to those occupations falling under the unskilled category such as woolsorters, bus conductors, labourers and weavers. This operational definition is very nearly equivalent to the C2 (skilled workers) and D (unskilled workers) classifications commonly used in English public opinion surveys. However, not

---

[1] Workers in Scotland and Wales are not included in the study.

[2] After considering all the recent changes in the social structure that have served to mitigate the importance of the division between non-manual and manual occupation, W. G. Runciman concluded that it remains 'the most important dividing-line in the British social structure, whether considered in the light of inequalities of status or of class'. *Relative Deprivation and Social Justice*: 1966, p. 51.

[3] The point that a particular definition of class should be adopted according to the use to which the concept is to be put has been aptly expressed by Heinz Eulau. 'Relevance to a theoretical purpose would seem to be crucial in the construction of a meaningful concept of class. Only in the framework of the theoretical objective of an investigation can it be determined which dimension or complex of variables is most adequate in the development of a concept of class—whether objective or subjective criteria are relevant, or on what level of society an inquiry into class-related conduct seems to be most fruitful. Otherwise class analysis will be redundant, arbitrary and irrelevant.' See 'Identification with Class and Political Perspective', *Journal of Politics*, May 1956, p. 233. A number of different possible definitions of class other than the one adopted as the defining one for the study as a whole (e.g. subjective class identification and working-class solidarity) are analysed in Chapter 7 above.

included in the present study, but sometimes found in the C2 category in public opinion studies, are office workers such as calculating machine operators, even though their work is essentially the same as that of many factory workers, and shop assistants, notwithstanding the fact that in terms of skill and wages they oftentimes rank lower than many factory workers. The reasons for the exclusion of such occupations is perhaps best symbolized by the fact that in each case these people do not wear blue collars to work; wearing white shirts and business suits they find themselves in a different work-place environment and tend to hold different conceptions of themselves in class terms than do the blue-collar workers. Or to make the point in a different way, following David Lockwood a differentiation is made between two types of class positions: 'market situation' and 'work situation'.[1] Both blue-collar and white-collar sales and clerical workers share the same market situation, 'that is to say the economic position narrowly conceived, consisting of source and size of income, degree of job-security, and opportunity for upward occupational mobility'. However, the two types of workers differ in their work situation, 'the set of social relationships in which the individual is involved at work by virtue of his position in the division of labour'.[2] And between the two types of class position it is the work situation which Lockwood finds to be 'the most important social condition shaping the psychology of the individual'.[3]

Secondly, it is thought that the working-class Tories living in urban areas present an especially interesting problem for analysis. In the rural areas of England, where the traditional social structure is still prevalent, Conservative voting within the working class is more easily understandable than in the cities. It may even be that a majority of those workers living in rural districts vote Conservative whereas just the opposite is true of the urban dwellers. Moreover, since only a small percentage of the English working class lives in rural areas, the inclusion of such people in the sample would be too small to allow for separate analysis, while grouping them together with the urban workers would complicate the analysis by including another set of variables. For these two reasons the study has been confined to the urban working class. Since the selection of any dividing

---

[1] David Lockwood, *The Blackcoated Worker*: 1958, p. 15.
[2] Ibid.
[3] Ibid., p. 205.

line between urban and rural areas is purely arbitrary, it need only be said that urban dwellers were defined as those workers living in cities of more than 70,000 population. In fact, the vast majority of the workers in the sample live in cities greatly in excess of this figure.

An important decision had to be made whether or not to include women in the sample. If it were possible to have constructed a sample numbering approximately 1,200 working-class respondents, this problem would not have arisen, but since our sample numbered only 717 informants, it was thought best not to include women. If women had been included the reliability of many of the findings would have been markedly reduced, having had to rely upon half the number of respondents for generalizations about men and women separately. Although the findings are consequently applicable only to the male half of the working class (at least in strict terms), their reliability is thereby enhanced. On the other hand, there is good reason to suppose that in many instances the women's political attitudes are simply those of their husbands' as reflected in a female mirror. Moreover, since one of the study's major goals is to suggest certain inter-relationships between non-elite attitudes and the contours of the political system, the data relating to the male manual workers is far more relevant given the fact that men are almost always more significant political actors than are women. Presumably then, if women were included in the sample not only would the data concerning them be of less significance for understanding the operation of the political system, the data would probably be much the same as that of the male workers except for a higher frequency of conservative and politically passive attitudes.

The fourth criteria of selection raises the problem of how to define a Tory supporter. If all those respondents who fulfilled the first three requirements were selected from the National Opinion Polls' surveys, the study would have included (besides Conservative and Labour voters) those workers who move from one political position to another, Liberal voters, and apathetic non-voters. In order to isolate those workers who were solid Conservative voters from these other groups, the Conservative supporters were operationally defined as those who replied in the National Opinion Polls interviews that they had voted Tory at the last General Election in 1959, and would do so again 'if there were a General Election tomorrow'. If a worker supplied only one Conservative response to the two questions, he was not included in the sample, not being viewed as a regular Tory voter.[1] In order to establish a control group with which the Tories could be compared the Labour supporters were defined in the same way as those workers who voted Labour in 1959 and who intended to repeat their performance at the next General Election. If the sample could have been doubled, Liberal voters, the uncommitted and the non-voters would also have been included; but not wanting to sacrifice the reliability of the findings to the inclusion of these groups, this was not done.

After selecting those respondents from the National Opinion Polls survey that met these four criteria, one further operation had to be carried out. If the sample were made up of Tories and Labour supporters in the proportions with which they were found in the actual working-class population there would have been approximately twice as many Labour as Tory voters in the sample. But given our focus upon the latter group it was necessary to utilize a weighting procedure to rectify this imbalance. This was done by placing the names of Labour supporters found in each of the six National Opinion Polls samples in alphabetical order and then randomly selecting every fifth name. The Conservative voters then constitute slightly over two-thirds of the resulting sample after every fifth Labour voter had been selected. Parenthetically, the need to locate a substantial number of working-class Tories who also fulfilled the other selection requirements necessitated the utilization of fully six national samples; if the primary goal of the study were the analysis of the working class as a whole rather than of a minority within it, only one or two national samples would have been needed.

Since only every fifth Labour respondent has been included in the sample, it is sometimes necessary to employ a weighting index in order to compensate for this factor. This need not be done when descriptive statements are made about the Tories and Labour voters separately (e.g. 23 per cent of the Conservatives and 50 per cent of the Labour voters favour a form of working-class solidarity). However, when a causal explanation is suggested, having as its dependent variable the workers' party preferences, it is necessary to multiply the number of Labour respondents by five. For example, in Table 43 on page 164, an attempt is made to relate the workers' class identifications to their voting behaviour. If the number of Labour supporters were not

[1] However, if a respondent was too young to vote in 1959, but said he planned to vote Conservative at the next election he was included in the sample.

multiplied by five, the resulting table of figures would not represent the actual distribution of working-class and middle-class identifiers in the working population; nor would it allow us to gauge the effect of this variable upon voting behaviour since the extent to which the two factors are inter-related among the Conservatives would be given excessive weight relative to their inter-relationship among the Labour voters. In order not to mislead the reader regarding the reliability of the data in which the number of Labour respondents have been multiplied by five, the figures representing the number of respondents found in each of the columns refers to the actual number of respondents in the sample rather than the inflated number of respondents after the size of the Labour group has been multiplied by five.

Before turning to the statistics of the sampling frame, one further point ought to be made about causal analysis. It is undoubtedly true that two requirements must be satisfied in the making of an explanatory generalization: a correlation between the independent and dependent variables must exist, and it has to be independently demonstrated that the two stand in a causal relationship to each other. In not a few instances a correlation between the two variables is found in the data, yet with the information at hand a causal relationship between them can only be established in a tenuous fashion. Notwithstanding such gaps, when the two variables *appear* to stand in an explanatory relationship to each other the data have been interpreted in this manner. It would therefore hardly be surprising to find that some of these hypotheses will be invalidated when future research produces the relevant data. Yet if these correlations were not stated in explanatory language—with the necessary *caveats* attached, of course—they would be nothing more than descriptive statements; they would not be hypotheses at all, but simply a factual reporting of the study's findings. As such they would be uninteresting statements (at least to this writer), whereas their statement as hypotheses entails analysis rather than description and allows for their future invalidation or confirmation by other social scientists.

As already mentioned, the respondents were originally interviewed by the National Opinion Polls in the spring and summer of 1963. The respondents selected from these national samples were then re-interviewed in the summer of 1964. With the exception of twenty-one respondents who could not be contacted at this time, the interviews were completed by September 1964. Since the General Election campaign began in earnest only after the interviewing was completed, the possibility that the respondents were inordinately influenced by the parties' heightened propaganda efforts was minimized. Those twenty-one workers who could not be contacted by the end of September were only interviewed in December of 1964 in order to permit the political environment to return to 'normal' after the exertions of the election campaign. The bulk of the field work was carried out by the British Market Research Bureau, with the present writer and one other person doing about one-fifth of the interviews.

The results of the interviewing process are summarized in the following statement:

Total attempts	717	100%
Completed interviews	473	66%
Refusals	79	11%
Not at home after three attempts	57	8%
Other reasons[1]	108	15%

Of the 473 completed interviews it was found that twenty-two respondents did not fit the criteria of the sampling frame. When originally interviewed by the National Opinion Polls, they replied to the two questions regarding past voting and voting intentions either as steadfast Conservatives or pro-Labour. In the interim some had apparently changed their voting intentions and in other instances the replies about their voting behaviour in the 1959 General Election did not correspond in the two interviews. These workers were therefore dropped from the analysis, leaving us with a sample of 447 workers, of whom 320 are Tories and 127 are Labour.

In order to supplement the largely quantitative data generated by the first-wave interviews a small second wave of open-ended interviews was carried out. These were done by the British Market Research Bureau's psychologically trained interviewers. From the 447 workers forty-five were selected as 'representative' of the three groups upon which the study is based—deferential Conservatives, pragmatic Conservatives and Labour supporters. Of the forty-five attempts only fifteen were successful. However, this relatively low response rate hardly invalidates the second-wave data. For these interviews are only

---

[1] Included here are those workers who were sick, who had died, who were not known at the address, who had moved, whose premises were demolished, and who could not be interviewed for administrative reasons.

used to illustrate, rather than substantiate, hypotheses suggested by the first-wave data, and to provide the writer with a more meaningful context within which to interpret the quantitative data. Unfortunately, the second-wave interview schedule was drawn up before the first-wave data had been analysed so that many of those areas which needed deeper exploration were not touched upon in the second wave.

CHAPTER 3

Political Leaders and Political Authority

BEGINNING with the break-down of feudalism a gradual transformation in the nature of political leadership has been taking place in the West. The acceptance of political leadership on the traditional basis of high social rank alone has now been very largely replaced by leadership legitimized on the basis of performance; ascriptive criteria of high status have given way to those of ability and knowledge. Even when people continue to accord authority to men with high ascriptive rank it is almost invariably justified (or rationalized) on the grounds that men of high social status are more likely to possess leadership abilities and skills, in contrast to a former unquestioning acceptance of authority because of social rank alone. A distinction ought then to be made between two historical patterns. First, there has been a growing influx of men with low social status positions into high governmental and political positions as achievement criteria have come to replace ascriptive standards in the selection of leaders. Secondly, when men with high social rank continue to occupy high political offices, their tenure is only indirectly legitimized by ascriptive criteria. It is thought that their social backgrounds have provided them with the experiences and opportunities that are especially useful for the development of political leadership attributes. In other words, the holding of high ascriptive rank is thought to develop high achievement capacities among political leaders. Perhaps more than in any other Western country, men of high status are frequently found in the English political and governmental elites, and as suggested in the introductory chapter, this is especially true of the Conservative Party. At the same time, there remains a widespread belief within the non-elite that the men residing in the upper reaches of the status pyramid are the best political leaders—that there is a close association between leadership abilities and high social rank.

In the first section of this chapter we shall examine the extent to which the workers continue to prefer aristocratic and upper-class leaders; how frequently political leadership attributes are still viewed as concomitants of high social rank; and also, how the believed association of these two attributes is explained.

Throughout this study comparisons will be made among three groups of respondents: deferentials, pragmatists, and Labour voters. The deferentials are those Conservative voters who manifest a strong preference for men of high status as their governmental leaders. They are deferring to the occupants of high social positions by allowing them, rather than the members of their own class, to enjoy positions of political leadership and governmental authority. It should be noted that the degree to which the deferentials are willing to submit to the judgement of such leaders, over and above expressing a desire to have them for leaders, is not used as a criterion in operationally defining the deferential respondents. The question of submission, which is often automatically associated with social deference, will be treated as a separate variable in order to test this common assumption. The pragmatist label will be used in a residual fashion to group together all those working-class Tories who are not deferentials. This is clearly not the most felicitous use of the term pragmatist, but for reasons of style it was thought best to substitute another term for that of 'non-deferentials'. Although the label itself may have few merits when used here in a residual manner, the frequency with which the data indicate a divergence in attitudes between deferentials and pragmatists suggests that the line chosen to divide the Conservative voters into two groups is indeed a significant, if not the most significant, one. When mention is made of the Conservative voters or the Tories the reference is to the deferential and pragmatist groups taken together. The Labour supporters are considered as one group throughout the study.

A hereditary peerage and a public school education (preferably Eton) are two signal marks of high social rank in England. They were therefore incorporated into the two questions used to separate the deferentials from the pragmatists. At the same time these two questions generated the data for the delineation of the respondents' attitudes towards the relationship between social rank and political leadership. The respondents were first asked which of two men having equal abilities and experience, and leaving party connections aside,[1] would

[1] It could be argued that the backgrounds of the two men make it perfectly

make a better Prime Minister: the man whose father was a member of the House of Lords, or the one whose father was a file-clerk in one of the ministries. A second question was asked, in the same form as the first, in which the respondents were asked to choose between a man who had gone to Eton and one who had attended an excellent grammar school.[1] The deferential group is then operationally defined as those respondents who said that they preferred *both* the peer's son over the clerk's son and the Old Etonian over the grammar school man as a Prime Minister. Of the 320 Tories in our sample, 28 per cent are grouped together as deferentials. The pragmatists' responses on

clear with which party they are associated, and the respondents might thus suspect that they were indirectly being asked which party they support or how strongly they feel themselves attached to their party. However, since half-a-dozen preceding questions in the interview schedule already elicited their party attachments, the possibility of the responses being skewed in the direction of the upper-class leaders for the Conservative supporters and in the opposite direction for the Labour voters is thereby minimized.

[1] The exact wording of these two questions is as follows: 'In the next set of questions I shall be asking you to choose between two candidates. In doing so completely forget about the parties of the candidates—their party connections should not influence your choice at all. Suppose there was an election which would decide which of two candidates would become the next Prime Minister. They are both equally good men, making it very difficult to choose between them either on the basis of experience or ability. Both of them seem to be excellent candidates. Yet the father of one of them was a member of the House of Lords, while the other's father was a file-clerk in one of the ministries. Do you think that the peer's son or the clerk's son would make a better Prime Minister? Why do you say this?

'Suppose now that there are two other men, one of them went to an excellent grammar school, while the other went to Eton. Which of the two men would make a better Prime Minister, the man who went to a very good grammar school or the man who went to Eton? Why do you say this?'

The structure of this question—asking the respondents to choose between two men—is borrowed from an item used by Robert T. McKenzie and Allan Silver in a paper entitled 'Conservatism, Industrialism and the Working-Class Tory in England', presented to the Fifth World Congress of the International Sociological Association, September 1962. McKenzie and Silver combined three attributes of the two men into one question—their father's status, their educational background and their positions in the Army. Here it was thought best to break this question down into two parts in order to allow the respondents to state their preferences for a particular type of governmental leader on the basis of status and educational criteria independently of each other. The fact that a sizeable proportion of pragmatists preferred the peer's son but not the Eton man, and vice versa, indicates that these two attributes are evaluated differently by many workers. The question was also broken down into two parts in order to provide two independent measures with which to define the deferential group, thereby providing a more meaningful operational definition for this group of workers.

3

these two questions could entail any combination of preferences for the peer's son, the Eton man (but not these two together), the clerk's son, the grammar school product, or such statements as 'both men are equally good' or 'it depends on other things than where they had their schooling'. Among the Labour supporters 13 per cent could be classified as deferentials, having selected both the peer's son and the Eton man as the preferable political leaders. Unfortunately this group is statistically too small in the present sample to allow for its separate treatment.

I. THE BASES OF POLITICAL LEADERSHIP

The data in Table 1 indicate that twice as many Conservative manual workers (41 per cent) prefer to be led by a peer than do Labour working-class people (20 per cent). Similarly, twice as many Tories (48 per cent) as Labour supporters (26 per cent) would like to have an Old Etonian at the head of Government. The fact that such a large proportion of Conservatives and a considerable proportion of Labour working-class men choose to have an aristocrat to lead them, when their way of life is so acutely different from that of the aristocracy that the latter cannot even serve as a reference group (imparting standards of behaviour) for the workers, when the workers are living in urban areas where the traditional social structure has always been less pervasive than in the rural areas, when their economic interests are often in conflict with those of the property-owning aristocracy, and when they are thereby implicitly relegating themselves to a position of political followership in a democratic age—when despite all these factors so many workers can still desire to be led by a peer, the importance attached to high status in the English political system is forcefully underscored.[1]

The workers' adherence to deferential attitudes are further underlined when it is noted that these attitudes are only being slightly eroded during an historical period characterized by egalitarianism, mass democracy, and further industrialization. It might have been expected that the proportion of deferentials among the older workers whose political attitudes were formed when English politics were more 'traditional' than they now are would be much larger than the

---

[1] Presumably if women were included in the sample the proportion of respondents choosing governmental leaders with eminent social positions would be somewhat larger. Alse see Bagehot, p. 83, op. cit.

TABLE I

Preferences for different types of political leaders

The Peer's Son v. The Clerk's Son

	Tories	Defs.	Prags.	Labs.
Peer's son	41	100	17	20
Clerk's son	25	0	35	47
Both equally good	23	0	32	21
Depends on other things	9	0	13	8
DK	2	0	3	3
Total per cent	100	100	100	100
Total number	320	90	230	127

The Eton Man v. The Grammar School Man

	Tories	Defs.	Prags.	Labs.
Eton man	48	100	28	26
Grammar school man	22	0	30	44
Both equally good	22	0	30	18
Depends on other things	7	0	10	5
DK	2	0	2	7
Total per cent	100	100	100	100
Total number	320	90	230	127

proportion of deferentials among the younger workers. However, the data in Table 2 indicate only small differences here. Whereas 21 per cent of the workers aged sixty and over are deferentials—preferring both the peer's son and the Old Etonian as governmental leaders—the proportion drops only slightly, to 16 per cent, among the youngest workers. Curiously enough, the Conservative and Labour voters manifest two almost contradictory generational patterns. Within the Tory group the highest proportion of deferentials is found in the thirty to forty-five year old age group, the proportion then declining among the older workers. These data indicate that the Conservatives' deferential outlook is not withering away over time—if anything, the data suggest just the opposite. In contrast, the generational differences among the Labour voters point to a decline in the number of deferentials among the younger and middle-aged workers. Apparently, the same historical events and similar alterations in the social structure, the economy, and the educational system are having almost the reverse impact upon the deferential attitudes of the Tory and Labour supporters.

TABLE 2

The proportion of deferentials according to age[1]

	21–29	30–45	46–59	60+
Among the Tories	18	43	28	21
	(28)	(80)	(98)	(114)
Among Labour supporters	14	8	15	21
	(7)	(52)	(39)	(29)
Among both Tories and Labour supporters[2]	16	15	20	21
	(35)	(132)	(137)	(143)

Having noted the high esteem in which socially eminent political leaders are held, we can turn to a discussion of the beliefs and evaluations which underly the perceived confluence between high birth and leadership abilities.

Traditionally, deference was offered to aristocrats on the basis of their upbringing which was thought to develop the personal qualities needed for political leadership and the exercise of governmental authority. When the workers in our sample were asked why they chose the peer's son as the preferable Prime Minister, this belief in the existence of an aristocratic training ground for governmental leadership continues to be one of the most frequent replies among both the Conservative and Labour supporters (see Table 3). Fully 67 per cent of the Tories and 39 per cent of those pro-Labour replied with such typical responses as 'He (the peer's son) has been taught to lead'; 'He has been brought up to it (i.e. governmental leadership) by his father'; 'It has been drummed into him from his early days'; 'Background always counts'; 'He has been brought up in the proper atmosphere'.

[1] The numbers in parentheses refer to the total N's.
[2] The number of Labour supporters have been multiplied by five according to the weighting index. The total N's, however, refer to the actual number of respondents.

In the second wave of interviews the workers were also asked about

TABLE 3

Reasons for prefering the peer's son as a political leader

	Tories	Defs.	Prags.	Labs.
Better education	48	41	64	42
Upbringing	67	67	67	38
Social connections	15	19	5	15
Wider experience	12	9	21	38
Greater intelligence	4	5	0	4
Other	4	0	0	4
DK	4	5	0	0
Total per cent	134	145	137	139
Total number of responses	193	132	61	37
Total number of respondents	129	90	39	26

their attitudes toward governmental leaders with differing social backgrounds: 'Thinking now of the different backgrounds the politicians come from, how do you feel a man from an aristocratic, very upper-class background, compares with a man from a more usual working-class background when it comes to taking positions of leadership in the government?' Again, the main theme struck by those workers who desire upper-class leaders is the belief that such men are trained to govern. In the words of one deferential, an unskilled worker in a Coventry motor car factory, 'The aristocratic man is more capable of taking leadership because this is something he has been trained for all his life and this is something he has been doing all his life. The man from the working-class background is still fighting his way up—he is too concerned in his own progress to make a really good leader. He can't give leadership his full attention. He is not used to it, and can't get people to do what he wants'. Another deferential, a twenty-one-year-old electronics apprentice from East London, echoed this last remark: 'Unless the working-class man is unusually gifted, and there have been such men, he doesn't command the respect that the aristocratic man does. Politics is in their blood so it comes more naturally.'

A somewhat different note is found in the comments of a retired engineer in the Royal Navy who is now living in Epsom, Surrey.

His deferential attitude is founded upon the belief that 'The aristocrat is best fitted to lead. The two men think on different levels. The
aristocrat has the knowledge. Moving socially among international
politicans the working man may never feel at ease. The aristocrat is
at ease on level terms with the others so he can concentrate on the job
in hand. They can't sway him with promises of wealth and power
since he already has it. A thing like that could be the downfall of a
working-class background man who's worked himself up from nothing.'
In all three interviews there is not only an appreciation of the peer's
son's special training, there is also a belief that a man with a working-
class background, even though he may be 'unusually gifted', would
not be able to exercise governmental leadership—he would continue to
promote himself, or possibly succumb to flattery and bribery, and even if
he were able to overcome these temptations, it is unlikely that he would
be accorded the respect needed for the proper exercise of authority.

Another set of replies to be noted in Table 2 are those referring to
the peer's son's wider experience with 'high class affairs', money
matters and foreign countries. There is a linear progression in the
proportion of workers mentioning this factor as one moves from the
deferentials (9 per cent), to the pragmatists (21 per cent), to the
Labour supporters (38 per cent). These workers are in effect suggesting
that the leadership qualities of the peer's son are not acquired through
his special training, either within the family or the school; rather, they
are a product of the wide-ranging opportunities open to aristocrats
allowing them to acquire a knowledge of those matters that are relevant for the exercise of governmental authority. The same point can
also be made about an unexpected set of explanations for the workers'
choice of the peer's son falling under the heading of social connections.
Some examples of these responses are: 'He (the peer's son) has more
contacts with higher ups'; 'If in doubt he can get advice from his father
and his friends'; 'The right people are behind him when he needs
advice or is in doubt'; 'He can get advice and help from top people'.
Among both the Conservative and Labour voters 15 per cent provided
this type of explanation for their choice of the peer's son. These
workers apparently believe that political leaders must frequently rely
upon others for advice and support, and that the best advice and the
most effective support comes from 'top people'—people whom the
peer's son is free to call on.

The passing of the 1944 Butler Education Act signalled the beginnings of important changes in the English social structure, and to a lesser extent, in the social origins of political and governmental leaders. Men with high social rank no longer have a monopoly on high office; there is competition from the first generation who have passed through the rejuvenated grammar schools and Oxbridge on government grants. Notwithstanding these first stirrings of change in governmental recruitment patterns, the structure of authority has almost entirely maintained its hierarchical form. In fact, Rose has speculated that the support for hierarchical and deferential attitudes may be increasing 'in so far as inequalities are now thought to represent fairly assessed intellectual differences'.[1] For an adequate test of Rose's hypothesis our data would need to be more extensive and intensive. Yet the striking amount of deference paid to the peer's son because of his presumed educational attainments—48 per cent of the Tories and 42 per cent of the Labour voters explained their choice of the peer's son on this basis—lends support to the argument by at least providing evidence underlining the significance now attached to education as a highly regarded attribute of leaders[2]—even aristocratic leaders.

The reasons provided by the respondents for explaining their choice of the Old Etonian over the grammar school product permit a more detailed analysis of the educational factor. A public school education is usually thought to confer two quite different types of training upon future leaders. There is the strictly intellectual training designed to develop the ability to handle any type of problem to be encountered in later life. Secondly, there is the training designed to develop the boys' leadership qualities—the ability to take command and the attainment of the Christian gentleman's virtues.[3] Traditionally, and

---

[1] Richard Rose, *Politics in England*, op. cit., p. 40. Elsewhere Rose has pointed out that 'Deference to educational achievement has supplemented but not entirely supplanted the traditional deference to social status and wealth'. See 'England: A Traditionally Modern Political Culture', in Pye and Verba, op. cit., p. 94.

[2] According to Mark Abrams, the parties are aware of this trend: 'Because housing, education, roads, industrial efficiency, etc., are the central issues of the propaganda battle, each party must prove that it alone has the skill, brains, competence, talent to carry out the programme effectively . . . Since the uncommitted voter has very little evidence on which to assess a political party's claims to technological efficiency, a long roster of professional names stands a good chance of serving as a substitute for evidence.' See 'Party Politics After the End of Ideology', in Allardt and Littunen, op. cit., p. 60.

[3] A third latent function of public school training in this connection is the acquisition of the elite's social *accoutrements*, thereby maintaining the elite's

perhaps until just the recent past, the training received at public school for the development of leadership abilities has been considered the schools' most important function. Intellectual training, where it did not degenerate into learning by rote memorization or where intellectual excellence was disparaged, was relegated to a secondary place.[1] To a large extent this is still applicable to the public schools today, especially to those schools which depend upon the reflected prestige of their more illustrious counterparts. However, as England is undergoing the alien, uncomfortable and somewhat disorderly process of having to adjust to her new status as a second-class power while meeting strenuous economic competition from abroad, the public schools are beginning to respond with a new devotion to intellectual, and even scientific excellence.[2]

In examining Table 4 it is seen that a related attitudinal change is taking place within the working class. When asked their reasons for selecting the Eton man over the grammar school product, by far the most frequent responses offered by the pragmatists (65 per cent) and those pro-Labour (67 per cent) refer to the better education to be had at Eton than that offered at an excellent grammar school—

---

homogeneity and the smooth functioning of intra-elite relations. By imparting to the system's products a particular manner of speech and social behaviour which cannot be readily acquired elsewhere, all but a few non-public school aspirants for elite positions are prevented from succeeding in their quest and the elite's *mystique* is protected by an outer veil of sharply delineated social mannerisms. In this latter connection it is interesting to speculate to what degree public school products feel that they have a responsibility never to let another public school man show himself to be a failure, for otherwise the non-elite would presumably lose much of its respect for the elite were too many of its members seen to be incompetent. In *Decline and Fall* Evelyn Waugh presents a caricatured illustration of this phenomenon in the person of the amoral Captain Grimes who manages to find a new teaching job after each of his failures, simply because of his public school credentials. Simon Raven tells of a comparable incident in his autobiographical *The English Gentleman*. His fellow public school officers succeeded in getting him an Army discharge before his gambling debts could cause him to be court martialled. Also see note 1, p. 95 below

[1] Glickman has rightly pointed out that the Tory defence of the public schools is largely based on the belief that 'leadership needs character more than brains', op. cit., p. 122.

[2] The boys themselves tend to recognize this development, even though some react against it. For example, there is the leader column of the *Eton College Chronicle*, June 24, 1966, which states: 'There is the side of an education which trains the mind, and the side which trains the character. Most schools in this world of exams and grades now appear to be concentrating more and more on the training of the mind. Unfortunately Eton is following in the general trend.'

for example, 'he has learned more at Eton', 'public school education is the best', 'it's a higher education'. Even among the traditionally oriented deferentials the largest proportion of workers mentioned the 'higher' education received at the public schools, thereby underlining the newly recognized importance of intellectual training as an essential attribute of governmental leaders. At the same time, the non-intellectual training received at Eton continues to be an important factor leading the workers to prefer the leadership of a public school product, with 58 per cent of the deferentials, 36 per cent of the pragmatists and 30 per cent of the Labour voters giving this as their reason. Here are found such comments as: 'Eton trains men to their duty'; 'The upbringing at Eton teaches them to be leaders'; 'The public schools train prime ministers'; 'They are educated to take the lead'.

TABLE 4

Reasons for prefering the Eton man as a political leader

	Tories	Defs.	Prags.	Labs.
Better education	54	47	65	67
Training at Eton	49	58	36	30
Social connections	12	18	5	3
Greater intelligence	5	4	5	9
Other	3	1	6	3
DK	0	0	0	0
Total per cent	123	128	117	112
Total number of responses	190	115	75	37
Total number of respondents	155	90	65	33

In the second wave of interviews both types of responses can be viewed in greater detail. In order to get a fuller picture of the workers' attitudes towards the public schools, the informants were first asked the broad question, 'How do you feel about public school education and the type of men who have been to a public school?' This was followed by a somewhat more specific question: 'How do you think politicians who have been to public school compare with those who have been to, say, a good grammar school?' A deferential Tory from Manchester expressed his admiration for the public schools with a good deal of certitude: 'Well, I think those places are very good. In every way they've got the brains. They're born with them and brought up in the right atmosphere'. When asked to compare politicians with public school backgrounds with non-public school politicians, this lorry driver replied that 'I don't think they do compare. Take Ernest Bevin for instance, who actually boasted of being a miner. How would he argue foreign affairs? What qualifications had he? They don't compare. You can pick them and every time the public school ones are streets above the others in every way.'

When asked to state his feelings toward the public schools, the deferential car worker from Coventry replied in a forthright manner: 'I think it is the finest thing that can happen to a man to have a public school education. It not only gives him book learning, it teaches him to work with and get on with his fellow men. It gives him a broader outlook on life. I think he is trained to be a leader and if he has it in him he will make a good leader. It makes him an honest, hard working, deep thinking man. I am all for it. I wish more boys could have the chance. They get something that no one can ever take away from them . . .' Referring specifically to politicians who have had a public school education, 'I think [such] men are better able to move in diplomatic circles and are not as worried by money and earning a living because he has usually come from a wealthy family. The education of these men is wider, they have a broader outlook. The man who went to grammar school will have the book learning, but he has lived a narrower life and hasn't got the family background.'

Without even being asked to relate a public school education to political leadership, the retired naval engineer expressed his admiration for these schools 'because they've produced the best men we've ever had. Times may be changing, but going back twenty or thirty years ago, they certainly produced the leaders—lots of statesmen, leading figures in the world, all from public schools. They're trained in leadership as were their fathers and grandfathers . . . so they must be the best type of men . . . After all, it's the purpose of the public schools to breed that leadership into them.'

The deferentials are thus seen to be the most tradition-oriented of the three groups by definition, having originally been grouped together on the basis of their desire for upper-class leaders. In comparison, the pragmatists have largely rejected the traditional political orientation. In a fundamental sense they ought to be viewed as the most 'modern' or 'contemporary' of the three groups. The achievement norm—the norm by which evaluations of others are made *solely* on the basis of their abilities and accomplishments—is commonly taken as the chief hallmark of modern societies. In our sample those who hold to this norm are the workers who, when asked to choose between two leaders with markedly divergent status positions, disregarded the available alternatives. Instead, they responded either that both are equally good men since they are equal in ability and experience according to the question's premises, or that their choice is dependent upon factors unrelated to the two leaders' family backgrounds and schooling. Some examples of these achievement-oriented responses are: 'I should not be influenced by what kind of fathers they had'; 'If they are clever enough, the school they went to doesn't make any difference'; 'If they've both got the same qualifications that's all that counts—it doesn't matter about the father or the school.'

Turning back to Table 1, it is seen that the pragmatists most frequently provided achievement-oriented responses: 45 per cent replied that both men are equally good, or that it depends on factors other than status, when asked to choose between the peer's son versus the clerk's son, and 40 per cent replied in this way when asked to choose between the Eton man and the grammar school product. In comparison, 29 per cent and 23 per cent of the Labour supporters disregarded the two questions' premises by offering achievement-oriented responses.

Although the pragmatists are largely achievement-oriented in their preference for different types of leaders, they also manifest a good deal of respect for political leaders with high status. Not only do 17 per cent and 28 per cent prefer to be led by the peer's son and the old Etonian respectively, the pragmatists' remarks during the open-ended interviews suggest that in some cases they adhere to a set of ambivalent attitudes; they recognize the desirability of having upper-class leaders, yet they believe that leaders ought to be chosen on the basis of their demonstrated abilities. And on the basis of this normative belief they are sometimes willing to criticize certain aspects of the public schools and the social stratification system.[1]

Most of the themes mentioned by the pragmatist group in their evaluation of different types of leaders are found in a second-wave

---

[1] It must be pointed out that the interpretation of the pragmatists presented in this paragraph is based primarily on the second-wave interviews. It would therefore be extremely hazardous to attempt to estimate the proportion of pragmatists to whom this interpretation is applicable.

interview with a foreman in a Birmingham electronics plant. This worker began his remarks by saying that 'I feel very happy about [the public schools]. I'd like to feel I could afford to send my child to one of them. It is the finest academic training a man can have, but not all the finest technical training. I think the biggest percentage of public school men turn out to be leaders of their professions. I also think that the few who take the wrong turn also turn out to be the biggest rogues. Either way they do well. You only have to look at a man and you can tell he's been to public school. He stands out—his dress, attitude to people and his speech.' He then went on to praise the 'eloquence of speech' and 'diplomacy' of public school politicians, which accounts for the fact that they are excellent diplomats, while the grammar school product might 'possibly fall flat on his face' as a diplomat. 'A public school (also) teaches a boy to be forceful; part of their training is to teach a boy to say what he wants to say and how. The public school teaches them a certain snobbery which, God help him, the working man respects.' But notwithstanding all the praise which this pragmatist has for the public schools, he concluded that 'the position of leadership should go to the best man regardless of schooling. If he is capable he will prove his status in the position he is holding.' And when asked to evaluate politicians according to their various social backgrounds this electronics worker replied: 'I don't think background has any bearing on leadership. It only has bearing on social position. Leadership is not made; it is born in a person of course. Two examples are Macmillan and Home. Both have the same background and so forth, but Macmillan could lead, and I don't think Home will ever be able to. Wilson can lead. I believe he's the best dramatist in politics . . .'

An equally strong adherence to the achievement norm is found in the comments of a pragmatist from Putney who works as a charge-hand in a tyre factory, although in this instance there is not any recognition of the value of a public school education in the formation of leadership qualities. He continuously distinguishes between boys who have been admitted to a public school because of their abilities and those whose fathers have bought their places. 'A public school boy, you often read in the paper is often a moron, and another brilliant. One has bought his way in and the other has earned his way . . . Almost the same thing applies [to politicians]. You can have a dud politician who's been through public school or grammar school, or a brilliant politician who has been to either . . . You hear that he has been to such and such a school, but you never hear what degree he's got. You just hear that he has been to Eton and Cambridge.' And when comparing politicians with differing social backgrounds, this respondent maintains his adherence to the achievement norm. 'When you have a son of a lord it doesn't mean to say he's going to be more brilliant than the son of a miner. There again it's the brains of the individual. If he's got the brains he's got the ability to get through . . . If a father was a big business man and put his son in as managing director, and you get a chap who works his way up—that's the chap I'd choose out of the two.'

TABLE 5

Reasons for prefering the clerk's son as a political leader

	Prags.	Labs.
In touch with ordinary people	64	70
Achievement	28	20
Anti-aristocracy	0	7
Other	9	7
DK	3	0
Total per cent	104	104
Total number of responses	82	62
Total number of respondents	80	60

In this latter instance, as in the case of a self-employed painter from Birmingham, the achievement norm is present, but in applying it these two workers express a preference for the man with a working-class background because it is assumed that he attained his position by merit compared to the other man who 'was born with a silver spoon in his mouth'. When asked to choose between the two men, the painter replied, 'I should say the man that's been to grammar school or that has had to use his brains to get there, and not just his father's money. The man who went to grammar school is the man who's gained it by merit.' Slightly more than a quarter of the prag-matists who opted for the clerk's son and the grammar school man did so for just this reason, believing that these two men gained their positions through their own achievements. (See Tables 5 and 6.)

Lastly, we might look at the remarks of a pragmatist who prefers public school leaders, but who is not willing to defer to upper-class

TABLE 6

Reasons for preferring the grammar school man as a political leader

	Prags.	Labs.
In touch with ordinary people	46	46
Achievement	29	34
Anti-Eton	0	14
Greater intelligence	4	4
Give him a chance	4	2
Other	16	5
DK	0	0
	—	—
Total per cent	100	105
Total number of responses	69	59
Total number of respondents	69	56

people simply because of their background. This respondent is now a pastry cook in Fulham, having previously worked as a cook at the Institute for Directors. According to him 'a man who has been to public school has more extensive and better chances to give guidance to manage things better. He has more confidence because of the very nature of public school activities. I like all the public schools stand for—the kind of life they live apart from the educational aspect.' Yet at the same time this informant did not hesitate in voicing his disapproval of 'the attitude that some ex-public school men have later on . . . Usually (these men) continue with the impression, because they've been to these schools, this entitles them to special consideration. I don't subscribe that they go around riding roughshod over everyone . . .' Referring to politicians having different educational backgrounds, 'I don't think it should be just a blind choice of the ex-public school boy to be the leader. But they generally are the leaders. All things being equal, they are probably better fitted to leadership because of their life in the public school.' Regarding 'people who come from wealthy families', these are also thought to be 'better suited to leadership. But there are exceptions of those who lose their warmth and humanity—those who lose touch with the ordinary men. Then they are not the right people for leadership. Gaitskell was much more fitted for leadership than Harold Wilson is. He was a much warmer, kinder, man. On the other side, Mr Macmillan and Sir

Winston Churchill are much more fitted for leadership than Sir Alec or Mr Eden. They both are most likely brilliant men, but so remote, without the warmth needed to be leaders of the country.'

Having characterized the deferentials as tradition oriented and the pragmatists as primarily achievement oriented, how characterize the Labour voters? Another glance at Table 1 shows that by far the largest proportion of them believe the clerk's son and the grammar school man to be the better governmental leaders. In both questions the Labour supporters selected these men almost twice as often as the upper-class leaders or the achievement norm. There is thus a marked tendency for the Labour voters to want men of similar origins to their own as governmental leaders, making it possible to speak of the Labour group's class orientation in this respect.

Further evidence in support of this interpretation is found in Table 5, where it is seen that fully 70 per cent of the Labour voters who prefer the clerk's son to the peer's son accounted for their choice with the remark that the clerk's son is in touch with ordinary people. Here are found such remarks as: 'He (the clerk's son) is more down to earth and in touch with the people'; 'He would have more understanding of my way of life'; 'He has tasted the rough side of life'; 'He has seen how working-class people live'; 'The peer's son doesn't understand other types of people.' In explaining their selection of the grammar school man the proportion of them referring to his contact with people like themselves drops to 46 per cent, but it remains the most frequent explanation of their choice of the grammar school product (see Table 6). And in the case of not a few Labour respondents, a significant number of responses classified under the achievement heading simultaneously imply a class orientation. Such remarks as 'He [the grammar school man] has done well', 'He is a self-made man', 'He starts from a more difficult position', all indicate a belief that the grammar school product will make a good Prime Minister because of his achievements. Yet at the same time such comments suggest that the respondents are proud that a man fit to be Prime Minister has arisen from a working-class background similar to their own.

One expression of the desire for leaders with a working-class background is found in the remarks of a Labour shop steward in London's Royal Arsenal. When asked to evaluate politicians with markedly divergent class backgrounds he registered a preference for men with working-class origins because they are 'more practical; they are more experienced in the way of life. The other man is more or less brought up with a silver spoon in his mouth. He's soft. I think you've got to rough it and know what you are up against. The aristocrat hasn't roughed it'.

In a reading of both the first and second wave interviews it is possible to detect a mixture of negative and positive attitudes towards men with upper-class backgrounds among individual Labour voters. They are at once expressing the concern of many people in their class with the perceived inequities of the social stratification system, while paying tribute to the predominant aristocratic and upper-class elements in the English political tradition. This confluence is exhibited by a Labour voter from Manchester, working as a machinery inspector for the Coal Board. According to him, the public schools have 'been a thorn in the side of the country for some time ... I think the person who has been to a public school is smiled on by a section of the community more than a person who's been to an ordinary school. When it comes to getting jobs, particularly on a good level, the public school boy has a better chance. It's not a good thing. I don't like this ... Someone who's been to public school gets the leader position [in government]. In this country in past generations politicians haven't come from the man in the street. They've been the aristocracy; they've been pushed on. Two men for the same post, and the public school man gets it. I don't think it's right, but it's happening all the time.' While criticizing the absence of open competition in English society due to the preferential treatment accorded the upper class, this Labour voter thinks that 'the aristocratic man is perhaps more equipped to represent people (than the man from a working-class family) by virtue of the fact of his background. His ancestors have ruled people. It's passed on; he inherits that quality. The other chappie gets on by perseverance, [but] this isn't always good enough. I'm talking contrary to my political convictions, but I do think that this is the case.'

This simultaneous adherence to, and divergence from, a major dimension of the English political culture is also apparent in the remarks of a Labour voter from Epsom who works as a post office sorter. 'In most of the public schools the fathers have been there and they say "I want my son to go there". They consider it important because they do get a better education. Later on, a man who has knowledge doesn't get the job by a board appointing him because he hasn't been to public school. They go on to look for someone

who's been to their school or one similar, even if he hasn't the knowledge of the other one. They have an old boys' association to help
each other into the best jobs. All the same, I think the public school
has more grounds for educating them for politics. All the grammar
schools are interested in is to get you to pass your G.C.E. . . . They
don't bother about politics.' This informant then went on to say that
'the aristocrat has been brought up to be a leader. Then again he
might not have it in him to take this position. A lot of aristocrats
are in business . . . dealing with ordinary people all the time. They
are bred and educated to lead (and) they know how to handle their
men that work for them as well as people on their own level. On the
other hand, the men who come into government through the trade
unions [also] have to know how to handle people at all levels—bosses
as well as the union members.'

The unmistakable conclusion which emerges from the discussion
up to this point is that the marked upper class and aristocratic strains
in the English political culture are strongly infused in the working-
class political culture. This conclusion is true by definition when applied
to the deferentials. It is also applicable, though certainly to a lesser
extent, to the pragmatists and Labour supporters. Not only do a
significant proportion of these two groups prefer to have men with
high status as political leaders. Even among those workers who subscribe to an achievement or class orientation, and who consequently
are prone to be critical of various aspects of the social stratification
system, there is a hardy respect and admiration for high born, well
bred and exclusively educated men as political leaders. At the same time,
it ought to be recalled that the workers who prefer leaders with high
status justify their preferences not with the assertion that such men
have a special claim to positions of authority, perhaps because they
have always held such positions;[1] rather, preferences for such leaders
are justified on the grounds of their presumed abilities, having acquired
these abilities through the particular experiences and opportunities
available to the upper classes.

---

[1] Compare R. C. K. Ensor's characterization of the two Tory leaders (Balfour
and Lansdowne) in the Edwardian period: 'They belonged to, they led in, and
they felt themselves charged with, the fortunes of a small privileged class; which
for centuries had exercised a sort of collective kingship, and at the bottom of its
thinking instinctively believed that it had a *divine right* to do so.' *England:
1870–1914*: 1936, pp. 387–388, italics added.

II. INDEPENDENT GOVERNMENTAL AUTHORITY

After analysing the working class attitudes towards the incumbents of governmental positions, the next area to be considered is the respondents' attitudes towards the authority of these incumbents. Authority adheres to a group or an institution when its actions are accepted by others in an unquestioning manner, sometimes entailing a suspension of one's own judgement and the abnegation of one's own interests. The presence of any form of persuasion, incentives, or coercion indicates that authority is not being completely respected.[1] In this sense of the term a signal measure of authority has been conferred upon British Governments. Indeed, as already noted in the introductory chapter, one of the most characteristic elements of the country's political culture is the wide scope of independent action allowed to the governmental elite. With respect to the working class, we want to be able to gauge the extent to which their orientations towards authority conform to the modal patterns of English political culture. Specifically, we are interested in the scope of independent action they allow governmental leaders, and the manner in which that authority is legitimized.

However, before proceeding in this direction it will be useful to distinguish between two broad types of authority according to the attitudes by which they are legitimized. Procedural norms legitimize governmental authority when its actions are thought to conform to the country's 'constitution'—the written rules or unwritten norms defining the manner in which decisions are taken and executed. Authority can also be legitimized on a personal (or non-institutionalized) basis when there is a strongly anchored confidence in the persons who are responsible for a Government's decisions; the governmental leaders are thought to be particularly capable, thereby inducing the non-elite to sanction independent action on their part.[2] In order to tap these attitudes towards governmental authority in the working-class political culture the respondents were presented with two situations. In one a Conservative, and in the other a Labour Government, were said to favour a policy thought by them to be for the good of the country;

[1] For a different definitional approach to the problem of authority, see Peter M. Blau, 'Some Critical Remarks on Weber's Theory of Authority', *American Political Science Review*, June 1963.

[2] The terminology employed here is an adaptation of Herbert J. Spiro's distinction between procedural and substantive authority. *Government by Constitution*: 1959, pp. 372–373.

yet a majority of the electorate does not agree with the Government's position. The respondents were then asked whether or not the Conservative and Labour Governments should carry out their policy, and their reasons for saying so.[1] Legitimization of Government action by procedural norms is then measured by the question in which the respondents are asked whether they approve or disapprove of action

TABLE 7

Approval or disapproval of independent Government action when taken by the workers' 'Own' Party or the 'Opposition' Party

| | The 'Opposition' Party Government | | | |
	Tories	Defs.	Prags.	Labs.
Approve	44	44	44	51
Disapprove	49	51	49	40
Depends	3	0	5	3
DK	3	5	2	6
Total per cent	100	100	100	100
Total number	320	90	230	127

| | One's 'Own' Party Government | | | |
	Tories	Defs.	Prags.	Labs.
Approve	64	81	58	71
Disapprove	31	19	36	25
Depends	3	0	5	2
DK	1	0	1	2
Total per cent	100	100	100	100
Total number	320	90	230	127

[1] These two questions appeared in the interview schedule in the following form: 'Let us say a certain issue arose, like raising taxes, on which a Labour Government had one opinion and the majority of the people had another opinion. The Labour Government thought it was doing the best thing for the country, even though most people did not think so. If this were to happen, do you feel that the Labour Government should go ahead with its policies? Why do you say this?'

'And how do you feel were a similar situation to arise under a Conservative Government. Should the Conservative Government go ahead with its policies which it believes to be for the good of the country even though the majority of the people do not agree with them? Why do you say this?'

in the face of majority opinion by the '*opposition*' Government—the Government staffed by the party which the respondents oppose.

In Table 7 the manual workers' recognition of the Government's procedural authority is seen in the following figures: 44 per cent of both the deferentials and the pragmatists think that a Labour Government should act as it sees fit even when its policy is opposed by a majority of the electorate, while 51 per cent of the Labour group exhibits the same reaction regarding a Tory Government. Thus in defining the procedural norms allowing for or circumscribing the Government's sphere of independent authority, nearly half the working class sanctions a wide sphere of Government authority to be used on its own initiative and responsibility—at least until the next General Election. Explicit support for this interpretation comes from the responses given to the second half of the question regarding the reasons for approving or disapproving of the Government's independent action. Of those respondents approving of an 'opposition' Government acting contrary to the majority's wishes, 90 per cent of the deferentials and pragmatists and 89 per cent of the Labour supporters gave as their reason some variation on the theme of Government leadership (see Table 8). The responses grouped together under this heading— e.g. 'The Government should do what it thinks right', 'We put them in power to get on with the job', 'The Government is there to lead'— are all expressions of the adherence to the procedural norm allowing the Government wide-ranging authority.

These data can be viewed as a striking confirmation of the hierarchical structure of the political system. Almost one-half of the working class sees fit to approve of a Government to which they are opposed acting contrary to the majority's wishes—a majority presumably constituted primarily by people with the respondents' own partisan attachments. And in such a situation as was hypothetically posed in the question, it is actually more than probable that the Government *would* act in the face of the electorate's wishes. Moreover, notwithstanding the Labour Party's 'democratic' ideology emphasizing popular control over the incumbents of authority positions, its working-class supporters are as willing as the Conservatives to permit an 'opposition' Government to act contrary to the voters' desires. The Labour supporters' attachment to the hierarchical strain in the English political culture in the face of their party's egalitarian and 'democratic' ideology is a recurring theme in this study.

TABLE 8

Reasons for approving of independent Government action when taken by the workers' 'Own' Party or the 'Opposition' Party

	Tories	Defs.	Prags.	Labs.
The 'Opposition' Party				
The Government should				
lead	90	90	90	89
Abilities of party leaders	2	0	3	2
Distrust the majority	8	8	8	5
Other, DK	3	5	3	5
Total per cent	103	103	104	101
Total number	141	40	101	65
One's 'Own' Party				
The Government should				
lead	60	52	64	82
Abilities of party leaders	35	44	31	15
Distrust the majority	5	3	7	3
Other, DK	4	7	3	2
Total per cent	104	106	105	102
Total number	206	73	135	90

When the workers' attitudes towards the scope of procedural authority are related to age, we find a further indication of both the Conservative and Labour voters' strong adherence to a wide definition of this authority. Instead of decreasing among the younger aged groups as might have been expected, the proportion of workers willing to allow the Government independent authority is inversely related to age (see Table 9). The age differences are especially marked within the Conservative group: 32 per cent of the oldest workers approve of an 'opposition' Government acting contrary to a majority in the electorate, with this proportion linearly increasing until it reaches 71 per cent amongst the youngest Tories. There is also a linear relationship in the case of Labour supporters, yet the percentage differences are far smaller. Although no explanation for the Tory-Labour differences of degree comes to mind, it is possible to suggest a sketchy interpretation for the correlation between age and attitudes towards governmental authority. It may be that the new economic responsibilities that the Government has taken up since 1945 have led the workers to conceive of the decision-making process as a highly involved affair requiring abilities, training and knowledge which only the political and administrative elites possess. As these economic problems—controlling inflation, planning for expansion, juggling the Sterling accounts—have forced themselves upon government there may have arisen a concomitant reluctance on the part of the workers to attempt to interfere with, and perhaps even to understand, governmental decisions. To a lesser extent, the same type of argument could also be made for defence and foreign policy; i.e. the newly arrived importance of future planning—strategic and scientific—in an age of instant war, has perhaps made the workers additionally reluctant to see themselves as competent enough to question governmental decisions.

TABLE 9

Attitudes towards independent Governmental authority according to age

	Tories				Labour			
	21–29	30–45	46–59	60+	21–29	30–45	46–59	60+
Approve	71	55	44	32	57	56	49	45
Disapprove	25	40	48	54	43	35	44	45
Depends	0	1	6	3	0	4	3	3
DK	4	4	2	3	0	6	5	7
Total per cent	100	100	100	100	100	100	100	100
Total number	28	80	98	114	7	52	39	29

In contrast to the workers who accede a broad plain of independent authority to the Government, there are those respondents whose more narrowly defined procedural norms do not allow for independent Government action. How then does this group of workers, constituting approximately half of the working class, explain their reluctance in this regard? For slightly more than 60 per cent of all three groups the Government is thought only to represent, rather than to represent and lead, the nation (see Table 10). Or to present a single statistic,

TABLE 10

Reasons for Disapproving of independent Government action when taken by the workers' 'Own' Party or the 'Opposition' Party

The 'Opposition' Party Government			
	Tories	Defs.	Prags.	Labs.
Majority rule	64	61	65	61
Inabilities of party leaders	25	39	20	6
Party bad for the country	3	0	4	20
Other, DK	8	0	12	16
Total per cent	100	100	101	103
Total number	158	46	112	51

One's 'Own' Party Government			
	Tories	Defs.	Prags.	Labs.
Majority rule	91	94	90	84
Inabilities of party leaders	0	0	0	0
Party bad for the country	0	0	0	0
Other, DK	9	6	10	16
Total per cent	100	100	100	100
Total number	100	17	83	32

in the case of slightly less than one-third of all the workers, their delimitation of the Government's independent sphere of action is summarized in the phrase 'majority rule', which underscores their conception of the Government as a representative institution. Here are found such comments as: 'The Government ought to take notice of what the people say'; 'The majority rules'; 'The Government should do what the country wants'; 'It would be undemocratic [for the Government to act independently]'. In attitudes such as these is found an important restraining element in the country's political culture, reinforcing the elite's responsiveness to the non-elite. It is this cultural pattern which England shares with the other Western democracies, but as was just seen, in the English political culture, these attitudes do not overshadow those allowing the Government to act as an independent, and not simply as a representative, institution. And again, even the ideology of the Labour Party which stresses the representative tradition, has not been able to infuse its working-class supporters with this emphasis; for the Labour supporters do not adhere to the 'majority rule' attitude more frequently than do their Tory counterparts.

There is, however, a significant difference between Conservative and Labour attitudes to be found in their reasons for disapproving of independent action taken by an 'opposition' Government. Of those Tories who would deny independent authority to a Labour Government 25 per cent explained their attitude by pointing to the perceived inabilities of the Labour Party leadership. In contrast, only 6 per cent of the Labour voters took a similar view of the Conservative leadership. Three possible explanations suggest themselves to account for these differing beliefs. It may be that the Conservatives take a more generally hostile or critical view of the Labour Party and its doctrines than does Labour of the Conservative Party. The Tories' greater distrust of the Labour leadership's abilities would then form one dimension of their more negative attitude towards the Labour Party as a whole. However, this explanation is vitiated by the data presented in a later chapter dealing with the workers' partisan attitudes; for there is a balance between the two groups of voters in the frequency with which they express negative beliefs about the 'opposition' parties. A second possible hypothesis refers to the fact that the survey was carried out at a time when a Tory Government had been in office for twelve years. Since the exercise of governmental authority accords the occupants of office additional prestige, this factor might account for the Labour supporters' not questioning the capacities of the Conservative leadership. At the same time, the Tory workers' lack of confidence in the Labour leadership may be attributable to the party's long spell in opposition when it was not able to demonstrate its leadership capacities. A third explanation relies upon that dimension of the English political culture in which governmental leadership capacities tend to be identified with high social status. Given the far higher status of the Tory leaders compared to that of the Labour leadership, this would account for those pro-Labour not questioning the Conservative leaders' abilities, while the Tory workers may believe the Labour leaders to be unqualified because they do not wear the trappings of high status. This interpretation is given further support when we note that the deferentials, who attribute greatest importance to the high status of governmental leaders, are more critical of the Labour leaders than are the pragmatists, who emphasize the leaders' visible achievement attributes.

Returning to the concept of the legitimization of independent governmental authority on personal grounds, the workers who subscribe to this attitude are those who approve of their 'own' Government acting in the face of majority opinion, *and* who give as their reasons an endorsement of confidence in the abilities of such a Government (see Table 8). Here are some typical expressions of confidence in the abilities of the workers 'own' Government: 'They know how to run the country'; 'What they do is for the good of the whole country'; 'They are reliable and don't make mistakes'; 'They can be relied upon because of their experience and training'; 'They are educated so that they will make wise decisions'; 'What they said has proved successful'. When a calculation is made of the number of workers in each of the three groups who would both grant their 'own' Government a wide sphere of independent authority *and* provide such reasons as the foregoing for their predispositions, it is found that 36 per cent of the deferentials, 18 per cent of the pragmatists, and 10 per cent of the Labour voters fall into this category.

The varying proportions of workers in the three groups who are willing to accord their 'own' Government personal authority indicates that they differ in their evaluations of their respective party leaders. The amount of personal confidence which the workers have in the leaders they support is greatest among the deferentials and lowest among the Labour voters, with the pragmatists standing between the two. Here again we find the identification of leadership abilities with high status influencing the workers' confidence in the two groups of political leaders. The Tories exhibit greater trust in their 'own' leaders than does Labour in theirs, presumably because of the higher status of the former. And within the Tory group it is the deferentials, with their especially strong desire for upper-class leaders, who manifest greater trust in the Conservative leadership than do the pragmatists.

At the same time, it ought to be stressed that the confidence that the workers have in their own political leaders does not overshadow their adherence to wide-ranging procedural norms in legitimizing governmental authority. It is calculated that the proportion of Tories legitimizing independent governmental authority on procedural grounds is approximately twice as large as the number doing so on personal grounds, with the ratio increasing to five to one amongst the Labour supporters. This point underlines the preponderance of 'constitutional' as opposed to personal and partisan considerations in the workers' attitudes towards governmental authority. It also means that the differences between Conservatives and Labour attitudes towards governmental authority are minimized; for the two groups differ not in the sphere of procedural values, but on the personal dimension which takes second place in providing the underpinning for independent governmental authority.

III. PERSONAL ACQUIESCENCE TO POLITICAL AUTHORITY

After analysing working-class attitudes which define the Government's sphere of authority, there remains a second dimension of the workers' orientations towards political authority—a dimension which centres about the *personal* submission or rejection of authority.[1] Whereas the first dimension allowed us to gauge the degree to which the Government is viewed in leadership as opposed to representative terms, the second dimension refers to the frequency with which the workers are ready to acquiesce to the demands of their party leaders. The respondents were presented with a situation in which the party they support adopted a policy which diverged from their own views; they were then asked if they would still favour their own position or take up the party's position, and their reasons for doing so.[2]

At the beginning of this chapter it was stated that the deferential group would be defined solely on the basis of a strong preference for political leaders enjoying high social positions; the common assumption that these deferentials are also politically submissive was not incorporated into our operational definition. At this point it is possible

[1] For purposes of explaining the operation of the political system a third dimension towards political authority is more significant; namely, the extent to which the workers believe that the electorate is able to influence governmental decisions, and the frequency with which they normatively sanction their perceived political impotence. This problem is treated in the following chapter.

[2] The wording of this question as used in the interviews reads as follows: 'You have stated that you tend to support the Conservative/Labour Party. Now suppose that on the issue of the size of old age pensions, for example, you favoured a position contrary to the one later adopted by the Conservative/Labour Party. In such a case, would you then still be in favour of your own position or would you take up the Conservative/Labour Party's position? Why do you say this?'

to test this hypothesis with respect to one type of political acquiescence. The figures in Table 11 do indicate that the assumed relationship between social deference and submission to the Conservative leadership is present, although at first sight the relationship is not a strong one: 66 per cent of the deferentials are willing to forego their own judgements by acceding to the party's position, compared to 53 per cent of the pragmatists. The relationship between personal political acquiescence and a preference for different types of political leaders does take on somewhat greater significance when it is recalled that the pragmatists are grouped together on a residual basis. When they are separated into two groups—those who manifest a measure of deference by having selected either the peer's son or the Eton man, and those who preferred neither—it is found that 63 per cent of the former and 44 per cent of the latter are willing to adhere to the party's position. A similar pattern also exists among the Labour voters, with 64 per cent of those who registered a desire to have either the peer's son or the Eton man as Prime Minister acceding to the authority of their party leaders, compared to 48 per cent of those Labour supporters who do not exhibit any social deference at all. To some extent then, validation is found for the hypothesis that those workers who prefer to be led by socially eminent politicians are more likely to maintain politically submissive attitudes.[1]

TABLE 11

The Workers' Probable Reactions when there is a divergence between their own views and their party's position

	Tories	Defs.	Prags.	Labs.
Maintain own views	32	21	36	36
Change to party's position	56	66	53	54
Depends	6	2	7	5
DK	6	11	5	6
Total per cent	100	100	100	100
Total number	320	90	230	127

However, the most significant aspect of the data is not the relatively acquiescent posture assumed by those workers preferring socially

[1] Also see n. 1, p. 117 below; but cf. n. 1, p. 101 below.

eminent leaders. For the data indicate that political acquiescence is frequently found throughout the working class. Only one-third of the respondents are predisposed towards the maintenance of their individual evaluations of public policies, while slightly more than half the workers are willing to forego their own views by acceding to their party leaders' authority.[1] What is significant here is the broad cultural setting typified by these acquiescent attitudes which serve as the underpinning for the country's hierarchical authority patterns. And while the deferentials are relatively more willing to accede to the various dimensions of political authority, this attitudinal difference is a quantitative rather than a qualitative one.

What then are the manifest reasons provided by the respondents to explain their politically acquiescent predispositions? Table 12 indicates that on this score there are not any significant differences between the deferentials and pragmatists; the same is not, however, true of the Tories and Labour voters. Nearly twice as many Conservative (66 per cent) as Labour voters (35 per cent) are ready to accede to their party's demands because of the confidence they have in the abilities of the party leaders to arrive at the right decisions. The Conservatives are imbued with the belief that 'they [the party leaders] know best', that 'they are more experienced and intelligent than me', and therefore, it ought to be left 'to them as they see fit'. Here, too, it is most probable that the greater amount of confidence in their party leaders expressed by the Tories is partly bound up with these leaders' higher social rank compared to that of their Labour equivalents. This difference between the Conservative and Labour supporters may also be related to the dual fact that the Labour Party's long period in opposition did not allow it to demonstrate fully the abilities of its leadership, these men concomitantly having to do without the prestigious mantle of authority.

The Tories' second most frequent explanation for acceding to their

[1] The acquiescent posture of the English workers is underscored when a comparison is made with a national sample of Frenchmen's responses to a somewhat comparable type of question. Just before the October 1946 referendum the respondent was asked first how he would vote if his party recommended that he vote *pour*, and then what his vote would be if his party recommended *contre*. Only 28 per cent of the respondents replied that their preferences would be altered by their party's recommendations, which is approximately half the number of English manual workers who said that they would change their position. *Sondages*, October 16, 1946, p. 239, cited in Duncan MacRae, Jr., *French Politics and Society*, forthcoming.

TABLE 12

Reasons for changing to the party's position

	Tories	Defs.	Prags.	Labs.
Abilities of party leaders	66	64	66	35
Party loyalty	4	3	4	22
Agree with most of party's policies	10	8	11	10
Party acts for the good of the country	15	19	13	6
Party helps the working class	2	3	1	19
Other	5	5	5	6
DK	1	2	0	1
Total per cent	103	104	100	100
Total number	180	59	121	68

leaders' wishes is the belief that their party acts for the good of the country as a whole, 15 per cent of the Tories and 6 per cent of the Labour voters responding in this manner. In comparison Labour acquiescence tends to be based upon a self-interested calculus, with 19 per cent and 2 per cent of the Labour voters and Tories respectively, adopting a 'followership' role because their parties' policies are thought to be of particular benefit to the working class. As will be seen in the chapter on partisan attitudes, this bread and butter socialism is the Labour voters' primary manifest reason for supporting the party. Lastly, it ought to be noted that 22 per cent of Labour, compared to only 4 per cent of the Conservatives, would acceded to their leaders' authority due to a feeling of party loyalty: 'the party line must be supported', 'I would stand by them', 'I have always supported the party'. Presumably Labour party loyalty is closely bound up with a preference for working-class political leaders and a sense of class solidarity, the party being viewed as representative of the working class in terms of both its personnel and its objectives. This interpretation gains additional plausibility when Tory and Labour attachments to the notion of working-class solidarity are contrasted in Chapter 7 below.

CHAPTER 4

The Elitist Political System
——

To what extent, and in what ways, does the working-class political culture support the country's elitist political system? It is this (assumed) relationship between working-class political attitudes and the structure and exercise of power that serves as the primary focus for the ensuing discussion. For example, we want to delineate the workers' beliefs and norms regarding the way in which power is distributed, and then go on to suggest certain relationships between such beliefs and the actual power structure. Bagehot was hardly unaware of the relationship between the two. According to him the monarch's most important function was to serve as a façade, hiding the real power holders from the inquisitive gaze of the masses and enveloping the exercise of power in the aura of reverence surrounding the monarch. In Bagehot's words, the monarchy 'acts as a disguise. It enables our real rulers to change without needless people knowing it. The masses of Englishmen are not fit for an elective government; if they knew how near they were to it, they would be surprised, and almost tremble.'[1] Bagehot was thus suggesting that the non-elite's perceptions of the power structure help to determine the direction in which power gravitates and the manner in which it is exercised. Before embarking upon such an analysis here, a few words ought to be said about the structure of power whose outlines are to be partly accounted for by the peculiarly English working-class political culture.

The English political system can be characterized as elitist in at least three respects, according to the manner in which authority is distributed, the boundaries within which the decision-makers can act in an independent fashion, and the style with which decisions are taken. In the introductory chapter it was shown that authority within the political system is distributed in a markedly hierarchical form, and that the Government is allowed a wide sphere of independent authority,

[1] Op. cit., p. 48.

leaving little doubt that it is the Government which is the system's energizing, initiating and directing element.

The English political system also merits the elitist adjective because of the private and informal decision-making style. The homogeneity of the elite—their common social and educational backgrounds[1]— allows them to operate in a rarefied atmosphere in which nuances of behaviour are immediately recognized for the political cues that they are.[2] Moreover, the pervasive familial and public school connections intertwining individual elite members with each other serves as an important communications network, allowing advice to be sought and decisions to be reached on an informal, club-like basis.[3] There is, in fact, a rough parallel between English club life and the decision-making process. English clubs have two purposes: to provide a conveniently informal meeting place, just as many important decisions are taken away from the formalized routine of committee meetings;[4] and to keep other people out, just as decisions relating to governmental policies are taken in considerable secrecy. According to Edward A. Shils, 'The secrets of the governing classes of Britain are kept within the class and even within more restricted circles. The British ruling class is unequalled in secretiveness and taciturnity . . . What is spoken in privacy is expected to be retained in privacy and to be withheld from the populace. When journalists are confided in, it is with the

[1] Lord Balniel has written that 'The cement of the [upper] class is not so much a sense of common purpose . . . as a sense of common experience . . . A common educational experience, not shared by the mass of the community, gives to the class a sense of mutual understanding, loyalty and tolerance'. See 'The Upper Class', in Rose, ed., op. cit., p. 72.

[2] An instructive example of a 'missed' cue occurred during the Tories' search for a new leader to replace Eden. A number of backbenchers publicly complained that they were not 'consulted' by the whips concerning their preferences for the succession. Perhaps the devices used to elicit their preferences were somewhat too subtle for them. If so, their inability to recognize the oblique processes by which 'soundings' are taken is a good indication that these MP's were not attuned to the informal and private decision-making style. For a discussion of the public interchange at the time this incident occurred, see R. T. McKenzie, op. cit., pp. 587–589.

[3] See the comments by Lord Chandos who thinks of the establishment as a communications network, with its 'tremendous interchange of information' about elite members. Quoted in Anthony Sampson, *Anatomy of Britain*: 1962, pp. 20–21.

[4] Witness Samuel Beer's comment that 'No formal arrangements of committees or staffs could quite free the British Government of its dependence upon the common rooms and lunch tables of the clubs of Pall Mall'. *Treasury Control*: 1957, p. 106.

expectation that the confidence will be respected.'[1] And what Sidney
Low said about the Cabinet more than fifty years ago is equally true
today. He did not find it surprising that the Cabinet operates as a
private committee; what impressed him greatly was that it is also a
secret committee, and in this respect it stands apart from nearly all
other governing bodies.[2] This pervasive secrecy finds its constitutional
expression in the criminal penalties of the Official Secrets Act, and
even more importantly, in the British version of ministerial responsibility. Although not originally designed for this purpose, it does
have the effect of preventing the public and the politicians from learning how important decisions are made, who actually made them, and
which civil servants are responsible for their execution and interpretation.[3] This private, secret and informal decision-making style
is not only a product of the system's hierarchical structure and the
social and educational homogeneity of the elite. It is also dictated by
the belief that the work of government can best be carried out with
a minimum of public attention, particularly while the decisions are
being worked out. Decisions can consequently be reached more
efficiently, points of view and candid statements of self-interest can
be expressed without public embarrassment, and compromise can be
effected without public loss of face.

Having briefly noted the political system's elitist characteristics,
it is now possible to analyse the cultural supports which they enjoy
among the manual workers—an analysis based on the assumption that
working-class support or acquiescence is a necessary condition for the
maintenance of an elitist system; for if public power is to be exercised
hierarchically and privately by a social elite in a democratic system,
it is necessary that the electorate's attitudes towards the distribution and
exercise of power be generally compatible with those held by the elite.[4]

---

[1] *The Torment of Secrecy*: 1956, pp. 49, 50. Also see Harry Street, *The Individual and the Law*: 1963, p. 85.

[2] Op. cit., pp. 35–37.

[3] The Crichel Down affair of 1954 is a great exception in two respects. First,
because the maladroit behaviour of some civil servants in the Ministry of
Agriculture was brought to light; and secondly, because the minister decided
to resign in order to give the civil service a salutary shock.

[4] The writer's definition of a democratic system, taken largely from Joseph
Schumpeter, does not pre-empt the possibility of public power being exercised
privately in a democracy; viz. a democratic system is one in which there is a
regular competition for control of the government through an electoral process
featuring universal suffrage. Also see below, Chapter 9.

I. THE POLITICAL INFLUENCE OF THE WORKING CLASS

The most important single feature of an elitist system is the relationship between the elite and the non-elite. Although it was argued that this relationship is a hierarchical one, it has not yet been shown that the *workers* view the political system in such terms. In order to elicit their beliefs about the relationship between the elite and the non-elite they were asked: 'Do you think that people like yourself have any say in how the country is run? Do people like you have a good deal of say, a little, or none at all?' Considering that 'people like yourself' are manual workers constituting two-thirds of the electorate, the responses not only refer to the worker's perceived political influence; they also imply a belief about the elite's responsiveness to the majority element in the population.

The data in Table 1 clearly indicate that the workers perceive themselves to be living in an elitist political system. Only 14 per cent of the Conservatives and 10 per cent of the Labour supporters replied that the workers have 'a good deal' of influence upon governmental decisions. Another 54 per cent of the Tories and 37 per cent of the Labour voters believe that the non-elite has only 'a little' influence in this respect. While one-third and one-half of the Conservative and Labour voters respectively, believe that the working class has no influence whatsoever in deciding how the country is to be run. When only slightly more than 10 per cent of the working-class population believes itself to have a good deal of political influence, it is hardly an understatement to say that the workers' beliefs are in accord with Amery's description of their political role as an 'essentially passive' one.

Although there is no way in which they can be validated, two plausible explanations may be suggested to account for the Conservative and Labour voters' differing perceptions of the non-elite's influence. During the preceding twelve years of Tory rule the Conservative Party has been identified as the Government whereas the Labour Party was tagged with the minority party label. The working-class Tories have seen their votes translated into effective parliamentary majorities while some of their economic and social values have been realized in the form of Tory legislation. In contrast, the Labour supporters have witnessed the defeat of their party in three successive elections—defeats which may have had a particularly significant impact on their beliefs about the non-elite's political influence, considering

4

TABLE 13

The perceived influence of 'people like yourself' upon Governmental
Decisions

	Tories	Defs.	Prags.	Labs.
A good deal	14	16	9	10
A little	54	48	68	37
None	31	34	23	50
Depends, DK	1	1	0	2
Total per cent	100	100	100	100
Total number	320	90	230	127

that most of the people with whom they come into contact voted
Labour. Consequently, Tory beliefs about the workers' political influence may have been shaped in a positive, and Labour's beliefs, in a
negative direction. Equally plausible, is the hypothesis that Labour
beliefs in this connection have been shaped by the party's ideology
which is critical of the elitist political system in which the 'privileged'
classes are said to have an excessive amount of power and influence.

These comments suggest two possible explanations for the different
beliefs held by the Tory and Labour voters. But they do not refer
to the reasons why different beliefs are maintained *within* each of the
two groups regarding the workers' political influence. In order to
analyse this problem we can turn to the political socialization process,
specifically, the respondents' experiences with parental authority
during early adolescence, for it is this experience which helps to account
for the workers' differing beliefs in this regard. Unfortunately this
entails a brief detour from the study's organizational structure since
the political socialization process is discussed at length in the following chapter. The reader is asked to bear this in mind, and if he so
chooses, to read the general comments on the political socialization
process at this point.[1]

The respondents were asked the extent to which they were allowed
to influence those family decisions which affected them.[2] These re-

[1] Pp. 123–126 below.
[2] The question reads: 'As you were growing up, let us say at about 13, how
much influence do you remember having in family decisions affecting yourself?
Did you have much influence, some influence, or none at all?' The question is
borrowed from Almond and Verba, op. cit.

sponses are then utilized as the explanatory variable in accounting for the workers' beliefs regarding the political influence of the working class. In Table 14 a significant relationship appears between the two variables, especially among the Conservative voters. Whereas none of the Tories who had 'much influence' upon parental decisions believe the working class to have no influence at all upon governmental decisions, 20 per cent of those who replied that they had 'some influence', and 46 per cent of those having had no influence at all upon parental decisions, believe that the workers have no voice in deciding how the country is run. This correlation is not, however, a linear one in the case of the Labour respondents. It is thought that the connection between these family experiences and adult attitudes, separated by time and setting, is affected by at least two processes. Those workers who were not allowed any influence in family decisions are unlikely to think that they have any influence upon government because their non-political adolescent experiences are generalized to, or projected on to, the political system, both involving relations between a subordinate and a super-ordinate authority. It may also be that those workers who did not enjoy any influence within the family developed the expectation that they would be in a similar position in relation to all authority figures. Not expecting to have any influence upon government, they believe themselves not to have any such influence.[1]

TABLE 14

Remembered influence upon family decisions and beliefs about the influence of 'people like yourself' upon Government decisions

	Influence upon Family Decisions					
	Tories			Labour		
	Much	Some	None	Much	Some	None
A good deal	15	16	13	29	14	6
A little	81	62	41	29	46	32
None	0	20	46	43	36	61
Depends, DK	4	2	0	0	4	2
Total per cent	100	100	100	100	100	100
Total number	27	117	160	7	50	66

[1] A third possibility—that the correlations are due to an artificial response set—cannot be completely discounted. See Almond and Verba, op. cit., p. 350, n. 18 and p. 357, n. 20.

II. REPRESENTATIONAL NORMS

We are not only concerned with the workers' beliefs about their own political influence; their normative predispositions towards the political role of the working class are even more significant. After having stated their beliefs regarding the political influence of people like themselves, the respondents were then asked: 'Do you think that this is the way things ought to be?' Since the key word in the question is 'ought', the respondents are not being asked how much influence they would be satisfied with, given such limiting conditions as the size, complexity and elitist features of the political system. Rather, the question is phrased in such a way so as to elicit the workers' representational norms irrespective of prevailing conditions which might make them extremely difficult to attain. Their responses presumably refer to the *ideal* measure of political influence they believe the non-elite should have in a democratic system. Considering the minimal nature of these norms, this point is particularly important because it underlines the circumscribed political role the working class thinks proper for itself even under ideal circumstances.

In Table 15 the respondents are divided into those believing people like themselves to have a little say in how the country is run and those thinking themselves to have no influence whatsoever. (Since the 12 per cent of the workers who believe themselves to have 'a good deal' of political influence are all contented with this situation, they have been dropped from the analysis.) When those respondents who believe themselves to have a little political influence were asked whether this is the way things ought to be, a majority of both Tories (79 per cent) and Labour voters (60 per cent) replied in the affirmative (see Table 15). Recalling that the largest proportion of Tories replied that the workers have 'a little' influence, it is now seen that by far the greatest number of these Conservatives are normatively content with the working class' minimal political influence. It is therefore possible to view this conjunction of beliefs and norms as the modal Tory attitude towards the non-elite's political role. The severely circumscribed representational norms which the workers adhere to are further highlighted by the responses of those workers who believe people like themselves to have no political influence at all. Fully a third of both the Conservative and Labour supporters registered their normative satisfaction with this perceived lack of influence. Here then is the strata of the working class which manifests an arch-typically pre-democratic attitude: it sees itself as politically impotent and sanctions it. Not only do these workers thus tend to agree with Amery that their political role is an 'essentially passive' one, they also agree with this former Tory cabinet minister that it should be.[1] As will be seen below, this acquiescent posture is in large part founded upon the diffuse sense of trust accorded the elite by the non-elite.

TABLE 15

Beliefs about the influence of 'people like yourself' and representational norms

| | Little Influence | | | | No Influence | | | |
	Tories	Defs.	Prags.	Labs.	Tories	Defs.	Prags.	Labs.
Satisfied	79	84	77	60	32	19	35	30
Unsatisfied	21	16	23	40	61	81	56	61
Depends, DK	0	0	0	0	7	0	9	9
Total per cent	100	100	100	100	100	100	100	100
Total number	172	61	111	47	100	21	79	64

The data in Table 15 indicate that the representational norms of the Labour voters are largely similar to those of the Tories. Among those workers perceiving themselves to have a 'little' political influence, Labour's norms are significantly less acquiescent than are the Conservatives', but among the workers believing themselves to have no influence at all, there is no difference between the two groups. Here is another indication that Labour attitudes towards authority tend to be in general accord with those characteristic of the English political culture, even when the latter sharply diverges from the egalitarian and 'democratic' ideology of the Labour Party. And taken together, the Tory and Labour data demonstrate the workers' minimal representational norms. In order to arrive at a single figure for summarizing the data in Table 15, it is possible to calculate the proportion of workers

[1] It is interesting to note that the deferentials are less accepting of complete political impotence on their part than are the pragmatists; 35 per cent of the pragmatists are satisfied with a purely passive role for the workers compared to 19 per cent of the deferentials. Unfortunately, the small number of deferentials in this group (N=21) does not allow for any extended analysis.

who see themselves as politically impotent, or nearly so, and who still offer their normative approval: 49 per cent of the workers fall in this category.[1] It is this cultural edifice which constitutes a singularly important support for the system's hierarchical structure of authority, the independence of the government from the non-elite, and the elite's private decision-making style.

What of those workers whose representational norms are not satisfied? How do they react to this situation? One relevant measure of their reaction is to compare their attitudes towards the Government's procedural authority with those of the respondents who are satisfied with the non-elite's perceived political position. It is then found that among both Conservative and Labour voters the proportion of workers allowing the Government an independent sphere of authority is 15 per cent smaller among those workers who are dissatisfied with the workers' political role. This figure suggests that a significant number of workers are unwilling to accord the Government a wide sphere of authority because they believe that the non-elite should have a louder political voice—or at least one that is listened to more often. But this 15 per cent difference is more important as it indicates that the workers' attitudes towards independent governmental authority are only partially affected by their displeasure with the workers' minimal political role; even unfulfilled representational norms do not have an overly important affect upon the readiness to grant the Government a wide range of independent authority.

Notwithstanding the pervasiveness of the workers' acquiescent representational norms, things appear to be changing. The younger generations are less likely to be content with a minimum of political influence than are the older ones. Among both the Conservative and Labour supporters who believe themselves to have either a little political influence or none at all there is a linear increase in the proportion of workers thinking this to be the proper distribution of power as age increases (see Table 16). Of those Tories aged 21 to 29 believing themselves to have a little or no influence upon government 43 per cent accept this distribution of power as 'proper', while 68 per cent of those aged 60 and over replied in this manner. Thus the older workers' traditional acquiescent attitudes towards the political elite are gradually being replaced by the younger generations' advocacy of

[1] In making this calculation the under-representation of the Labour voters was taken into account by utilizing the weighting index. See pp. 59–60 above.

a more assertive (or directive) role for the working class. However, it may be that the apparent rate at which this change is taking place is exaggerated by the presence of a psychological factor—the conservatizing effects of increasing age. Although there is preciously little evidence to support the claim, it is often said that older people tend to develop conservative attitudes which, in this instance, would lead them to adopt an acquiescent posture *vis-à-vis* the elite, thereby inflating the apparent rate of generational change in Table 16. With the available data the possible effects of the age-cycle upon political attitudes must remain a moot point. Yet despite this gap it is undoubtedly warranted to suggest that at least a large part of the generational changes indicated by the data follow from historical events and alterations of social, economic and educational patterns. As such, it may be expected that the future will see a reversal in the existing predominance of minimal over assertive representational norms. However, the diffusion of the two other authority variables examined in this study—attitudes towards independent governmental authority and acquiescence to the demands of party leaders—do not appear to be decreasing over time. In the case of the former there is a definite increase among the younger and middle-aged voters, while the latter appears to be unrelated to age.

TABLE 16

Those workers believing people like themselves to have little or no influence upon Governmental decisions and their representational norms according to age

	Tories				Labour			
	21–29	30–45	46–59	60+	21–29	30–45	46–59	60+
Satisfied	43	57	63	68	29	36	42	56
Unsatisfied	52	41	33	30	57	59	52	41
Depends, DK	4	3	4	2	14	5	6	4
Total per cent	100	100	100	100	100	100	100	100
Total number	23	74	75	102	7	44	33	27

III. THE EXISTENCE OF EXCESSIVELY POWERFUL GROUPS

The belief that certain powerful groups are able to manipulate the government for their own ends, when these ends are detrimental to the majority's welfare, is a pervasive belief among French and Italian workers. Numerous groups and individuals are thought to have an inordinate amount of power which is fully exploited in the service of selfish ends. This diffuse mistrust is especially directed towards members of the political class, which goes a long way in explaining why France and Italy have failed to adopt a tradition of authority allowing the political elite the wide sphere of independent action which is eminently conducive to the stability and decisional effectiveness of democratic government.[1]

In order to gauge the English workers' attitudes in this regard, and then to relate their attitudes to the functioning of the political system, the sample was asked: 'One sometimes hears that some people or groups have so much influence on the way government is run that the interests of the majority are ignored. Do you agree or disagree that there are such groups?' Half of the Tories and 69 per cent of the Labour voters registered their agreement with the statement, indicating that a majority of the male working-class population believes in the inordinate and selfishly exploited power of certain groups (see Table 17). Even among the Conservative supporters, who are least affected by Labour Party propaganda denouncing the inequities of the power structure, almost half hold to such a critical view.[2]

The belief that the democratic process is impaired due to the self-interested action of particular groups or individuals is not an uncommon one amongst both workers and middle-class people in a great many

---

[1] See the present writer's 'Democratic Stability and Instability: The French Case', *World Politics*, October 1965, and the references cited there, and Chapter 9 below, pp. 246–50. For Italy, see Edward Banfield, *The Moral Basis of a Backward Society*: 1958; Almond and Verba, op. cit., *passim*; Joseph La Palombara, 'Italy: Fragmentation, Isolation, Alienation', in Pye and Verba, op. cit., pp. 288–292.

[2] It is tempting to view these beliefs as part of the workers' general tendency to regard the middle and upper classes in a cynical and distrustful light—what Richard Hoggart summarizes as the 'Them/Us' dichotomous picture of society. However, analysis of the Almond and Verba data (from which the interview question is borrowed) indicates that the middle class perceives the existence of inordinately powerful groups just as frequently as does the working class, which hardly supports the hypothesis drawn from Hoggart, *The Uses of Literacy*: 1961, pp. 62ff. Another hypothesis, that the beliefs in the existence of these powerful groups are related to pre-1939 experiences with an unmodified capitalism, can also be rejected; for the older workers believe in the existence of such groups less frequently than do the middle-aged and younger voters.

TABLE 17

Beliefs in the existence of inordinately powerful and selfish groups acting contrary to the majority's interests

	Tories	Defs.	Prags.	Labs.
Exist	50	53	48	69
Don't exist	40	38	41	19
DK	11	9	11	12
Total per cent	100	100	100	100
Total number	320	90	230	127

countries. For the present analysis such beliefs are not of any great significance in and of themselves; it is the effect which these beliefs have upon the non-elite's support for the political system that is important in understanding the system's contours. Specifically, do such beliefs lead to a general disenchantment with, or alienation from, the political system? Or do the workers simply accept this perceived inequity as an inescapable aspect of the democratic scrimmage? Or are the workers dissatisfied with the imbalance in the power structure but not to the extent that their support for the elitist system is undermined? From the available evidence it appears as if the latter is the best interpretation.

Political alienation may be manifested by the transference of responsibility for one's personal dissatisfactions to the political system. If the belief in the existence of inordinately powerful groups were to entail a measure of political alienation there ought to be an association between the holding of this belief and personal economic dissatisfactions. Presumably, those workers who are less satisfied with their economic positions will more frequently believe in the existence of excessively powerful groups, blaming the perceived inequities of the power structure for their own economic dissatisfactions. In order to test this hypothesis the respondents were divided into those who are economically 'satisfied', 'fairly satisfied', and 'unsatisfied'.[1] It was then found that the posited relationship does exist, although it is not strong

[1] The respondents were asked: 'Thinking about the economic situation of your family in general—the money you earn, the chances for advancement, etc.—do you think it is satisfactory or not?' The open-ended responses were then placed in one of the three categories.

enough to suggest that political alienation is an important element in the working-class political culture. Among both Tories and Labour supporters there is a 14 per cent difference in the proportion of workers perceiving an inequitable distribution of power among those who are economically satisfied and dissatisfied.[1]

Secondly, if the workers who believe that power is inequitably distributed have consequently become somewhat disenchanted with the elitist political system, they should more frequently express dissatisfaction with the non-elite's influence upon the elite than those workers who do not recognize the existence of such groups. In Table 18 it is seen that those workers who replied that the majority's interests are being subverted by powerful groups are less frequently satisfied with the political influence of the non-elite than are those workers who do not perceive the existence of such groups, there being 21 and 25 per cent differences within the Tory and Labour groups respectively. These differences indicate that beliefs about the inequitable distribution of power produce a fairly widespread sense of political disaffection within the working class; those workers who believe in the existence of excessively powerful groups apparently want the non-elite's influence to be increased as a counter to the inordinate power of these groups.

TABLE 18

Beliefs in the existence of inordinately powerful groups and representational norms

	Tories		Labour	
	Exist	Don't exist	Exist	Don't exist
Satisfied	52	73	42	67
Dissatisfied	43	26	53	33
Depends	1	0	2	0
DK	4	2	2	0
Total per cent	100	100	100	100
Total number	159	128	88	24

[1] It should be mentioned that the association between the two variables is not a linear one in the case of the Conservative supporters, thereby raising some doubt about even the presumed small effect of these beliefs as they lead to a measure of political alienation.

Up to this point the discussion has presumably not contained any surprises; it is expected that negative beliefs about the power structure would lead to a measure of political disaffection. Certainly this is what we would expect to find in an analysis of the French and Italian working classes. The English working class, however, does not fit the continental pattern in a singularly important respect.

On an *a priori* basis it might well be assumed that those workers who are dissatisfied with the distribution of power would consequently not only desire a greater role for the non-elite, they would also opt for a type of governmental authority which is limited in scope. Yet this second assumption is not supported by the data. The proportion of workers who allow the Government a wide sphere of procedural authority is almost identical among those workers who believe in the existence of inordinately powerful groups and those who do not share in this belief—a finding which is true of both the Conservative and Labour voters. Thus negative attitudes towards the distribution of power do not lead the workers to desire the Government's authority to be circumscribed, which might otherwise weaken the workers' support for the system's hierarchical features.

The lack of effect which these negative beliefs have upon the workers' willingness to accord the Government a wide sphere of authority appears to be due to two factors. Because of the traditionally strong support given to Governments when acting in an independent fashion, this procedural norm is not questioned even when it is thought that the power structure is skewed in an inequitable direction. Secondly, unlike the French and Italians, the English workers do not perceive the political class to be using the power at their disposal for selfish ends. This point is substantiated in the responses to the follow-up question asked of those workers who replied that the majority's interests are being neglected due to the excessive power of certain groups. When asked, 'Which people or groups have such influence?' only two respondents in the sample named the Conservative Party, the Labour Party or any of the leaders of these parties. The members of the political class are then not viewed as men having an inordinate amount of power, who are willing to sacrifice the public interest for their own private ends—something which can hardly be said of the French and Italian workers' attitudes towards their political leaders.[1] It is this

---

[1] For example, in February 1952 a national sample of Frenchmen ($N=1381$) was asked the following question by the Institut Français d'Opinion Publique:

diffuse sense of trust enjoyed by the political elite which prevents the workers from delimiting the Government's procedural authority even when they are dissatisfied with the inordinate power of certain groups. And it is these attitudes that also go a long way in accounting for the workers' adherence to a set of minimal representational norms for themselves.

To summarize, negative beliefs regarding the distribution of power do lead to a significant measure of disenchantment with the political system. However, those workers who are somewhat politically alienated are neither led to protest against that aspect of the elitist political system which allows the Government a wide sphere of procedural authority, nor to question the good intentions of the political class. Thus in the English political system, the political dissatisfactions which are to be found among the non-elites in all societies, are not transformed into a set of attitudes which undermine its elitist structure—or in broader terms, which are dysfunctional for the stability and efficient operation of the democratic system.

Having noted that it is not the political class which is thought to have an excessive amount of power which it uses for private ends, which groups are seen in this light? In Table 19 it is seen that business groups are singled out most frequently by the Conservative and Labour voters. The power of 'industrial combines', 'big monopolies', 'capitalists', 'businessmen', etc., were alluded to by 41 per cent of the Conservative and 39 per cent of the Labour voters. Surprisingly, then, an equal proportion of Conservatives and Labour supporters singled out the business interests as having an excessive amount of power which they are thought to use in a manner detrimental to the majority's interests. The Tories are not led to view the business groups in an especially favourable light because of their close connections with the Conservative Party; nor is Labour predisposed in an exceptionally negative direction due to party attacks upon the power and excessively self-interested motivations of some of the large industrial and financial concerns.

Within the Conservative ranks there is an important difference

---

'Do you think that the present government is made up of a majority of honest men, of a minority of honest men, or of men who are all dishonest?' Of the male manual workers living in urban areas (N = 173) only 20 per cent replied that the majority are honest, 44 per cent said that only a minority are honest, 21 per cent remarked that all of them are dishonest, while 15 per cent felt unable to answer the question.

TABLE 19

Identification of those groups thought to have an inordinate amount of power which is used contrary to the majority's interests

	Tories	Defs.	Prags.	Labs.
Business groups	41	58	33	39
The rich	9	13	7	19
The upper class	6	6	5	15
The Conservative Party	0	0	0	1
Trade Unions	28	23	31	11
Other	16	23	14	19
DK	11	4	14	6
Total per cent	111	127	104	110
Total number of responses	177	61	116	97
Total number of respondents	159	48	111	88

between the deferentials and pragmatists in this regard, with 58 per cent of the former and 33 per cent of the latter singling out the business groups. Considering that the deferentials continue to prefer the type of leaders identified with a past generation when Tory politicians adopted an outwardly vigorous hostility towards industrial and commercial interests, it is plausible to interpret their attitude as a contemporary manifestation of the anti-business ideology created in the second half of the nineteenth century by Disraeli and Randolph Churchill. They helped construct an ideological synthesis between an hereditary upper class and the manual workers—a synthesis which portrayed the Liberal industrialists as crass self-seekers whose interests were diametrically opposed to those of the working class. These two Tories successively sought to inculcate the idea that property and wealth are to be legitimized only through the acceptance of social responsibility and public service. The Tories were said to conform to this ideal, in contrast to the Liberal businessmen who failed to concern themselves with the workers' needs and who did not see fit to make any sacrifices in the cause of public service. It is presumably this ideological hang-over amongst the deferentials which accounts for their strong hostility to the business groups; this type of hostility and a preference for leaders of high social rank have apparently been inter-related for the last century amongst some working-class Tories. Although

the Conservative Party has continually been absorbing business elements into parliamentary and leadership positions, starting with
Bonar Law, there remains a distinct Disraelian aversion to the purely
business ethic in the modern party. Anthony Eden gave vent to this
view at the 1947 party conference that approved the *Industrial Charter*:
'We are not the Party of unbridled, brutal capitalism, and never have
been. Although we believe in personal responsibility and personal
initiative in business, we are not the political children of the laissez-
faire school. We opposed them decade after decade.'[1]

*   *   *

Taking all the data in this chapter together, the conclusion emerges
that the Conservatives adhere to a quantitatively different set of
beliefs and norms regarding the distribution of power within the
political system compared to those maintained by the Labour voters.
Relative to the latter, the Conservatives believe the working class to
have a somewhat greater influence upon government, and among those
workers who believe themselves to have 'a little' influence, the Tories
more frequently accept this situation as 'right'. Moreover, the Tories
less often perceive the existence of powerful groups subverting the
majority's interests. Yet the differences between the two groups are
not nearly so wide as to justify the use of such adjectives as a 'cleavage'
or a 'marked divergence' to describe them. The most striking and
important feature of Tory and Labour attitudes towards the system's
power structure is their convergence rather than their divergence;
for notwithstanding a number of differences, both Tory and Labour
attitudes lend support to the political system's elitist features. And
even when the Tories and Labour supporters differ in their beliefs
and norms regarding the pattern of power, the more critical attitudes
of the Labour supporters are not translated into a marked disaffection
from the political system nor into a reduction in their support for
its elitist contours.

[1] 1947 *Conservative Party Conference Report*, p. 42, cited in Beer, op. cit.,
p. 271.

CHAPTER 5

Patterns of Potential Activism[1]

In THE previous discussion of the political culture approach it was said that a political culture consists of a number of attitudinal dimensions. Preferences for different types of leaders, predispositions towards personal political acquiescence, beliefs and norms regarding the scope of governmental authority and the political role of the non-elite are the dimensions which have already been explored. In this chapter we shall be looking at the activist element in the working-class political culture. The two variables which shall serve as the foci for the analysis are subjective competence—the belief that one *could* do something to influence the government on a particular issue—and potential activism—the belief that one *would* actually make the attempt. Primary attention will be devoted to potential activism, but it will be seen that subjective competence is a necessary precondition for its development.

It is realized that there is a yawning gap between potential activism and actual behaviour. Only one-fifth of the workers who said that they would attempt to influence the government if it were acting in a harmful or unjust manner reported that they have ever made the attempt. And it is safe to surmise that only a literal handful of this group met with any degree of success in their endeavours. But this is hardly reason to question the importance of activist predispositions as opposed to activist behaviour.

In a democratic system the non-elite does not only assume political influence through its disposal of the ballot. In the years between elections the elite commonly remains attuned to the electorate. This is due not only to the knowledge that to disregard the voters' wishes

[1] This chapter contains a most liberal helping of the concepts developed by Almond and Verba. Although analysis of the data proceeds along different lines and the findings are used to explain different variables, with but one exception and some modifications, all the central interview items upon which this chapter is based are borrowed from their work. Op. cit., Chapters 7 and 9.

is to court future electoral disaster. The action of the elite is also circumscribed by the knowledge (or myth) that the non-elite is more
or less likely to protest against decisions that are thought to be particularly unjust or harmful. It is the *anticipation* of such behaviour—
whether it be done through the writing of letters, the lobbying of
MP's, organizing demonstrations, or exerting pressure through local
party organizations, civic-minded voluntary associations or pressure
groups—which contributes to the elite's attentiveness to the non-
elite in the inter-election years.[1] The elite is on notice that the non-
elite is able, willing, and perhaps likely, to bring sanctions to bear
if its expectations are flouted. This can occur through the loss of confidence in the elite's abilities, a questioning of its prerogatives, a loss
of prestige, the tabling of parliamentary questions detracting from a
minister's reputation and thus his chances for future promotions, and
the public embarrassment produced by newspaper publicity.[2]

Even leaving aside its effects on the operation of the political system,
activist predispositions are of interest in themselves, for they are an
important element in the working-class political culture. We want to
know how widespread these predispositions are and how they are
distributed between Tory and Labour supporters. A third objective
of this chapter is to examine the behavioural correlates of potential
activism—the extent to which the activists are better informed politically, take part in political discussions with their friends, and participate in associational activities—at the same time suggesting certain
interconnections between these variables. Lastly, the roots of activist
attitudes will be sought for in the political socialization process,

---

[1] 'The rule of anticipated reactions' was originally stated by Carl J. Friederich
in his *Constitutional Government and Democracy*: 1941. Friederich illustrated
this 'rule' when he wrote: 'Once, when being asked (in private) how much
English public opinion influenced the conduct of English foreign affairs, Sir
Eyre Crowe, a keen permanent official of the Foreign Office, replied that there
is only one instance, the Venezuela imbroglio, when the Foreign Office had been
obliged to change its policy in response to public opinion. The implication of
this statement was that the influence of public opinion is very small. Sir Eyre
Crowe forgot that almost daily the policy-making officials deliberated upon
what would be the reaction of the public to this, what the reaction of Parliament
to that move. By correctly anticipating these reactions, the Foreign Office
avoided getting embroiled and having to reverse its course; but was it therefore
free from being influenced by Parliament and the public?' (p. 589).

[2] For a discussion of the general problem of 'linkage' between public opinion
and governmental action, see V. O. Key, *Public Opinion and American Democracy*: 1961, pp. 411–535.

specifically in the workers' experiences with the authority of parents, teachers and employers.

I. SUBJECTIVE COMPETENCE

In order to operationalize the concept of subjective competence the respondents were asked, 'Suppose a regulation were being considered by Parliament or the local council which you considered very unjust or harmful, what do you think you could do about it?'[1] The respondents were placed in this hypothetical 'stress situation' because it is only under such circumstances, when the individual perceives the government to be sharply impinging on his life in an undesired manner, that he is likely to think about making an attempt to influence the government. Those workers who said there are things which they *could* do in such an instance are termed subjectively competent. The distribution of this attitudinal variable is reported in Table 20, where it is seen that more than two-thirds of both the Conservative and Labour voters register attitudes of subjective competence. This finding is significant in at least two respects. The frequency with which subjectively competent attitudes are found throughout the working class means that the workers' view of the political system is not a rigidly elitist one. Within this system the workers perceive a large number of possible conduits through which their personal views can be brought to the attention of political leaders. These men may still have the last word, but at a minimum the opportunity to communicate with them is available.

Secondly, the fact that identical proportions of Conservative and Labour voters register attitudes of subjective competence indicates that the two groups' perceptions of the political system as it is open to formally non-political individuals is very similar. Having previously seen that the Labour supporters more frequently believe in the

---

[1] Almond and Verba asked the same question twice, once referring to Parliament and once to the local council, whereas here the two are combined in order to reduce the length of the interview. They found that subjective competence (which is also their term) is more frequently found with respect to the local council than towards Parliament (op. cit., pp. 185–186). The frequency of subjectively competent responses in the present study falls at the midpoint between the rates of subjective competence exhibited towards the national and the local legislative bodies amongst those male manual workers living in urban areas found in the Almond and Verba sample, thereby lending additional confidence to the present data.

TABLE 20

Subjective competence: the belief that one could do something to
influence a Governmental decision in a stress situation

	Tories	Defs.	Prags.	Labs.
Political competents	70	68	71	69
Political non-competents	27	29	27	28
DK	3	3	2	3
Total per cent	100	100	100	100
Total number	320	90	230	127

existence of powerful groups which are able to subvert the majority's
interests than do the Tories, and that the Labour voters somewhat
less frequently believe the working class to have any significant influence on governmental decisions, here it turns out that the two
groups contain nearly identical proportions of subjective competents.
It thus seems warranted to argue that the Labour group's often expressed belief that they could act to influence the government if they
chose to do so has the function of further integrating them into the
political system; otherwise, their beliefs regarding the existence of
powerful minority interest groups and the holding of unfulfilled representational norms would tend to make them marginal, if not alienated,
members of the political system. This point is further buttressed
when it is noted that the Labour voters' estimation of the likelihood
of *success* if they attempted to alter the course of the government is
actually somewhat more optimistic than that of the Conservatives.[1]
In short, the Labour voters' dissatisfactions with the operation of the
political system are not acutely felt partly because they believe that
channels of protest are open to them if the government were to act
improperly.

The data go on to suggest that the working class as a whole conceives
of the political system as relatively open. While 70 per cent of the workers believe that channels of protest are available to them under stress
conditions, more than a third estimate that the probability of their

[1] The wording of this item is: 'If you made such an effort to change this
regulation, how likely is it that you would succeed?' Whereas 32 per cent of the
Tories answered in a positive fashion, saying that success would be at least
moderately likely, 39 per cent of the Labour voters replied in a similar manner.

actions influencing the government to change its policy is either very likely, moderately likely, or likely if others joined in. The holding of both these beliefs by relatively large numbers of workers serves to integrate them into the elitist political system. When dissatisfied with governmental decisions, the belief that *if* one wanted to do something about them, it would be possible to do so, yet waiting to act until things become really unbearable, is an effective device for psychologically submerging or dissolving negative political emotions. It is an even more effective psychological device for those workers holding an inflated estimate of their chances for success in altering government policy.

What of those workers, making up 28 per cent of the sample, who believe that they are impotent to do anything about changing the course of governmental policy? Does this figure represent a significant streak of working-class political alienation? Or are these workers simply realistic enough to conclude that there actually is nothing they could do to bring about a change in government policy, thereby acknowledging (and accepting?) the political impotence of non-elite individuals when faced with the imposing complex of governmental institutions? In order to decide between these two interpretations it is necessary to posit a condition which would have to be satisfied if the first hypothesis best accounts for the data; and if this condition is not met, it would enhance the plausibility of the second hypothesis. Hence, if the workers who feel themselves to be politically impotent are politically alienated—if they do not accept their perceived impotence—they should normatively object to the small or insignificant political role they attribute to the working class. However, this is not the case. Among those workers believing people like themselves to have little or no influence at all on governmental decisions, those respondents believing themselves to be politically impotent as individuals are somewhat more often satisfied with the working class' minimal political role than are the subjectively competent workers.

The evidence then indicates that notwithstanding feelings of personal political powerlessness on the part of more than one-quarter of the workers, these workers are not politically alienated. Rather, it seems as if they accept their impotence as an inevitable consequence of the individual's weak position and limited resources in contrast to the resources and complexity of the government. Moreover, the higher frequency with which those workers who are not subjectively competent subscribe to minimal norms regarding the working class' political role in comparison to the subjective competents, suggests that they may in some instances even think that individuals ought not to protest against government policies, either because the government is viewed as the repository of all authority, or because of an overriding faith in the correctness of all government actions—actions that might un-justifiably be interpreted as injurious by uninformed individuals. But whatever the underlying reason, the fact that those workers who believe that there is nothing they could do in the face of government action, instead of being resentful, willingly submit to the dictates of the political system, indirectly provides the elitist system with another layer of popular support.

II. POTENTIAL ACTIVISM

To ask a man if he could do anything in a political stress situation is not the same as to ask him how likely it is that he *would* do something. The former question elicits the respondent's beliefs regarding the possibilities for non-elite protests; the latter question measures poten-tial activism—the subjective likelihood that the individual will actually make the attempt to block an unjust or harmful regulation.[1] The two are not, however, unrelated. The belief that one could protest against a governmental decision is a necessary pre-condition for the develop-ment of activist predispositions. Only 2 per cent of the workers be-lieving that there is nothing they could do in a stress situation replied that it is likely that they would make the attempt.

The assumption of an acquiescent or inactivist posture in the face of injurious government action may be interpreted as a pre-democratic attitude towards authority; it strongly implies that the individuals are willing to be acted upon by the government without adopting the reverse attitude in which *they* attempt to act upon the government, even under stress conditions. But political passivity, or non-partici-pation, is not always equivalent to the assumption of an acquiescent stance towards governmental authority, necessarily entailing a respect for that authority. For non-participation may be found together with a thorough-going political cynicism, political alienation or a refusal

---

[1] After being placed in a hypothetical stress situation, the respondents were then asked the following question as an indicator of potential activism: 'If such a case arose, how likely is it that you would actually do something about it?' 'Very likely', 'moderately likely', and 'likely if others joined in', are the types of responses which are taken as indicators of potential activism.

to accord the governmental system legitimacy. However, in the case of the English manual workers, it is possible to interpret non-participation as nearly equivalent to acquiescent attitudes given the minimal extent to which the workers are politically alienated. If this interpretation is accepted, and then turning to the data presented in Table 21, we find another dimension of attitudes towards political authority in which the Conservative and Labour voters manifest distinct similarities. In fact, if the data are accepted at face value, it is the Labour supporters who are actually more acquiescent than the Tories: 43 per cent of the former compared to 34 per cent of the latter replied that they would passively accept the government's actions. Yet it must be recalled that the interviews took place while a Conservative Government was in office, which probably accounts for the Labour voters' somewhat greater reluctance to exert their political influence. We have here another attitudinal dimension which allows us to speak of a common or unified working-class political culture, in which the two parties' conflicting ideologies and traditions with respect to the political role of the non-elite have not succeeded in forcing a division between their working-class supporters.[1]

TABLE 21

Potential Activism: the belief that one would make an attempt to influence the Government in a stress situation

	Tories	Defs.	Prags.	Labs.
Potential activists	61	50	65	56
Potential non-activists	34	40	32	43
Depends	1	3	0	2
DK	3	7	2	0
Total per cent	100	100	100	100
Total number	320	90	230	127

Potential activism is one attitudinal dimension in the non-elite's orientation towards governmental authority. How then does its distribution within the working class relate to the distribution of comparable

[1] A significant difference that cannot be explained away by the presence of a Tory Government does appear between the deferentials and pragmatists, with the deferentials adopting a pre-democratic attitude somewhat more frequently than the pragamatists. (See Table 21)

dimensions? Namely, how valid is the assumption that the potential activists tend to subscribe to attitudes delimiting the government's procedural authority since they are apparently ready to take action against the elite in stress situations? One might also expect that amongst those workers perceiving the working class to have only a modicum of influence upon the government the potential activists amongst them would less frequently ratify this situation as normatively proper. However, neither of these assumptions is verified. The potential activists register nearly identical attitudes towards the scope of governmental authority and maintain the same set of representational norms as do the non-activists. This finding indicates the presence of an important balance in the working-class political culture. The government is not subject to intensive pressures from the workers which would be the case if the potential activists also insisted upon a restriction of governmental authority and a greater political role for the working class, i.e. if participatory demands and activist predispositions were cumulative so that the groups with political demands also contained a particularly high ratio of activist to non-activists. On the other hand, the non-activists are not simply opting out of the political game by their refusal to make any attempts to direct the flow of government policy in stress situations; for they are just as likely as the potential activists to believe in the delimitation of governmental authority in favour of the non-elite and to subscribe to norms dictating a larger role for the workers in the decision-making process.

III. POTENTIAL ACTIVISM AND ACTIVIST BEHAVIOUR

While 18 per cent of the potential activists replied that at one time or another they had actually attempted to influence government policy, not one of the non-activists replied in the same manner. Clearly then the potential activists are more likely to engage in political activity then are the non-activists. Yet an attempt to influence the government directly is not the only form of political activism, though it is the most demanding in terms of the effort and personal resources involved. Taking the time to inform oneself politically, discussing politics with friends, and in some instances, joining voluntary associations and trade unions also involve political activity. We want to know how and to what extent these 'lesser' forms of political activity are related to potential activism. If the measure of potential activism is a valid and reliable one, an association ought to be found between the latter and these other variables; individuals who say that they would make a protest to the government should also manifest a higher frequency of other types of activist behaviour.

In order to measure political awareness or cognizance the respondents were asked two questions: to name three leaders of the Conservative Party, three Labour Party leaders, and one leader of the Liberal Party, and also to name at least five cabinet positions.[1] The number of correct answers were added together to provide a single measure of political awareness, the respondents then being classified as high, medium or low scorers.[2] As expected, both Conservative and Labour supporters who are potential activists score higher on this scale than do the non-activists; 52 per cent of the potential activists compared to 32 per cent of the non-activists are high scorers, indicating that the former devote a greater amount of time to informing themselves politically.[3] This would appear to be a better, though not a complete, explanation for the correlation between the two variables than the reverse argument that political awareness results in potential activism. It is difficult to see how being 'interested' in gaining political information can lead to activist tendencies; at the most, high political awareness can strengthen the resolve to influence the government by suggesting the best strategy to be employed. Further support for the proposition that it is activist attitudes which lead to the acquisition of political information is found in the application of quasi-experimental techniques to survey analysis. Two sophisticated social scientists concluded that attitudes lead to the acquisition of knowledge, rather than the level of information playing a role in the development of attitudes.[4]

[1] These two items appeared in the interview schedule in the following form: 'We are also interested in how well known the national leaders of the various parties are in this country. Could you name three leaders of the Conservative Party (the Labour Party, and one leader of the Liberal Party)?' The second question reads: 'When a new Prime Minister comes into office, one of the first things he must do is appoint people to cabinet positions and ministries. Could you tell me what some of these cabinet positions are?'

[2] Since the two questions refer to the most elementary pieces of political information, the operational definition of high scorers was limited to those workers supplying 11 or 12 correct answers out of a possible perfect score of 12. Otherwise the scores would not effectively discriminate among the respondents.

[3] In making this calculation and the one following, the weighting index was employed, the number of Labour respondents being multiplied by five.

[4] H. Hyman and P. Sheatsley, 'Some Reasons Why Information Campaigns Fail', *Public Opinion Quarterly*, 1947–48, pp. 412–423.

The potential activists not only register a higher degree of political cognizance, they also talk about politics somewhat more frequently than do the non-activists. Whereas 48 per cent of the potential activists discuss politics with their friends 'sometimes' or 'often', only 36 per cent of the non-activists exhibit similar behaviour.[1] These two variables stand in a complex inter-relationship with each other, both being part of what might loosely be called the political participation syndrome—a set of attitudes and behaviour indicating political involvement. However, one aspect of the relationship can be clearly stated: discussing politics with one's friends reinforces activist tendencies in a number of ways. It often provides experience and training in shaping the opinions of others and in organizing support for one's own views within the peer group. Secondly, discussing politics is a form of political participation which engenders confidence in one's persuasive abilities and thereby increases the likelihood of activist behaviour. A circle of friends with whom the individual has political contacts is also a potential resource which can be utilized under stress conditions, whether it be as a readily available source of signatures on a petition or as the support of numbers in lobbying the local MP.

Workers join voluntary associations for a variety of reasons, but since only a small percentage of organizations in the working-class community have purposes which could be termed civic or political,[2] most of these reasons are unrelated to political activism. Yet the two are related in a latent manner. Once having joined an association, any prior activist tendencies are given a further impetus, while in other instances potential activism may originate with associational membership. This point is evidenced in Table 22 in which organizational membership is utilized as the explanatory variable. Of the Conservatives who are group members 80 per cent are potential activists, while only 53 per cent of the non-members are such. The Labour supporters show a significantly smaller difference (one of 12 per cent) in the proportion of potential activists between members and non-members. The stronger relationship between organizational membership and activist

[1] This question was asked in the following form: 'Do you discuss politics with your friends often, sometimes or hardly at all?'

[2] Trade union membership (which does have distinct political overtones) is not included in the discussion at this point as can be seen from the wording of the question referring to organizational membership: 'Are you a member of any organized group—social groups, sports clubs, religious organizations or any other type of organized group besides trade unions?'

predispositions among the Tories is possibly related to the lower rate at which they join associations (28 per cent) compared to the Labour supporters (43 per cent). The Conservatives' lower rate of membership reflects their minority position in the working-class community. There are fewer associations to which they are attracted and feel comfortable in, especially with respect to those working-class associations in which politics is a subject of conversation.[1] It would therefore take more of what might be roughly called an activist personality to join an association if one is a working-class Tory; it is a more meaningful indicator of activist behaviour for a member of a minority to join an association than it is for a member of the majority to do so. Hence the 80 per cent of Tory group members who are also potential activists is partly accounted for by the activist personality traits needed for Conservatives to become group members—a requirement which is not equally applicable to the Labour voters.

TABLE 22

Group membership and potential activism

	Tories		Labour	
	Member	Non-member	Member	Non-member
Potential activists	80	53	63	51
Potential non-activists	19	41	35	48
Depends	1	1	2	1
DK	0	5	0	0
Total per cent	100	100	100	100
Total number	93	227	54	73

In attempting to explain the difference in the strength of the group membership—potential activism relationship between the Tory and Labour groups it was just suggested that activist personality traits— and thus potential political activism—are the independent variables affecting the membership rate. But in accounting for the relationship within the two groups the reverse is also true. Associational membership is likely to develop activist tendencies due to the structural similarities between the political system and voluntary organizations. The decision-making process in voluntary associations has certain affinities with that

[1] See below, Chapter 7, for a discussion of this point.

of the political system, while their smaller size provides greater opportunities for the members to participate in that process. Associational membership provides the members with a certain amount of political training and experience in their relations with the associational leaders, consequently enhancing the workers' skill in influencing governmental decisions. Such experiences in an embryonic political system also provide the members with the necessary confidence in themselves as participants if they are to become potential activists within the larger political system. Further, the greater proximity and control of the non-elite over the elite within most associations serves to increase the value placed upon, and the expectations regarding, the non-elite's role in the political system, as values are transferred from one to the other.

It was thought best to analyse the effects of trade union membership upon potential activism apart from membership in other types of voluntary organizations. Trade union membership is not always voluntary in the strict sense of the word, and it is expected that membership would have different effects upon the political attitudes of Conservative and Labour voters given the close connection between the trade unions and the Labour Party. Both these assumptions are born out by the data. For the Conservatives, trade union membership has no effect whatsoever in developing activist tendencies. The absence of a relationship here is due both to the sometimes involuntary nature of the Tories' membership, being pressured into joining a trade union by their peers, the 'closed' shop[1] and by the dictates of economic advantage, and to the Conservatives' weaker trade union identification because of the unions' connections with the Labour Party, entailing a smaller amount of interest and participation in union affairs than in the case of the Labour voters.[2] Trade union membership consequently has no effect in developing the Tories' activist predispositions. On the other hand, a significant relationship between these two variables is found among the Labour voters: 59 per cent of the members compared to 44 per cent of the non-members are potential activists. The previous remarks relating organizational membership to potential activism would then appear to be applicable to trade union affiliations among the Labour supporters. However, here too the frequently involuntary nature of the member-

[1] For a discussion of compulsory unionism, see W. E. J. McCarthy, *The Closed Shop in Britain*: 1964.

[2] For a comparison of Tory and Labour trade union membership rates and activities, see pp. 198–208 below.

ship plays a part in lessening the activist effects of membership. Assuming that the training and attitudes developed in organizations with political objectives are more directly relevant to the formation of activist tendencies than are experiences in non-political organizations, we should have found a stronger relationship between trade union membership and activist attitudes than between voluntary association membership and activist attitudes. Since this is not the case, it would seem that the heightened effects of membership in a quasi-political trade union are often neutralized by the involuntary nature of the membership—even among the Labour supporters who at least tacitly support the connections between their unions and the Labour Party.

IV. POLITICAL SOCIALIZATION

Political socialization is a broadly inclusive term referring to the inculcation or learning of political attitudes and behaviour, whether this be done in a latent or overt manner. The political socialization process begins in the first years of life when the child enters into dependence-authority relations with his parents; the process picks up momentum during the early school years as the child learns to distinguish between governmental and non-governmental authority figures, generalizing from the latter to the former; the adolescent begins to develop partisan feelings and sometimes experiences overt political socialization in the form of 'citizenship' training provided at home and in the school; and the adult's political attitudes are oftentimes modified by his work-place experiences.

Here we are only concerned with one aspect of the political socialization process, namely, those factors which contribute to the development of activist political attitudes. This predisposition is essentially one involving the relationship between the individual and his government; his willingness and readiness to question and to act against particular expressions of governmental authority. It therefore follows that the aspect of the political socialization process that is most crucial for the formation of activist tendencies is the experience with non-governmental authority figures. More specifically, we have in mind the workers' readiness to question and protest against the authority of parents, teachers and work-place supervisors. It is these authority figures which generally have the strongest influence on the formation of adult attitudes towards the relationship between the individual and his government. Relations with non-governmental authority figures are thought to be the latent matrix within which attitudes towards governmental authority are developed because the former are not only more pervasive than the latter (they are part of the individual's immediate and continuous environment), they are also more acutely experienced by the individual than are the distant and intermittent relations with governmental authority. This relationship is not a direct one as is often assumed. For example, having an overbearing authority figure as a father does not directly result in an adult political submissiveness. The environmental factor (in this instance the father's excessive strictness) is first instrumental in the development of certain adolescent predispositions *vis-à-vis* parental authority. It is these predispositions which are then transferred to political authority figures in the adult years. Latent political socialization thus takes place in at least two steps: the non-political environment shapes non-political attitudes which in turn help pattern adult political attitudes.

What are the motivational links connecting experiences with non-political authority figures and attitudes towards governmental authority? There appear to be at least four paths by which experiences in one sphere pattern behaviour and attitudes in another sphere separated from the first by time and setting. In the first place, experiences with authority in non-political settings are likely to be projected on to the political system. For example, in a study of American school children it was found that attitudes towards the President are the same attitudes that were previously directed towards the children's fathers. The President is perceived as standing in a similar position to the children's fathers and communities as does the father with respect to his children, thereby resulting in the projection of attitudes from non-political to political authority figures.[1] Secondly, expectations regarding the proper relationship between the person possessing authority and the person over whom that authority is exercised are engendered in a non-political setting and generalized to the political system. If the individual is able to influence the decisions of parents, teachers or employers when they make decisions affecting his interests, he is likely to *expect* to be able to influence the wielders of governmental authority under similar circumstances. Thirdly, the factor of psychological congruence might dictate a convergence of attitudes towards political and non-political

---

[1] Robert D. Hess and David Easton, 'The Child's Changing Image of the President', *Public Opinion Quarterly*, Winter 1960, pp. 632–644.

authority figures. A marked divergence in attitudes towards the same type of object in two different settings, unless neutralized by a tension management device, may set up a psychological strain; e.g. when an individual is acted upon by his employer while assuming an activist role towards governmental authority. This factor is particularly relevant to the relationship between attitudes towards the employer's authority and that of the government because the two sets of attitudes are being held simultaneously, which is not true of attitudes towards parental and governmental authority, for example. Lastly, experiences with non-political authority serve as a training ground for the individual's citizen role. They provide the opportunity to develop a facility for self-expression, confidence in oneself as an activist, and the ability to bring together (or work together with) a group of peers in pursuance of a goal— goals involving the making of demands upon authority figures being especially relevant.

Potential activism has been defined as a readiness to protest against a particular exercise of governmental authority. The three key questions employed here with respect to socialization experiences in the family, school and on the job are also measures of activist tendencies. In fact, the structure of these three questions closely parallels that of the question utilized as a measure of potential activism; in each instance the respondents were asked to state the likelihood of their protesting about a decision which they found disagreeable to the authority responsible for that decision. Thus to measure the presence or absence of activist tendencies in the family, the respondents were asked: 'As you were growing up, let us say at about thirteen, if a decision were made by your parents which you didn't like, did you feel free to complain, did you feel a little uneasy about complaining, or was it better not to complain?' Before analysing the data produced by this question, it must be noted that, especially in the case of the older workers, the respondents are being asked to recall a period in their lives dating back many years. Clearly there is room for some error in their responses as there is in the responses to a similar question referring to the respondents' former school teachers. There is both the problem of memory and the possibility that current adult attitudes unconsciously pattern recollections of adolescent experiences; that the past is seen through the skewed lenses of the present. However, the reliability of the data is enhanced because the patterns fit our knowledge of changes in child rearing practices and teacher-pupil relations since the beginning of the twentieth century.

The workers were asked to characterize the strictness with which they were treated by their parents and teachers. When the sample is then divided into four age groups, a linear increase is evidenced in the proportion of workers with strict parents and teachers as age increases. (See Table 23)[1]

TABLE 23

The proportion of workers with very strict fathers and teachers according to age[2]

	21–29	30–45	46–59	60+
Very strict fathers	11	16	29	38
Very strict teachers	22	30	61	85
Total number	35	132	137	143

In Table 24 the responses to the above question regarding activist tendencies during early adolescence serve as the independent variable in the relationship with potential political activism. Among the Tories 60 per cent of those who reported that they 'felt free' to complain to their parents exhibit adult activist predispositions, compared to 32 per cent of those who 'felt uneasy' or thought it 'better not to complain'. Adolescent activist tendencies are an equally strong explanatory factor among the Labour voters. The data clearly point to these adolescent attitudes towards parental authority as an important factor in the formation of adult attitudes towards the relationship between the individual and governmental authority. Unfortunately it is not possible to specify the relative importance of the four possible paths linking these adolescent and adult attitudes. To do so would require an elaborate study combining experimental and survey data. But with the data at hand we can answer another question of equal importance. The analysis can be taken one step further *back* by inquiring into the factors which made some respondents feel free to complain to their parents while others felt uneasy or thought it better to dismiss the idea entirely.

The answer to this question clearly lies in the familial pattern of authority experienced by the adolescents—the manner in which parental authority was exercised and the extent to which the adolescents were

[1] See below, pp. 128, 132, for the wording of the two questions.
[2] The weighting index, according to which the number of Labour respondents are multiplied by five, is employed here.

TABLE 24

Remembered freedom to protest parental decisions and potential activism

| | Tories | | Labour | |
	Felt free	Uneasy or better not	Felt free	Uneasy or better not
Potential activists	60	32	68	41
Potential non-activists	36	65	32	55
Depends	0	1	0	4
DK	4	2	0	0
Total per cent	100	100	100	100
Total number	173	138	72	51

allowed to share in that authority. In order to measure the latter, the respondents were asked to what extent their parents permitted them to influence those decisions affecting themselves.[1] The responses are then used as the independent variable in accounting for the adolescents' felt freedom to protest parental decisions. The data clearly indicate that this element in the familial pattern of authority plays a crucial role in the development of activist adolescent predispositions (see Table 25).[2] Of those respondents whose parents allowed them a 'good deal' of influence in deciding matters affecting themselves, 92 per cent replied that they felt free to complain when decisions were made with which they disagreed, the proportion falling respectively to 78 per cent and 34 per cent among those having 'some' influence and no influence whatsoever on family decisions. It ought to be stressed, that despite possible appearances to the contrary, the two variables in Table 25 are independent of each other; to be consulted by someone in authority is not the same thing as protesting a decision taken by that authority. In one instance influence is voluntarily shared by the parents, and in the other demands are being voiced by the adolescents.

A second variable in the development of activist tendencies within

[1] The question reads: 'How much influence do you remember having in family decisions affecting yourself? Did you have much influence, some influence, or none at all?'

[2] Here and in Table 26 the Conservative and Labour patterns are virtually identical; they have therefore been combined.

TABLE 25

Remembered influence upon parental decisions and the felt freedom to
protest against parental decisions[1]

| | Influence Upon Parental Decisions | | |
	Much	Some	None
Felt free to protest	92	78	34
Uneasy and better not	6	21	64
Don't remember, DK	3	1	2
Total per cent	100	100	100
Total number	36	171	227

the family is the manner in which parental authority is exercised. To
get at this factor the respondents were asked: 'How did your father
generally treat you when you were about 13 years old? Was he very
strict, fairly strict or rather easy?' A linear increase is found in the
proportion of activists within the family as the father's reported
authority becomes more lenient. Only 36 per cent of the respondents
having very strict fathers are likely to make protests to their parents,
compared to 52 per cent and 70 per cent of those workers with fairly
strict and rather lenient fathers respectively (see Table 26). Adolescents
with stricter fathers are clearly penalized for protesting against their
decisions. An identical question was also asked in reference to the
manner in which authority was exercised by the mother, but here there
is only a 5 per cent difference in the proportion of actively predisposed
respondents between those having very strict and rather easy going
mothers. This finding is somewhat surprising considering the predominant role which is commonly attributed to the working-class
mother. Hoggart calls her 'the pivot of the home'.[2] But apparently in
this regard the male adolescent's behaviour is more often shaped by the
father's exercise of authority than by the mother's, even though the
father does not make the decisions relating to the punishment of the
children more frequently than does the mother.[3] It would thus seem

[1] See note 2, p. 127.
[2] Op. cit., p. 38.
[3] The sample was asked how decisions were made regarding the punishment
of children for misbehaving. Nearly identical proportions of respondents said
that the father made such decisions and that the mother made them.

that the father's greater effect on the adolescent's activist tendencies is due to a combination of his pre-eminent position of authority in the home—he is clearly the 'Mister' in the working-class family—and to the harsher psychological effects of patriarchal as opposed to matriarchal authority.

TABLE 26

Strictness of father and the felt freedom to protest against parental decisions[1]

| | Father Reported to be: | | |
	Very strict	Fairly strict	Rather Easy
Felt free to protest	36	52	70
Uneasy and better not	62	47	28
Don't remember, DK	2	2	2
	—	—	—
Total per cent	100	100	100
Total number	111	161	137

Having found strong correlations between the frequency with which the adolescents were consulted by their parents when making decisions affecting them and the strictness of the father on the one hand, and activist predispositions within the family on the other, we ought to be able to turn these correlations into plausible explanations by suggesting how the latter variable is patterned by the other two. There appear to be at least three inter-connections here. It was previously stated that two factors inter-relating non-political adolescent attitudes with adult attitudes towards governmental authority are the acquisition of expectations regarding the proper exercise of authority, and the training received for inter-acting with authority wielders. These two linkages are presumably equally relevant for understanding the correlation between the familial pattern of authority and the development of activist pre-dispositions within the family. When adolescents are permitted a role in the making of family decisions expectations and training are presumably engendered which would lead them to protest against undesirable decisions. Similarly, given a lenient father, expectations about relations with other authority figures are developed, while the give-and-take relations one has with an easy going father serve to develop the adolescent's abilities for influencing other authority figures. A third

---

[1] See note 2, p. 127.

5

intervening factor has already been alluded to at the beginning of this chapter, where it was pointed out that a necessary condition for the formation of adult activist political tendencies is the belief that there is something the individual *could* do to protest a governmental decision. This argument is also relevant for the present analysis. Both the role which the adolescent is allowed to play when family decisions are made and the degree to which the father is a strict and overbearing parent closely determine the extent to which the adolescent thinks that he could do something to complain about a parental decision, thereby affecting the likelihood that he would register a protest.

The school is the second sphere in which the young adolescent comes into contact with authority figures. Schools are almost universally a system of institutionalized dominance and submission, necessitated by the conflict of interests and values between the 'governed and the governors'. The teachers represent the adult world, purposefully attempting to curb spontaneity; they also support the formal curriculum which the students have to accept, or at least abide by; and they are responsible for upholding the established order of the school against student unruliness. Moreover, in the case of our working-class sample, the teachers are the representatives of middle-class authority, feeling it incumbent upon themselves to inculcate the values of their own social class. As an institution, the school expresses little of working-class life. It is a middle-class institution whose utility and authority tend to be questioned because it entails the imposition of an alien culture; education is something to be endured rather than desired.[1]

In order to contain the conflict of interests and to impose a foreign culture upon the usually undisciplined students it is necessary for the teachers to be particularly strict.[2] One writer has characterized the 'typical school in Great Britain' as a system in which the relationship between teachers and pupils is 'essentially a dominance-submissive one in which information is "given" by the teacher and accepted by the pupils. Pupil activity is minimal, and docility and "order" are the

---

[1] This conflict between middle-class teachers and working-class students could also be considered in the context of the particularly accentuated hierarchical patterns governing inter-class relations that were discussed in the introductory chapter.

[2] Needless to say, teachers are exceptionally strict and the students especially undisciplined in urban slum areas where the conflict between middle-class and working-class cultures is most marked. For a discussion of the school in a slum district, see B. M. Spinley, *The Deprived and the Privileged: Personality Development in English Society*: 1953, pp. 53ff.

criteria of behaviour. Punishment as a technique of control is much more widespread and severe than is usually admitted.'[1] Presumably this statement is especially applicable to the technical, secondary modern, and comprehensive schools where working-class students predominate. Our data provide further substantiation for the point that the teachers are commonly strict authority figures. Whereas a sizeable proportion of parents chose not to exercise their prerogatives in an overly strict manner, this is rarely the case amongst teachers operating within an institutionalized and culturally divided system of conflict; 30 per cent of the sample reported having fathers who were somewhat lenient in their exercise of authority, but only 6 per cent reported having teachers who were similarly disposed. It is within this setting that the school acts as a socializing agent in the development of working-class attitudes toward governmental authority.

The relationship between the felt freedom to protest to the teacher, when it was thought that the teacher did something unfair or said something with which the student disagreed,[2] and adult potential activism is reported in Table 27. Among those Tories replying that they felt free to talk to the teacher about a matter with which they disagreed 71 per cent are potential activists, compared to 52 per cent of those feeling uneasy about talking to the teacher or thinking it better not to do so. These figures indicate that the school experience plays a part in the development of adult attitudes towards governmental authority, but its effects are not as strong as are experiences with parental authority. It may very well be that attitudes are more readily shaped by social objects belonging to the same culture than by those of an alien culture. In the former instance the socializing agents are better understood (the nuances of behavioural cues are more easily recognized) and the value placed upon these behavioural cues is increased because the socializing agents tend to serve as a valued reference group. In contrast, when the socializing agents are members of a different culture their influence is mitigated by the communications difficulties involved, while the flavour of an imposition of values is imparted to individuals when the socializing

---

[1] Ben S. Morris, 'Education and Human Relations', *Journal of Social Issues*, Spring 1947, p. 42. As indicated by our data, this generalization becomes somewhat overdrawn when applied to the contemporary schools.

[2] This variable was measured by asking the respondents, 'If you had been treated unfairly in some way, or disagreed with something the teacher said, did you feel free to talk to the teacher about it; did you feel a bit uneasy about talking to the teacher; or was it better not to talk to the teacher?'

agents belong to a socially superior cultural strata. This general hypothesis is certainly applicable to the present analysis since the respondents' parents belong to the same cultural strata as do the respondents, whereas the lower middle-class teachers (even though a sizeable proportion originally come from working-class families) not only belong to an alien cultural stratum, but a socially superior one at that.[1] The hypothesis' plausibility is enhanced when it is noted that the correlation between potential activism and the comparable attitude towards the teacher's authority is twice as strong among the Tories than among the Labour voters. This is what we would expect since it is the Labour voters who more frequently view the middle-class teachers as culturally and socially alien; the Labour voters place a greater value upon working-class solidarity and communality,[2] thereby setting middle-class people apart in a distinctly different social *milieu*.

TABLE 27

Felt freedom to talk to the teacher and potential activism

	Tories		Labour	
	Felt free	Uneasy or better not	Felt free	Uneasy or better not
Potential activists	71	52	61	51
Potential non-activists	24	44	39	46
Depends	1	0	0	3
DK	4	4	0	0
Total per cent	100	100	100	100
Total number	143	169	44	80

Since teacher-pupil relations in working class schools are ordered on a strictly hierarchical basis, the workers were not asked to state the amount of influence they were accorded by the teachers; the number of positive responses would probably be close to zero. But they were asked to characterize the degree of strictness with which they were treated by most of their teachers.[3] Just as the manner in which the father exercised

[1] Even among working-class students in the grammar schools, the teachers rank them lower than their middle-class peers in terms of their 'integration into the school'. Glass, op. cit., p. 159.

[2] See below, Chapter 7, for a presentation of the relevant data.

[3] This question reads: 'What were your teachers like? How strict were they —very strict, moderately strict, or lenient?'

his authority was seen to be associated with the respondents' felt freedom to complain to their parents, the teachers' style of authority helped produce or discourage the expression of dissatisfactions in the classroom. Of those workers reporting that they had moderately strict or lenient teachers[1] 54 per cent replied that they felt free to talk to the teacher if they thought they had been treated unfairly or disagreed with something the teacher said. In comparison, only 30 per cent of the respondents having very strict teachers developed this felt freedom to protest in the classroom. Thus the manner in which the teacher's authority is exercised influences the activist predispositions of those subject to that authority.[2] Again, the two variables are presumably inter-related by the expectations *vis-à-vis* authority figures engendered by the style with which the teacher exercises his authority, by the opportunities for developing one's abilities as an activist, and by the presence or absence of the pre-condition for the formation of activist attitudes—the belief that one could attempt to exercise influence.

The political socialization process does not come to an abrupt end when adolescents become adults. Even though political attitudes frequently harden in their pre-adult mould after adolescence, political socialization continues to effect important changes. Attitudes and behaviour alter as adults come into contact with various types of authority figures in voluntary associations, trade unions, the church and in the military. However, the most continuous and pervasive, and therefore the most psychologically significant, authority relations are those experienced on the job. And as already mentioned, attitudes towards the authority of the worker's supervisor are particularly relevant in the development of attitudes towards governmental authority since the two

[1] The two types of teachers are grouped together here because of the small number of reportedly lenient teachers.

[2] Here we are analysing the activist attitudes of our respondents during early adolescence. Similar attitudes are already found to be related to the teacher's authority among eight-year-old American children. A number of statistically significant behavioural differences were found between children having an 'integrative' teacher and those having a 'dominative' one. The former more frequently made voluntary suggestions, voluntarily indicated that they wished to do something, and in responding to the teacher's questions, voluntarily told about their personal experiences. (H. H. Anderson, *et al.*, *Studies of Teachers' Classroom Personalities*, II, Applied Psychological Monographs, 1946, pp. 70ff.) Although these forms of behaviour do not reflect activist attitudes which are as strong as those entailing a protest to the teacher, the subjects being studied are only eight years old as contrasted with the thirteen-year-old reference point used in the present survey.

are held simultaneously; the two sets of attitudes must approach congruence if a psychological strain is to be avoided, unless of course, a tension management device is available.

In order to tap their activist predispositions on the job the workers were asked to state their reactions to a decision affecting their own work with which they strongly disagreed.[1] In Table 28 the responses generated by this question serve as the independent variable in accounting for potential activism. It is seen that 64 per cent of the Conservatives who feel free to complain about work-place decisions, compared to 39 per cent of those feeling uneasy about doing so or thinking it better not to protest, are potential activists. There is an even stronger correlation between the two variables among the Labour supporters.

TABLE 28

Felt freedom to complain about work-place decisions and potential activism

	Tories		Labour	
	Feel free	Uneasy or better not	Feel free	Uneasy or better not
Potential activists	64	39	62	29
Potential non-activists	32	56	38	65
Depends	1	0	1	6
DK	2	5	0	0
Total per cent	100	100	100	100
Total number	252	41	104	17

Taking the analysis one step further back, as a measure of the worker's role in the factory authority structure, the respondents were asked how often they are consulted by their supervisors when decisions are made affecting their own work.[2] A linear relationship is then found between

[1] The question reads: 'If a decision were made affecting your own work that you disagreed with strongly, what would you do—would you feel free to complain, would you feel uneasy about complaining, or would it be better to accept these decisions and not complain?'

[2] Here the respondents were asked: 'When decisions are made affecting your own work do those in charge ever consult you about them? Do they usually consult you, do they sometimes consult you, or are you never consulted?' Self-employed workers have been excluded.

the frequency with which the workers are consulted—whether they are 'usually consulted', 'sometimes consulted' or 'never consulted'—and their activist attitudes towards the supervisor (see Table 29).[1]

TABLE 29

Frequency with which consulted by superiors and the felt freedom to complain about work-place decisions

	Frequency with which Consulted		
	Usually	Sometimes	Never
Feel free	97	83	65
Uneasy and better not	2	17	32
Depends	0	0	2
DK	1	0	0
	—	—	—
Total per cent	100	100	100
Total number	201	95	124

However, the second variable which was thought to be influential in shaping the workers' attitudes towards their supervisors, namely the manner in which the supervisor exercises his authority, is seen to have no appreciable effect; having a 'very strict, moderately strict, or somewhat easygoing' superior does not affect the workers' readiness to protest against the particular exercise of his authority.[2]

To be consulted by one's supervisor is a significant factor patterning the workers' attitudes because they are not able to demand such consultation; it is almost entirely up to the supervisor whether or not to seek the advice of his subordinates. There is thus a close parallel between this aspect of worker-supervisor relations, and the adolescent's relations with his father and teachers, which allows us to assume the existence of the same three linkages between the frequency with which advice is requested from the subordinate and his activist predispositions towards the superior. On the other hand, when a supervisor attempts to exercise his authority in a very strict manner the workers' position

[1] Since the Tories' and Labour supporters' manifest virtually identical response patterns the two have been combined in Table 29.

[2] The respondents were asked: 'What is the authority of your immediate supervisor like? Would you consider him to be very strict, moderately strict, or somewhat easygoing?'

of strength obviates their acceptance of such a relationship. A full employment economy has given the workers the bargaining power readily to stand up to their superiors, while the protection (if not immunity) provided by trade union membership provides security for the free expression of dissatisfactions. And thirdly, the 'human relations' spirit beginning to permeate management ranks legitimizes genuinely inspired worker protests against overbearing authority. Taken together, these factors make the workers immune to the overly strict exercise of authority by their supervisors, indicating why the presence of overbearing superiors has no effect in shaping the workers' activist predispositions on the job.

CHAPTER 6

Patterns of Partisanship

COMPARED to non-voters and independents, all the respondents in the sample are partisans: they have supported their respective parties in the 1959 election and continued to do so in the months before the 1964 election. Taking a walk to the voting booth on election day is clearly the *sine qua non* of partisanship. But to characterize a partisan solely by virtue of his having voted for a particular party is surely too broad a definition. Consequently, the first part of this chapter is designed to refine this encompassing category by specifying its various dimensions. It will then be possible to compare the three groups of voters in the sample with respect to each dimension, and then to combine the latter into an overall measure of partisanship.

Partisanship is commonly used to denote the voters' attachment to a particular party. Their continued electoral support over a long period of time, their identification with the party's leaders and symbols, and their willingness to contribute time and money to the party, are all measures of this attachment to the party. However, it is thought that the behavioural tendencies actually being measured in these instances refer to party loyalty or identification, rather than partisanship as conceived here. In this study partisanship is employed as an analytical concept referring to the perceived political distance separating one's own party from the opposition party. Partisanship is thus defined in a negative fashion: the degree to which the opposition party is viewed as undesirably different from one's own party. The term which comes closest to characterizing this conception of partisanship is the German *Gegnerschaft*, roughly translated as 'oppositionship'.

I. THE DIMENSIONS OF PARTISANSHIP

There are numerous ways in which this negative concept of partisanship could be operationalized. Here the partisanship scale is based

137

upon the responses to three questions referring to the perceived motivations of the opposition party, the extent to which the parties are thought to differ in their policies, and a general evaluation of the opposition party.

In order to tap the workers' beliefs about the motivations of their own party and those of the 'opposition' party they were asked: 'When people talk about politics some say that political parties try to get laws passed just to get votes, while others say that political parties have the best interests of the country at heart. Do you think that a Conservative Government usually has laws passed just to get votes, or for the good of the country?' The same question was also asked of a Labour Government. Those responses referring to the motivations of the 'opposition' party shall be utilized as our first dimension of partisanship. But before looking at these responses it would be useful to examine the workers' beliefs regarding their own party's motivations, even though these beliefs are indicators of party identification rather than partisanship as conceived here. The ensuing discussion of the first part of Table 30 then becomes something of a detour before returning to the workers' beliefs about the 'opposition' party's motivations.

One measure of the voters' party identification is the degree to which they attribute public spirited motives to their party leaders. In this respect, the data clearly show that the pragmatists are least often swayed by party loyalties in evaluating the goals of their party. Whereas 20 per cent of the pragmatists replied that the Tories are out to get votes, only 3 per cent of both the deferentials and Labour voters view their respective parties in this fashion. In Chapter 3 it was seen that the pragmatists are less acquiescent (or 'loyal') towards the party leaders when there is a policy divergence between the latter and themselves than are the deferentials—a finding which dovetails with the present one, indicating that the pragmatists maintain a less idealized and weaker attachment to the Conservative leaders than do the deferentials.

The most striking aspect of Table 30 is the frequency with which both the Tories (72 per cent) and Labour (95 per cent) adhere to the idealized belief that their own parties are primarily concerned with the country's welfare. This frequent idealization of one's own party is also brought out in the second wave of interviews. The respondents were asked what it is that leads Conservative and Labour MP's to go into politics. One deferential trade unionist from Coventry provided an eloquent answer to the question regarding the Tory MP's: 'They wanted very sincerely to help people, to help the country and to keep the Commonwealth going. It is born in them, a sort of tradition of service to Queen and country—and it is in all the good families in the land. It is part of their life to be concerned for the ordinary people of the country and to help them in every way; to give them good working

TABLE 30

The perceived motivations of the workers' 'Own' Party and the 'Opposition' Party

The Workers' 'Own' Party			
	Tories	Defs.	Prags.	Labs.
Get votes	16	3	20	2
Good of the country	72	80	69	95
Both	12	17	10	0
Depends	0	0	0	3
DK	0	0	0	0
Total per cent	100	100	100	100
Total number	320	90	230	127

The 'Opposition' Party			
	Tories	Defs.	Prags.	Labs.
Get votes	59	56	61	50
Good of the country	23	23	23	36
Both	12	14	11	8
Depends	1	0	1	2
DK	4	7	3	4
Total per cent	100	100	100	100
Total number	320	90	230	127

conditions, full employment and a good chance of educating themselves.' On the other side of the political divide, a post office sorter from Epsom had this to say about his party's MP's: 'I think you'll find that a lot of Labour MP's have been TUC members. They feel in themselves that it's up to them to run the country, and they must have the country at heart to do this. They go into it for the betterment of the country. They see a lot of the faults in the industry they've been in so they feel they

can serve the best interests of the working men they represent by
going in to be MP's'.

A minor point to be brought out from Table 30 is that a small proportion of Conservatives are sophisticated enough to recognize a
confluence between individual self-interest and the interests of the
country as a whole in regard to party leaders. In their view the two
types of motivations need not be mutually exclusive, whereas the Labour
voters seem unable to conceive of this idea. While a small number
of Tories (12 per cent) chose to answer the question regarding the
motivations of Tory politicians in terms other than those provided
in the question's phrasing, replying that these politicians are motivated by *both* the country's interests and their own, not a single Labour
supporter replied in this vein. This relatively sophisticated streak
within the Tory group—the recognition that the interests of the part and
of the whole may be complementary rather than mutually exclusive—
also appears in two other parts of the study. In a first wave question the
Tory respondents were asked to describe the kind of people who run
the Conservative Party. Three of the open-ended replies are particularly relevant at this point. The Tory leaders are described as 'people
who have their own interests to consider and who would suffer if
England lost its strength'; 'people of breeding who have money and
benefit from the country if it is kept strong and healthy'; 'business
people who would be hurt if England were to become weak'. When
asked why the Tory MP's became interested in politics, a deferential
who is a retired maintenance worker for British Railways, replied:
'We know the Conservative side is really the money side. I suppose
they go into it (politics) for the love of the thing and the love of looking
after their wealth and the wealth of the country'. Another deferential,
a long-distance lorry-driver from Manchester, answered the question
in a similar manner: 'What I can see of them (the Tory MP's) they've
got the money. I think the interest of the country is their financial
interest so it's up to them to keep the country prosperous because it's
to their own advantage'. He went on to say that this overlap is not
applicable to the Labour MP's because they do not have any financial
interests to protect, and are therefore only out for personal power as
evidenced in the Labour Government's schemes to control the economy
and the people.

Not only are the Tories sometimes sophisticated enough to recognize the possible confluence of self-interest and selflessness, they are

also realistic enough to realize that the Tory MP's can more often afford to be selfless than can the Labour MP's because of their secure economic and social positions. One pragmatist thinks the Tories go into the House 'for the good of the country because they already have money'. Another pragmatist, the foreman working in a Birmingham tele-communications plant, thinks that the Labour MP's go into politics because of their 'egotism', their self-interested desire to move up from the trade union movement into the political limelight. But in reference to the Tory MP's he said that 'there isn't any egotism in the Conservative Party. Most of them have made their mark before they go into Parliament so they have no need for egotism'. This line of reasoning finds a distinctly similar echo in the writings of one modern Tory apologist. According to A. K. White, 'Responsible government demands certain privileges in the way of leisure and culture . . . Only those who are economically secure can acquire the culture which . . . enables (them) to rule responsibly.'[1]

Turning to the second part of Table 30, we find the data which serves as our first measure of negative partisanship: the interpretation placed upon the motivations of the opposition party. On this dimension the Tories are at first sight slightly more partisan than the Labour voters, with 59 per cent of the Tories replying that the Labour Party is out to get votes, compared to 50 per cent of the Labour voters who maintain this same belief about the Conservative Party. Yet even this small difference loses its significance when we take into account the 16 per cent of the Conservatives who also hold this view about their own party, while only 2 per cent of the Labour voters think that their party is out to get votes. Partisan scores are assigned to those respondents who believe that the opposition party is out to get votes, but who do not subscribe to the same belief with respect to their own party; for our definition of partisanship stresses the perceived *differences* between one's own party and the opposition party. There is thus almost a perfect balance between the Conservative and Labour voters on this partisan dimension.

The second dimension of partisanship refers to the perceived distance separating the two parties in terms of their policies. The respondents were asked: 'Considering the policies of the Labour and Conservative Parties, would you say that there is a good deal of difference between their policies, some difference, or very little difference?' In constructing

---

[1] *The Character of British Democracy*: 1945, pp. 17–20, cited in Beer, op. cit., p. 94.

the partisanship scale those responses which refer to the large policy differences between the parties are taken as indicators of partisanship. As set out in Table 31, the responses indicate that the deferentials maintain the highest degree of partisanship of the three groups, with the pragmatists and Labour voters exhibiting almost identical patterns. But when the Tory group is considered as a whole there is very little difference in the amount of partisanship expressed by the Conservative and Labour voters. The data also indicate that within the Tory and Labour groups there is a balance between the number of workers who believe there to be a wide policy divide separating the two parties and those who see relatively small differences separating them, each group constituting approximately half of the Conservative and Labour supporters.

TABLE 31

The perceived differences between Conservative and Labour Party policies

	Tories	Defs.	Prags.	Labs.
A good deal	47	57	43	43
Some	28	33	25	24
Very little	26	10	32	29
Depends, DK	0	0	0	2
Total per cent	100	100	100	100
Total number	320	90	230	127

The third dimension of partisanship is a general evaluation of the 'opposition' party. The workers were asked what they 'like' and 'dislike' about each of the two parties.[1] At this point we are only interested in those respondents who replied that there is 'nothing' they like about the 'opposition' party, which is a fairly reliable indication that these workers believe the two parties to be separated by a deep political divide.[2] Again, the deferentials manifest the strongest degree of parti-

[1] See p. 257 below for the wording of these four questions.
[2] However, this interpretation of the data is at least partly questionable. Presumably some of the respondents replied that there is nothing they like about the 'opposition' party because they could not think of any other response to this open-ended question. This factor is relevant in gauging the absolute levels of partisanship within our three groups, but there is no reason to believe

sanship, but when the two Tory groups are combined there is almost no difference between them and the Labour supporters on this dimension of partisanship (see Tables 39 and 41).

In Table 32 the respondents' replies to the previous three questions are integrated into one partisanship scale. The strong partisans are those who replied to all three questions in a partisan manner. The medium partisans provided one or two partisan responses, and the weak partisans did not answer any of the three questions as partisans, i.e. their partisanship is limited to voting for one party or another. Although the deferentials are somewhat more partisan than the pragmatists, the most striking aspect of the data is the emergence of a virtually symmetrical pattern of partisan attitudes when the Tories and Labour supporters are compared—the nearly identical partisan configurations for both groups of voters. The other important point to be noted about Table 32 is the large proportion of respondents falling into the medium partisanship category—three times as many as are in the strong or weak partisanship groups. This finding indicates that there is a limited partisan polarization; the Conservative and Labour supporters are indeed negatively oriented towards the 'opposition' party, but these attitudes are tempered by a respect for the 'opposition' party leadership and a partial agreement with the 'opposition' party's policies.

TABLE 32

Partisanship Scores

	Tories	Defs.	Prags.	Labs.
Strong	23	29	21	20
Medium	62	57	63	61
Weak	15	14	15	19
Total per cent	100	100	100	100
Total number	320	90	230	127

The working class partisan attitudes are thus balanced in two crucial respects: there is a balance (or close similarity) between the two groups of voters in terms of the intensity with which they subscribe to partisan

that it detracts from a comparison of partisanship levels among them; i.e. there is no reason to think that the proportion of workers answering 'nothing' and doing so for lack of a different response varies *within* the three groups.

beliefs; and within the Tory and Labour ranks the influence of the strong and weak partisans is balanced by the high proportion of medium partisans. These two findings are indirectly, but fundamentally, linked to the operation of the political system. The balanced and limited partisanship of the Tories and Labour voters indicates that there are no sharp substantive (and probably procedural) cleavages separating the two groups of voters, and that a low emotional content attaches to the workers' negative attitudes towards the 'opposition' parties. If partisan attitudes were emotionally charged and highly negative, it would only be a small further step to the formation of mass movements and the fragmentation of the political system. At the same time, such a politics of high emotional content and sharp cleavages would be incompatible with an acquiescent orientation towards governmental authority—an orientation pre-supposing a respect for the government and a willingness to subordinate partisan feelings to its legitimate demands no matter which party is in power. And as will be suggested in the concluding chapter, it is just this acquiescent strain in the political culture that is a necessary condition for stable and effective democracy.

II. PARTISANSHIP AND POLITICAL ACTIVITY

In order to gain both a better understanding of the workers' partisan beliefs and to analyse their effects upon the political system, it would be well to examine the relationship between these beliefs and various types of political activity.

It was previously pointed out that political awareness is an indicator of political activity since it measures the amount of time and energy devoted to the mass media's reporting of political news. In relating partisanship and political awareness we specifically want to know whether those workers who are strong partisans are also the workers who manifest the greatest degree of political awareness? The answer to this question is found in Table 33.

Among the Conservatives it is the strong partisans who exhibit the lowest measure of political cognizance, which is to say that among these voters strong partisan attitudes are based upon a cursory amount of political knowledge. And even though the Labour data show a positive correlation between increasing partisanship and political awareness, to a large extent the same conclusion is applicable to this group. For

TABLE 33
Partisanship and Political Awareness

	Partisanship Scores					
	Tories			Labour		
	Strong	Medium	Weak	Strong	Medium	Weak
High wareness	36	47	48	38	35	13
Medium awareness	40	35	30	35	35	21
Low awareness	24	18	22	27	30	67
Total per cent	100	100	100	100	100	100
Total number	75	195	50	26	77	24

only 38 per cent of the strong Labour partisans are high scorers on the political awareness scale—a scale based upon a set of questions referring to the most elementary pieces of political information. Thus with only 36 per cent and 38 per cent of the strong Tory and Labour partisans respectively, registering high scores on the political awareness scale, it is clear that strong partisanship is not founded upon any extensive amount of political information. If only a little more than a third of the strong Tory and Labour partisans can name seven national political figures and five cabinet offices, it is most improbable that they have enough knowledge even to *begin* to evaluate the opposition parties' motivations and policies.

It would therefore seem that highly partisan attitudes are largely a result of a pre-determined set of emotional dislikes through which the activities and policy statements of the 'opposition' party are prejudicially filtered. Or to state the matter somewhat differently, the data imply that the strong partisans unthinkingly accept the black and white view of the two parties painted by the propagandists of their own party. For without a far greater amount of political information than they possess, it is impossible for the strong partisans to separate the parties' propagandistic chaff from the objectively accurate wheat. Regarding the medium and weak partisans, it can at least be said that they do not automatically accept the necessarily tainted picture of the 'opposition' party as portrayed by their own leaders, although even this refusal would appear to be based upon a pre-determined set of emotionally neutral predispositions towards the opposition party rather than even a minimal storehouse of political information.

A second measure of political activity is the frequency with which the workers talk about politics with their friends. We want to know whether or not partisan attitudes predispose the respondents towards more frequent political discussions. Table 34 indicates that amongst the Labour voters the strong partisans carry on political conversations with their friends more frequently than do their less partisan equivalents, with 31 per cent of the strong Labour partisans 'often' discussing politics, compared to 12 per cent and 13 per cent of the medium and weak partisans respectively. There is preciously little in either the first or second wave data to suggest that the workers who discuss politics do so in order to convince their friends of their own partisan views. Rather, it would seem plausible to suggest that the workers who are the most dissatisfied with political conditions, in this instance the strong Labour partisans, will most often become involved in political conversations because they have the most to complain about. This hypothesis fits well with the fact that twice as many strong Labour partisans frequently discuss politics (31 per cent) as do strong Conservative partisans (16 per cent). Since it is reasonable to assume that the strong Labour partisans, voting for an ideologically reformist party, are more dissatisfied with the state of political affairs than the strong Tory partisans, especially during the tenure of a Conservative Government, we would expect the former to be more often involved in political discussions than the latter. This interpretation would also account for the fact that there is only a weak relationship between partisanship and involvement in political conversations among the Conservatives. Since the Tories are voting for a largely *status quo* party, there is little reason to expect their partisan beliefs to be related to dissatisfactions with the state of political affairs, especially when the Labour Party is out of office. On the basis of these data the general hypothesis may be offered that individuals who are politically dissatisfied will more frequently engage in political conversations in order to give vent to their dissatisfactions than will politically contented individuals.[1]

---

[1] The general hypothesis that individuals who are politically dissatisfied will more often engage in political conversations in order to voice their complaints is given further support when the workers' beliefs about the existence of inordinately powerful groups are related to the frequency with which they discuss politics. Among the Tories, 50 per cent of those who believe in the existence of such groups discuss politics 'often' or 'sometimes', compared with 29 per cent of those who disagree that there are such groups. The equivalent percentages for the Labour supporters are 53 per cent and 29 per cent.

Examination of the inter-connections between partisanship and the frequency of political discussions permits analysis of another question: Who are the workers that set the tone and pace of political discussions? More specifically, how strong are the partisan leanings of those workers who discuss politics most frequently compared to those who do not take part in these conversations? In order to answer this question the positions of the two variables in Table 34 have been reversed to form Table 35. Among the Labour voters those who 'often' discuss politics are somewhat more partisan than those who talk politics 'sometimes' or 'hardly at all'. However, the differences are hardly of such a magnitude to suggest that the characteristic tone of Labour political conversations is heightened by strongly held

TABLE 34

Partisanship and frequency of political discussions

	Partisanship Scores					
Discuss politics	Tories			Labour		
	Strong	Medium	Weak	Strong	Medium	Weak
Often	16	9	12	31	12	13
Sometimes	27	31	28	19	36	29
Hardly ever	57	60	60	50	52	58
Total per cent	100	100	100	100	100	100
Total number	75	195	50	26	77	24

partisan beliefs. This is even more true of the Conservatives, since the group that talks about politics most frequently is slightly weaker in its partisan leanings than are their less talkative equivalents. This finding is significant to the extent that it helps to explain the presence of a limited partisanship among the Conservative and Labour voters. If the workers who 'often' talk politics were particularly strong partisans their negative attitudes towards the 'opposition' parties would be more broadly distributed throughout the working class. By engaging others in political conversations they would presumably have succeeded in infusing their own partisan beliefs among their less partisan friends.

The third aspect of political activity to be related to partisanship is potential activism. Are the strong partisans also those workers who are most frequently predisposed to attempt to influence the government under stress conditions? The data indicate there to be no relationship between the two variables. And it is just this absence of a correlation that helps to account for the orderly and unemotional style in which working-class politics are conducted. If the strong partisans who are most antagonistic towards the opposition party were also predisposed to act upon their beliefs, those workers with the loudest political voices would be mouthing the most radical partisan demands. Moreover, under such circumstances there might well be a divergence in the policies of the two parties as they attempt to satisfy their more activist and extremist supporters.

TABLE 35

Frequency of political discussions and partisanship

	Politics Discussed					
Partisanship	Tories			Labour		
	Often	S'times	Hardly	Often	S'times	Hardly
Strong	26	21	20	26	18	17
Medium	40	61	63	63	63	63
Weak	34	19	17	11	18	20
Total per cent	100	100	100	100	100	100
Total number	38	97	179	27	49	81

III. PARTY POLICIES AND WORKING-CLASS INTERESTS

Turning away from the particular conception of partisanship employed here, the balance of this chapter will centre upon the reasons provided by the respondents in accounting for their preferences for one party and their disinclinations towards the other.

Observers of English politics have often wondered about the connection between the Conservative Party—a party primarily representing the middle and upper classes—and their working-class supporters. Do the working-class Tories believe their material interests to be satisfied by the party's policies, or are they voting Tory in the belief that the Conservatives are the best party for the country as a whole? In order to elucidate this problem, the respondents were asked the following question in reference to both parties: 'Do you feel that a

Conservative/Labour Government does more to better the lot of the workers than it does for other people?' As can be seen in Table 36, fully 49 per cent of the Tories think that their party is *particularly* concerned with the workers' interests. This is an unexpectedly high proportion considering that Conservative propaganda does not claim that the party is concerned with the interests of one class more so than with those of another, and certainly not the interests of the working class. In Harold Macmillan's words, the Labour Party is 'a class party . . . They build on division. We are a national party. We build on unity'.[1]

TABLE 36

'A Conservative/Labour Government does more to better the lot of the workers than it does for other people'

	Conservative Government		Labour Government	
	Tories	Labour	Tories	Labour
Agree	49	5	41	89
Disagree	14	86	45	3
Same for all	37	9	9	7
Depends	0	0	2	0
DK	1	1	3	1
Total per cent	100	100	100	100
Total number	320	127	320	127

In attempting to account for this set of responses we run up against a formidable problem, for the most plausible of explanations do not hold up under closer analysis. It was thought that the widespread Tory belief that their party is particularly partial to the 'lot of the workers' might stem from the new found prosperity which these workers enjoyed under successive Conservative Governments. The workers have not only witnessed a large improvement in their own standard of life, it may also have appeared to them that their economic gains during the 'fifties' and early 'sixties' were proportionately greater

[1] *Conservatism*, 1945–50: 1950, p. 102, cited in Beer, op. cit., p. 102. The Disraelian echo from the Crystal Palace speech of 1872 is manifested even more clearly in Ian Macleod's speech at the 1957 party conference: 'If we are not a national party, representing both trade unionists and employers, we are nothing.'

than were those of the middle and upper classes, leading them to think of themselves as the special beneficiaries of Tory measures. But an examination of the data does not bear out this hypothesis. Neither the Tories who are economically satisfied, nor those who earn above average incomes, believe the Conservative Party to be particularly attuned to the workers' desires more frequently than do their less satisfied and less prosperous counterparts'.[1]

Although we are not able to explain why it is that half the Tories believe that their party is especially concerned with the workers' interests, this is not to question the validity of the data. If the meaning of the question or its particular wording were improperly understood by a significant number of respondents, thereby invalidating this surprising finding at the outset, then a far larger number of respondents ought to have rejected the question's premises by answering either 'don't know' or 'depends'. Of the 320 Tory respondents only two of them replied in this vein. It should also be noted that notwithstanding the unexpectedness of this finding, it is not an overly important one. For as will be seen momentarily, the belief that the Conservative Party is especially concerned with the workers' interests is not an overly important electoral factor, since only one-fifth of the Tories manifestly support the party in the hope of material betterment.

In the second part of Table 36 the Conservatives' beliefs regarding the beneficiaries of Labour policies are set out. The data show that 45 per cent of the Tories do not believe a Labour Government to be especially attuned to the workers' desires. The Labour Party wants to attract middle-class votes, but its appeal is unmistakably directed to the workers; its propaganda underlines the inequalities and injustices of a capitalist economy and a hierarchically ordered social structure as they impinge upon the lower strata. How is it then possible for nearly half the Conservatives to believe that the Labour Party does not do more to 'better the lot of the workers than it does for other people'? In a sentence, these Tories believe the Labour politicians to be untrustworthy. They may make all manner of promises to the workers but these are usually not kept, for the Labour politicians are simply out for themselves.

When asked what they dislike about the Labour Party, 44 per cent of the Tories who disagreed with the statement that the Labour Party

---

[1] This disconfirmation of the hypothesis is also applicable to the pragmatists alone.

is especially attuned to the workers' interests replied that the party leaders are either untrustworthy in the sense that they do not keep their promises (e.g. 'it's all talk to get into power'), or that Labour politicians are self-seeking (e.g. 'they are too much for themselves', 'most of them are after a good job', 'they only want power').[1] In contrast, only 9 per cent of the Tories who registered their agreement with the statement believe the Labour politicians to be untrustworthy and egotistically motivated. Similarly, when asked whether the Labour Party is out to get votes or whether it is concerned with the good of the country, 73 per cent of the Tories who disagreed with the statement that the Labour Party is particularly concerned with the workers' interests replied that it is out to get votes, compared to 44 per cent of the Tories who agreed with the statement. It is probably these beliefs about the Labour politicians' motivations which fail to convince a large number of Tory voters in the sincerity of their concern with working-class interests, and by extension, spells the ineffectiveness of the Labour Party's most effective appeal among the workers.

On the other hand, there are the 41 per cent of the Tories who accept the Labour claim that they are particularly oriented towards the working class. Which is to say that these workers believe that they would benefit materially from a Labour Government, yet they continue to vote Conservative. Leaving aside that one-third who believe that the Conservative Party is also particularly concerned with the workers' desires, we are left with 28 per cent of the Tory voters who believe that they would more often be materially favoured by a Labour than a Conservative Government. Presumably these workers find other attractions in the Conservative Party, or faults with the Labour Party,

[1] A recurrent theme struck by the Tories interviewed in the second wave revolved around the belief that the Labour MP's jumped out of the TUC and into the House in order to obtain additional power and money. One pragmatist, an electrician from Wimbledon, believes that the Labour MP's went into the House after they 'got as far as they could through the trade union movement. They took that step over to get that extra bit, but with a lot of them it is also power seeking'. A deferentially-oriented materials' handler from Coventry stated the matter in these terms: 'I like to think the Labour men came into Parliament because they like to hear themselves talk. They came up through the trade unions and got used to hearing themselves talking and then they wanted power to make themselves bigger, and this is how they get it. I don't deny that some of them worked hard to get where they are, but I think it is personal power they are looking for. And they can only find it in politics because they have no real training for other things, like business, where they might be powerful'.

which over-ride any 'extra' material benefits which they think will accrue to them under a Labour Government.

Approximately half the Tories believe that both the Conservative and Labour parties are particularly heedful of the workers' desires. Whereas 86 per cent of the Labour voters do not think that the Conservative Party is especially solicitous of the workers' interests, while 89 per cent said that this is true of the Labour Party. Furthermore, while 37 per cent of the Tories replied that Conservative policies benefit all classes equally, only 7 per cent of the Labour voters believe their party to be equally partial to all classes. These findings clearly suggest that the Labour voters support their party primarily for bread and butter reasons, only a few crumbs being available from the Conservative table.

This point finds its confirmation in the Labour supporters' forthright replies when asked 'What are the things you like about the Labour Party?' A majority referred to the special benefits accruing to the workers: 53 per cent provided responses such as 'the Labour Party has the common man's interests at heart' and 'they are more inclined to see the workers' point of view' (see Table 41). And the second most frequent set of responses (17 per cent) refers to the expected increases in old-age pensions under a Labour Government— a benefit which is clearly most desired by working-class people. When we add to these two sets of responses others of the same type—those referring to prosperity, housing and the health service—it is found that nearly four-fifths of the Labour voters support their party in the belief that it will provide them with additional material benefits. When this same calculation is made for the Tories—adding up the number of workers who gave as their reasons for supporting their party the belief that it will provide them with material benefits— only one-fifth are found to fall into this category. To which might also be added the previous finding that 28 per cent of the Tories believe that their lives would be materially better under a Labour than a Tory Government, yet voting Conservative all the same.

The argument that Labour supporters are first and foremost concerned with the material advantages accruing to the working class under Labour rule is further underlined upon examination of their criticisms of the Conservative Party. When asked what they dislike about the Conservatives, 24 per cent of Labour replied that Tory measures are detrimental to the workers' interests (see Table 40).

A whole array of responses indicate the depth of this belief: 'They (the Tories) don't understand what a few extra shillings mean for the working man', 'they don't care about the happiness of the workers', 'they don't always understand what the very poor people have to stand', 'they wouldn't help out an ordinary working fellow'. Another 27 per cent of the Labour supporters expressed similar thoughts in an indirect fashion by replying that the Conservative Party serves special interests: 'They look out for the monopolies', 'they give money to those that have money', 'they only look out for themselves and don't bother with poor people'. These typical responses suggest that for many Labour voters the Tories' pandering to special interests is not only thought to be unfair in and of itself, but is also harmful to the workers' interests. To which might be added another 17 per cent of the Labour supporters who think that the Conservative Party is overly niggardly in its pensions policies. Thus Labour's basic complaint against the Tory Party is the belief that it would short change the workers when distributing the *largesse* of the welfare state, while permitting the middle and upper classes to rely on the Government's resources and influence in order to enrich themselves further.[1]

In order to gain a better understanding of the workers' differing types of attractions for the two parties, we might ask why it is that the Labour voters place a very much greater importance upon the governmental distribution of material benefits than do the Conservatives. The first explanation that springs to mind is the possibility that Labour incomes are generally lower than are those of the Tories, thereby making them more dependent upon the welfare state. However, the data indicate that the Labour supporters actually earn somewhat higher wages than do the Conservative voters (see Table 37). But even though the Labour supporters earn slightly more than the Tories, it is still possible that they are less satisfied with what they do earn. This point emerges from Table 38. At each of the three income levels— i.e. amongst those workers earning roughly the same amount of money— the proportion of Labour voters who are economically satisfied is smaller than the corresponding proportion of Conservatives. And this is

---

[1] It ought to be noted that the Labour voters are not critical of the Conservative Party because of the invidious class distinctions it is sometimes said to represent and engender. Only 8 per cent of the Labour voters replied that they didn't like the Conservatives for reasons centring about the theme of class distinctions; e.g. 'they are all Eton and Harrow types', 'they are only hunting, shooting and fishing people', 'they put on airs'.

especially true of those workers earning above average incomes. Whereas 70 per cent of the Tories who earn £16 or more a week replied that they are economically satisfied, the figure drops to 46 per cent among the affluent Labour supporters. Thus the Labour voters tend to have significantly higher economic expectations or criteria of economic satisfaction, making them more frequently dissatisfied with their economic lots than are the Conservatives. Relating this finding to the problem at hand, it would seem to be just these relatively high criteria of economic satisfaction that lead the Labour voters to place such value upon the material benefits that can be supplied by the welfare state, whereas the Tories are more readily satisfied economically, leading them to attribute a lesser importance to this aspect of the two parties' programmes.

TABLE 37
Income Distribution[1]

	Tories	Labour
£10 and below	31	22
£11 to £15	41	47
£16 and above	28	31
Total per cent	100	100
Total number	298	124

TABLE 38
Income and personal economic satisfaction

	£10 and below		£11 to £15		£16 and above	
	Tories	Labs.	Tories	Labs.	Tories	Labs.
Satisfied	33	26	37	35	70	46
So-so	32	7	22	29	18	26
Unsatisfied	27	67	40	33	12	28
DK	9	0	1	3	0	0
Total per cent	100	100	100	100	100	100
Total number	92	27	123	58	83	39

[1] It might be relevant that 7 per cent of the Tories refused to disclose their income compared to 2 per cent of the Labour supporters.

IV. THE SPECIFICS OF PARTISANSHIP

Up to this point we have utilized the responses to the four questions regarding the workers 'like' and 'dislikes' about the two parties in order to support a number of hypotheses about the relationship between the parties' policies and working-class interests. This short section will simply serve to describe some of the more significant sets of specific responses to these questions (see Tables 39, 40, 41 and 42).

TABLE 39

Those features of the Conservative Party that the workers 'like'

	Tories	Defs.	Prags.	Labs.
Able leaders	14	17	13	3
Leaders' educations	10	13	9	1
Leaders' social status	3	0	3	1
General: did a good job	24	21	25	2
Business virtues	10	12	10	1
Do what is best for the country	17	26	13	2
General: like their ideas	9	9	9	3
Free enterprise	15	12	17	2
Foreign policy	6	13	3	4
Defence policy	2	2	2	4
'They have the money'	2	0	3	0
Prosperity	12	9	13	6
Housing policies	8	4	9	6
Welfare policies	4	0	5	4
They are trustworthy	9	3	11	1
Education policies	2	0	3	2
Nothing	1	1	1	58
Other	5	5	5	6
DK	1	0	1	4
Total per cent	154	147	155	110
Total number of responses	490	134	356	138
Total number of respondents	320	90	230	127

Focusing upon the workers' more specific 'likes' and 'dislikes' about the two parties, only one significant difference emerges between

TABLE 40

Those features of the Conservative Party that the workers 'dislike'

	Tories	Defs.	Prags.	Labs.
Class distinctions	6	9	4	8
Serve special interests	3	2	3	27
Lack of trust	1	2	0	7
General: dislike policies	1	2	2	8
Old fashioned	4	2	6	2
Not enough prosperity	3	0	5	6
Taxes too high	3	2	3	6
Pensions policies	7	4	8	17
Housing policies	3	2	3	3
Bad for working class	2	2	2	24
Foreign policy	1	0	1	3
Defence policy	1	4	0	2
Nothing	52	47	54	11
Other	15	22	12	15
DK	0	0	0	3
Total per cent	102	100	103	142
Total number of responses	338	90	248	179
Total number of respondents	320	90	230	127

the deferentials and pragmatists. The deferentials give somewhat greater emphasis to the patriotic or national values embodied in the Conservative Party, whereas the pragmatists are more concerned with the material benefits to be derived from Tory rule. When asked what they like about the Conservative Party twice as many deferentials as pragmatists replied that the party acts for the good of the country as a whole—e.g. 'they (the Tories) are fair to all and put the country first', 'they run the country for all people and not just one class', 'they have the well-being of the country at heart'. Secondly, 13 per cent and 3 per cent of the deferentials and pragmatists respectively, mentioned the party's handling of foreign affairs as one of its attractive features. There are two types of responses which fall into this category, those which stress the party's ability to handle foreign affairs (e.g. 'their management of foreign affairs is admirable', 'they have a better understanding of the international situation'), and those which refer to the hardy dose of patriotism in the Tories' foreign policy equation (e.g. 'they are pro-British abroad', 'they try to keep Britain strong'). In contrast, the pragmatists more often stated their preferences for the Tories in terms of bread and butter benefits. Taking comments about prosperity, housing and welfare policies together, 27 per cent and 13 per cent of the pragmatists and deferentials respectively, paid their respects to these aspects of Conservative policy.

TABLE 41

Those features of the Labour Party that the workers 'like'

	Tories	Defs.	Prags.	Labs.
Able leaders	4	0	5	2
Leaders' educations	1	0	1	2
Leaders' social backgrounds	1	0	1	6
Trustworthy	1	0	2	6
General: like their policies	5	10	3	11
Nationalization and planning	1	0	1	7
Humanitarian	3	3	3	4
Prosperity	0	0	0	4
Pensions policies	5	2	6	17
Health services	5	2	6	4
Housing policies	2	0	3	6
Education policies	1	1	1	1
Good for all the people	1	2	0	8
Good for the working class	10	13	9	53
Foreign and Defence policies	1	0	1	2
Nothing	58	69	54	0
Other	3	0	4	7
DK	3	0	4	1
Total per cent	105	102	104	141
Total number of responses	328	93	235	169
Total number of respondents	320	90	230	127

Turning to the Tory voters' criticisms of the Labour Party, its nationalization policy is singled out most frequently (38 per cent). Next in importance comes the belief that Labour politicians are untrustworthy and self-interested—25 per cent of the Tories replying

TABLE 42

Those features of the Labour Party that the workers 'dislike'

	Tories	Defs.	Prags.	Labs.
Too aggressive	10	10	10	2
Leaders' lack of education	5	4	5	2
Unable to run the country	8	9	8	0
Untrustworthy and self-interested	25	30	22	4
Don't do what is good for country	2	4	0	0
General: dislike policies	3	4	2	0
Nationalization and planning	38	40	37	9
Financial laxity	11	11	10	2
Trade union connections	5	3	6	2
Internal party disruption	3	6	2	6
Foreign policy	4	9	3	2
Defence policy	3	2	3	1
Nothing	9	9	9	50
Other	9	8	10	19
DK	3	0	4	1
Total per cent	138	149	131	100
Total number of responses	435	135	300	127
Total number of respondents	320	90	230	127

that the Labour politicians are mainly out for votes, money and power. It will be recalled that it is these beliefs which are particularly injurious to the Labour Party's appeal as the defender of working-class interests, this appeal appearing as a façade behind which the Labour politicians are acting out their self-interested drama. Third in importance are the related beliefs that the Labour Party is financially lax (10 per cent) and that they are unable to run the country (8 per cent). Here are found such comments as: 'they (the Labour leaders) don't know where they are going, just governing from day to day', 'they don't have the ability to carry out their policies', 'they spend the country's money without thought', 'the country goes bankrupt when they are in power'.

Having noted the Conservatives' frequent disparagement of the nationalization programme, what is the Labour reaction to this issue? When asked what they like about the Labour Party only 7 per cent of the Labour voters mentioned nationalization and governmental planning—a figure which hardly indicates a sizeable amount of grass roots support for this section of Labour's electoral platform, especially since another 9 per cent of the Labour voters referred to nationalization and planning when asked what it is that they *dislike* about their party. Moreover, the tepid manner in which that 7 per cent of Labour support nationalization is no match for the strident opposition of the large group of Tory critics. This is clearly seen in a sampling of the latter's reactions to nationalization: 'they (the Labour Party) are next door to communism with their state ownership', 'it is all regimentation and control', 'it isn't fair to take a man's business away from him', 'there is no freedom with all this nationalization'.

Lastly, it might be noted that only a small proportion of both Tory and Labour voters attach any importance to the parties' foreign and defence policies—and this notwithstanding the importance Sir Alec Douglas-Home attributed to these issues in the months before the 1964 election, continually returning to his twin themes of Britain's great power status and the independent nuclear deterrent. Only 8 per cent of the Tories had anything positive to say about their party's foreign and defence policies, with 7 per cent criticizing Labour on this score. And among the Labour supporters, only 2 per cent mentioned the party's foreign and defence policies in a positive manner, with another 2 per cent voicing their disagreement with the party over its position on the nuclear deterrent. Parenthetically, the emphasis placed upon foreign policy issues by the Conservative Leader when contrasted with the indifference shown by Conservative and Labour supporters alike, points to an important gap in the existing literature on English politics: the congruity or discongruity between the electorate's concerns and the party leaders' perceptions of those concerns.[1]

---

[1] But see the forthcoming study of the 1964 and 1966 General Elections by D. E. Butler and Donald Stokes in which this problem is explored.

CHAPTER 7

Class Identification, Class Conflict and Social Relations

―

IN THE last ten years political scientists have come to attribute major significance to people's self-evaluation of their class position as this influences their voting behaviour. The influence of subjective class identification upon the workers' electoral behaviour, with special reference to those workers who consider themselves middle class, has received a good deal of attention in England. However, as Goldthorpe and Lockwood have pointed out, the hypotheses relating the workers' subjective class to their voting behaviour have not been developed in a systematic way, nor are these authors ready to place much reliance on the manner in which subjective class has been measured.[1] Here an attempt will be made to analyse some of the possible inter-relationships between subjective class and voting behaviour in a systematic manner, but before launching into this problem it is necessary to outline the methodology used in assessing the respondents' subjective class position.

There are basically two possible strategies to be followed. The respondents may simply be presented with a list of social classes and asked which class they belong to. This method is followed in the great majority of survey studies; it requires the minimum of time and expense. The second strategy relies upon a series of intensive and broad ranging interviews of an open-ended nature. Information is gathered about the respondents' perceptions and evaluations of the entire class and status systems, which then serves as the relational context within which the respondents' own subjective class position can be located. This method is expensive and requires a great deal

---

[1] John H. Goldthorpe and David Lockwood, 'Affluence and the British Class Structure', *The Sociological Review*, Vol. XI, No. 2, July 1963. However, this assertion was made before the appearance of Runciman's study, op. cit.

of the respondents' time. However, it is a more powerful and valid tool of social analysis than is the former method relying solely upon a completely structured interview schedule. Most importantly, a frame of reference is provided for interpreting the respondent's *meaning* when placing himself in a particular class. For example, some workers who define themselves as middle class may have as their frame of reference not the entire class system, but only the objective working class, and within that strata they believe themselves to be 'middle class', i.e. they are in the 'middle' of the working class. Or to take another example, some workers assign themselves middle-class status when that term is taken to refer to all those people who 'work for a living', and since they too are working people, they define themselves as middle class. Someone using the first method would conclude that these two types of workers are claiming objective middle-class membership for themselves, having identified themselves as such, but this would immediately appear to be an unwarranted interpretation to the social scientist using the second method.

While admitting that the second method is the optimum one if it could be applied to a sufficiently large sample,[1] in a national survey the problem becomes one of maximizing the validity of the interpretations placed upon the respondents' class identifications, while minimizing the proportion of the interviewing session devoted to this problem. The survey strategy employed here is something of a hybrid, combining the main features of the two basic methods. Following the usual procedure, the respondents were asked: 'Here is one type of list of the various social classes found in this country. People are sometimes placed in these classes. Which one would you say you belonged to?' The list contained five classes: labouring working class, skilled working class, lower middle class, middle class and upper middle class.[2] In order to minimize the possibility of these responses being misinterpreted the sample was also asked to describe the class

---

[1] In one of the leading studies employing an extensive and intensive series of interviews only twenty husband and wife couples constituted the sample. See Elizabeth Bott *Family and Social Network*: 1957. So far as this writer is aware the intensive method has never been applied in a large survey study.

[2] Another difficulty in using a structured list of responses is that the class appearing at the bottom of the scale might take on negative connotations in the respondents' minds. This usually happens when the terms 'unskilled working class' or 'lower class' are used. It was therefore thought best to employ the term 'labouring working class' which does not usually imply a negative valuation.

6

structure, mentioning the number of classes to be found in England and the types of people making up each class.[1] The free answers given to this question served as the frames of reference within which the workers' subjective class positions were interpreted, i.e. given a meaning. In 10 per cent of the cases there was a clear-cut divergence between the respondents' definitions of the working and middle classes and the common definitions given these terms by social scientists. For example, some workers conceive of the working class as 'people who live off the government', as 'lazy lay-abouts', or 'rough and ready types', and when asked which class they belong to they replied 'middle class'. Such responses were then altered to subjective working class.[2] In another instance, a man who defined the middle class as 'just ordinary people of the world', consequently assigning himself to the middle class, was also placed in the subjective working-class category. In these instances the respondents' frames of reference regarding the class structure were markedly different from the frame of reference used by most social scientists, and when subjectively placing themselves in the class structure they consequently have in mind a different conception of their class position than indicated by the terms working class and middle class as they are commonly employed. In order to take this discrepancy into account, the respondents' frames of reference were first aligned with the one used by social scientists, and their subjective class positions were then altered accordingly. This hybrid method of identifying the respondents' subjective class position both reduces the danger of misinterpreting the responses to the single subjective class question, and allows its application to a large sample.[3]

[1] The wording of this item is: 'People usually agree that there are such things as social classes. Now if a friend of yours from Australia were to ask you to describe the different social classes in this country, how would you do it? You would want to tell him how *many* different social classes there are, and what *kind of people* are in each class.'

[2] It is recognized that in some cases of this sort the respondents are indeed attempting to elevate their own status by defining the working class in such a way as to differentiate themselves from its less desirable elements, and by positing the existence of a class lower than the one to which they belong. Yet an attempt to raise one's status through an invidious comparison does not necessarily entail the desire to be recognized as a member of the middle class.

[3] Runciman has also recognized the difficulty of assigning any particular meaning to subjective class identification given the fact that a significant number of people define the working class and the middle class in terms that are most peculiar to social scientists. He has attempted to get around this problem by employing a technique similar to the one used here. The respondents were

I. THE 'MIDDLE-CLASS' TORIES[1]

A perusal of English voting studies will show no lack of comments about the observation that manual workers who think of themselves as middle class vote Conservative more frequently than do those workers whose subjective and objective class positions coincide. As with the findings of other surveys, the data in Table 43 indicate that middle-class identification strongly predisposes the workers to vote Conservative. More than twice as many working-class identifiers vote Labour as vote Tory, whereas among the 'middle-class' workers a slightly larger proportion actually vote Conservative. To be more specific, 29 per cent of the working-class subjectives compared to 53 per cent of the middle-class identifiers vote Tory. However, to note the correlation between these two variables is only the beginning. If this phenomena is to be properly understood and its political relevance appreciated, it would be necessary to know what it is about subjective class which affects voting behaviour (i.e. what leads 'middle-class' workers to vote Tory); and to take the analysis back one step further, there is the fundamental problem of specifying the factor(s) that lead manual workers to think of themselves as middle class (i.e. deciding what it is about middle-class membership that allows some workers to identify themselves in this way).

Within academic, journalistic and Labour Party circles it has been argued that either economic affluence or status aspirations have induced a sizeable proportion of workers to claim middle-class membership for themselves; and at the same time, their perception of themselves

---

asked 'What sort of people do you mean when you talk about the middle class (the working class)?' After a careful analysis of these responses, Runciman concluded that subjective class is a meaningless concept when applied to about 10 per cent of the respondents—the exact figure which appears in the present study. There is, however, one important difference between the two techniques for handling this difficulty. Given the relatively small proportion of respondents involved, Runciman thought it best to carry out his analysis of subjective class without either dropping the 10 per cent from the analysis or altering their subjective class identifications to conform to the more orthodox definitions. In the present study it was decided to do the latter. In Runciman, op. cit., pp. 152–164, and esp. p. 177, it is seen that the correlation between Conservative voting and middle-class identification does not hold among those workers who maintain a peculiar definition of the middle class.

[1] Whenever the respondents are described as 'middle class' in quotes this should be taken as a shorthand reference to the manual workers who replied that they are middle class.

TABLE 43

Class identification and voting behaviour[1]

	Working class	Middle class
Conservative	29	53
Labour	71	47
	—	—
Total per cent	100	100
Total number	340	99

as middle class has led the larger proportion of these workers into the Tory fold. Yet notwithstanding the attention that this subject has received, until the recent appearance of Runciman's work its sociological meaning has hardly been touched upon in any rigorous analysis. In the estimation to two careful students of the problem, 'There is in fact as yet little evidence which would help in deciding how far the Conservative vote of the manual worker (excluding the "deference voter")[2] is due to his conception of himself as "middle class" simply in material terms (the hypothetical "prosperity" voter), or how far it represents a claim to be accepted as a middle-class person in a full social sense (the hypothetical "identification" voter)'.[3]

The first interpretation of the relation between middle-class identification and Conservative voting to be tested is the most commonly accepted one amongst English political scientists and sociologists: a significant proportion of the manual workers actively aspires to become members of the objectively defined middle class;[4] and since one

---

[1] The weighting index, according to which the number of Labour respondents has been multiplied by five, is used here.

[2] The authors do not state why the deferentials are disregarded in this connection. The implication is that the deference voter is thought to be content with his traditional place in the social hierarchy and therefore middle-class identification is not characteristic of him. However, our data indicate this not to be the case; deferentials and pragmatists exhibit almost identical rates of middle-class identification. McKenzie and Silver, op. cit., and Seymour M. Lipset also make this unwarranted assumption. He suggests that except for the deferentials, all Tory manual workers are middle-class aspirants. ('Must Tories Always Triumph?', Socialist Commentary, November 1960.)

[3] Goldthorpe and Lockwood, op. cit., p. 145.

[4] In the words of D. E. Butler and Richard Rose, they are 'on the threshold of the middle class'. (The British General Election of 1959: 1960, p. 15. Also see p. 2.) According to Ferdinand Zweig, 'The whole working class finds itself on the move, moving towards new middle class values and middle class exis-

mark of middle-class status is Conservative voting, these workers support the Tories in order to better their claim for such status and to allow themselves to identify with the middle class. In the words of Mark Abrams, 'They see themselves as merging with the middle class and, by voting Conservative, they hope to consolidate their new class (i.e. status) aspirations.[1]

On an *a priori* basis this argument ought to be approached in a sceptical manner. Notwithstanding the overlap between the incomes of the highly paid workers and those of the lower middle class leading to certain common consumption patterns which certain writers have interpreted as an indication of status-seeking—it does not appear overly plausible that a significant number of manual workers are actively aspiring for middle-class status.[2] The workers' increasingly widespread adoption of what was previously considered a lower middle-class life style is hardly an indication of status strivings on their part; televisions, cars and washing machines may be bought to make life easier and more pleasurable, not to imitate a higher status. Even if an innate aspiration for higher social status were found among manual workers its expression would be very much discouraged. The peer-group pressures felt by workers putting on middle-class 'airs';[3] the formal and informal work-place segregation of the manual 'works' people from the non-manual 'staff'; and the high acceptance barriers

tence.' ('The New Factory Workers', *Twentieth Century*, May 1960). For additional references, see Goldthorpe and Lockwood, op. cit.

[1] 'Party Politics After the End of Ideology', in Allardt and Littunen, op. cit., p. 57, parenthesis added.

[2] Although writing of a less prosperous working class than that of the middle 'sixties', Richard Hoggart thinks that the workers are concerned with avoiding the 'Fall' into the depths of the unrespectable working class, rather than with pushing themselves up to middle-class heights. 'Cleanliness, thrift and self-respect arise more from a concern not to drop down, not to succumb to the environment than from an anxiety to go up . . . Even the urge for children to "get on" and the respect for "booklearning" is not most importantly produced by the wish to reach another class out of snobbery. It is associated much more with the thought of a reduction in the numerous troubles which the poor have to meet, simply and because they are poor.' Op. cit., p. 67. Josephine Klein stresses the 'contempt and disapproval' which the workers have for the "unrespectable" working class, and their fear of becoming part of that group. *Samples From English Cultures*: 1965, Vol. I, p. 5.

[3] 'Acting beyond the ideas of the group "acting posh", "giving y'self airs", "getting above y'self", "being lah-de-dah", "thinking y'self too good for other people", "being stuck up", "turning y'nose up at other people", "acting like Lady Muck"—all these are much disliked and not very sensitively discriminated.' Hoggart, op. cit., p. 73. Also see Klein, op. cit., p. 89.

erected by the lower middle class against any aspirations for middle-class membership on the part of manual workers[1]—these are only some of the factors mitigating against any manifest strivings for middle-class status on the part of the working class.

The belief that a working man cannot appreciably elevate his status, thereby making any such aspirations unrealistic, even if he had money or a responsible position, finds expression in a number of second-wave interviews. When asked 'How do you feel about people moving from one class to another?', a Birmingham house painter who votes Tory replied: 'Quite frankly, I don't think they can move. I'm working class now, but if I won the pools tomorrow I might have a swimming pool in the garden, but I'd still be working class.' A deferential respondent living as an old-age pensioner in Putney believes that with 'good qualifications you can rise up in the firm you work for—from worker to manager. I'd say yes to this. But the man oughtn't to go into a club (that) his manager belongs to. The manager can't hold his usual conversation and neither can the worker. None of them can be truthful. They've got to build up their conversation.' The fact that this particular worker thinks of himself as lower middle class, while denying the possibility of social as opposed to occupational mobility, foreshadows one aspect of the conclusion we are moving towards.

These responses are cited simply as two examples of the workers' beliefs about social mobility—beliefs whose representativeness need to be established by testing the hypothesis of the middle-class identi-fication voter with the first-wave data. It is reasoned here that if the 'middle-class' workers are concerned with becoming *bona fide* members of the middle class, they should exhibit certain attitudes having a decidedly middle-class flavour more frequently than do the working-class identifiers. They would hold such attitudes in order to 'prove' their status claims both to themselves and to others, and because the middle class would serve as their normative reference group to whose values they would conform in anticipation of their entry into that social strata.

---

[1] Peter Willmott and Michael Young, *Family and Class in a London Suburb*: 1960, p. 122. At times the high acceptance barriers are replaced by an even more effective device; the status conscious middle class sometimes simply move out of the predominantly working-class neighbourhood. See Peter Willmott, *The Evolution of a Community*: 1963, Chapter V.

One attribute of a middle-class life style is a respect for education, both as a status symbol and as a means for social and economic mobility. In order to measure the value placed upon education the respondents were asked: 'If you had your life to live over again, would you have tried to stay on in school longer than you did?' Since only a small fraction of the respondents attended secondary school, they are being asked whether they would have desired such an education, presumably for reasons of economic or social betterment. The data indicate that the middle-class identifiers answered with the proper middle-class reply only to a slightly greater degree than the respondents who see themselves as working class, only 6 percentage points separating the two groups on this measure.[1] A similar finding emerges from the data collected by F. M. Martin in his study of the subjective aspects of social stratification. After dividing the manual workers in his sample into those who identified as working class and middle class, the respondents were asked: 'Up to what age would you like to see your children continue full-time education?' The mean age selected by the 'middle-class' workers was 16·7 years, compared to the 16·6-year mean of the working-class subjectives.[2] Taken together, these two findings indicate there to be only an insignificant difference in the importance and desirability attributed to education by the two types of workers.

A second way in which middle-class aspirations can be gauged is to ask the respondents what kind of social connections they would desire for their children. Even if the manual workers cannot hope to achieve middle-class status themselves, if this ambition were present they could entertain it for the next generation. The workers were asked: 'Let us say that you have a son at a grammar school. Would you prefer that he become friendly with the son of a cabinet maker or the son of a bank clerk?' Among the working-class subjectives 6 per cent replied that the bank clerk's son would be preferable, compared to 7 per cent of the 'middle-class' workers. These figures can then hardly be said to support the middle-class identification hypothesis.[3] In fact

---

[1] This applies to both Tory and Labour voters. Wherever the two groups are combined it may be assumed that there are no differences between them.

[2] F. M. Martin, 'Some Subjective Aspects of Social Stratification', in Glass, ed., op. cit., p. 68. The mean age selected by the professional middle class was 18·8 years and 17·5 years for the salaried middle class.

[3] It must be admitted that the response pattern might have been different if a bank manager had been substituted for a bank clerk in the formulation of the question.

they show the working class as a whole to have few aspirations for middle-class social status—even for their children.[1] However, these data must not be interpreted to mean that only some 7 per cent of the male manual workers want their children to 'rise' out of the working class through their own efforts and achievements. When asked what *occupation* they would prefer for their sons, fully one-third of the workers interviewed in the Martin study indicated their choice of a clerical, business or professional occupation.[2] What is claimed here is that only a small percentage of workers are concerned with the social status aspects of middle-class membership for their children (i.e. associating with people of higher status as opposed to becoming middle class through occupational mobility), and that there is no difference in this regard between the working-class and middle-class identifiers. And even when we examine the workers' occupational preferences for their children the middle-class identifiers turn out not to have any greater aspirations than the working-class subjectives; there is only 2 per cent difference between the two groups in the proportion desiring non-manual occupations for their children.[3]

If the commonly held assumption that women are more status conscious than men is accepted, then we find further evidence for the argument in another survey study. Runciman reports that the proportion of men and women in the working class who described themselves as middle class is exactly the same.[4] But if middle-class identification were a manifestation of status strivings, the data ought to have indicated a higher proportion of 'middle-class' women than 'middle-class' men.

Taking all these data together, it is clear that the 'middle-class' workers do not think of themselves in such terms because of any stirrings for membership in the middle class.[5] It then also follows that the tendency for the middle-class subjectives to vote Conservative is not due to a desire on their part to increase their social status. Since they do not view the middle class as a reference group, imparting its

---

[1] This set of responses is treated more fully below in the section on working-class solidarity, pp. 179–183.

[2] Op. cit., p. 69.

[3] Ibid.

[4] Op. cit., p. 166.

[5] W. G. Runciman reaches this conclusion by a different path in his ' "Embourgeoisement", Self-Rated Class and Party Preference', *The Sociological Review*, July 1964, pp. 144–145.

standards of behaviour to the workers, there is no reason to believe that these workers vote Conservative in order to appear middle class. The hypothetical 'identification' voter is then just that—hypothetical.

The second factor which is commonly used to explain social up-grading and Conservative voting is the working class' new-found affluence. On the face of it this hypothesis is eminently plausible. Compared to the 'traditional' pre-1939 working class whose primary concern was the maintenance of a minimal standard of living, the contemporary workers' relative prosperity obviates any untold concern for income and economic security.[1] Furthermore, compared to the pre-1939 situation when a significant gap separated working-class wages from lower middle-class salaries, there is today an overlap between the two, with not a small percentage of skilled workers earning more than the lower-echelon 'black-coated' and 'white-collared' workers. Then, too, with the coming of the welfare state, the beginnings of voluntary pension schemes and a full-employment economy, the workers are approaching the degree of economic security enjoyed by the lower middle class. And finally, the combination of high wages and opportunities for hire purchase has resulted in the workers' acquiring a standard of life comparable to that of many lower middle-class people. Thus it would seem plausible to argue that the workers' new-found prosperity (in absolute and relative terms) has led many of them to identify as middle class, and having achieved their new level of prosperity under the *aegis* of Conservative Governments, they have been ushered into the Tory fold.

The obvious test of the latter half of the argument is to relate income to voting behaviour in order to see whether or not the more prosperous workers tend to vote Conservative. This is done in Table 44, where the hypothesis is clearly seen to be unwarranted. The rate of Tory voting does not increase as income increases. In fact, just the opposite is true: 39 per cent of the workers earning below average incomes vote Conservative, compared to 30 per cent of the above

[1] Notice should be taken of the warning given by David Lockwood about such comparisons. When contrasting the pre-1939 working class with its post-1950 counterpart, the error of comparing the most distinctive part of the 'old' working class (the unemployed) with the most distinctive section of the 'new' working class (the £20-a-week wage earners) is an easy one to fall into. For an 'unemployed society people are interested in how the worker survives in poverty; in a full employed one how he reacts to prosperity.' ('The "New Working Class"' *Archives Européenes de Sociologie*, 1960, Number 2, p. 251.)

average earners.[1] The 'prosperity' voter, as such, who enters the polling booth with a thank-you note in his pocket addressed to Central Office is clearly not a significant factor in English politics.

Since the hypothesis that higher incomes result in Tory voting is based on a crude economic determinism there ought to be little surprise in its disconfirmation. Material prosperity alone does not shape party preferences. It is only after material prosperity is related to personal economic expectations, resulting in economic satisfaction or dissatisfaction, that income level helps to pattern voting behaviour. The crucial variable is not income, but the degree to which the workers

TABLE 44

Income and Voting behaviour[2]

	£10 and below	£11–£15	£16 and above
Conservative	39	31	30
Labour	61	69	70
Total per cent	100	100	100
Total number	115	184	121

are satisfied or dissatisfied with their economic situation. Table 45 indicates that greater economic satisfaction does help to explain Conservative voting behaviour. The rate of Tory voting increases from 26 per cent among the economically dissatisfied, to 34 per cent among the partly satisfied, to 40 per cent of the economically contented workers.

On the one hand we have found Tory voting to decrease as income increases, and on the other, to increase with greater economic satisfaction. These seemingly contradictory patterns are accounted for by the higher economic expectations held by the Labour supporters,

---

[1] In his study of West German workers Juan Linz also found an inverse relationship between income and voting for the Socialists. See *The Social Bases of German Politics*: unpublished Ph.D. thesis, Department of Sociology, Columbia University, 1958, p. 325. For similar data on the French working class during the Fourth Republic, see Richard F. Hamilton, *Affluence and the French Worker*: 1967.

[2] The weighting index, according to which the number of Labour respondents has been multiplied by five, is used here.

which consequently remain unfulfilled more often that the Conservatives' economic expectations. The evidence for this argument is found when income is related to economic satisfaction. In the preceding chapter it was seen that within all three income groups the proportion of Labour voters who are unsatisfied is greater than the corresponding proportion of Conservatives.[1] Thus given the fact that it is more difficult to satisfy the Labour voters than the Conservatives' economic expectations, notwithstanding the somewhat higher average income of the Labour voters, affluence alone does not lead to an increase in Tory voting.

Having shown that economic satisfaction is associated with the workers' Tory preferences, it remains to be seen how the other half

TABLE 45

Economic satisfaction and Voting behaviour[2]

	Satisfied	So-so	Unsatisfied
Conservative	40	34	26
Labour	60	66	74
Total per cent	100	100	100
Total number	194	104	139

of the argument—the effect of subjective class upon voting behaviour —is related to this finding. It is then first necessary to specify what it is that leads a sizeable proportion of workers to think of themselves as middle class. The overlap between the more prosperous workers and the lower economic strata of the middle class suggests that the 'middle-class' workers think of themselves in these terms because of their absolute and relative affluence. This hypothesis is partly supported by the data; there is a relationship between income and class identification (see Table 46). None of the Labour voters earning below average incomes identify as middle class, the proportion increasing to 18 per cent of those with above average incomes. Thus affluence does tend to induce them to view themselves as middle class. Presumably they conceive of themselves as such because middle class people are thought

[1] See Table 38, p. 154.
[2] The weighting index, according to which the number of Labour respondents has been multiplied by five, is used here.

of as prosperous types, and seeing themselves in this light, they too become middle class.

This conclusion is not, however, applicable to the Conservatives, even though there is a correlation between income and subjective class among these workers. For in Table 47 it is seen that economic satisfaction is a more powerful explanatory variable in accounting for middle-class identification than is income alone. Of those Tories who are economically contented 39 per cent are middle-class subjectives, the proportion dropping to 15 per cent of those who are economically dissatisfied. The weaker correlation between the Tories' income and their class identification then becomes only a limited explanation; for it is the sense of economic well-being rather than income alone

TABLE 46

Income and class identification

	Tories			Labour		
	£10 and below	£11– £15	£16 and above	£10 and below	£11– £15	£16 and above
Working class	80	69	66	100	88	80
Middle class	17	28	31	0	11	18
DK, other	4	3	2	0	2	3
Total per cent	100	100	100	100	100	100
Total number	88	127	83	27	57	40

which leads the Tories to identify as middle class. The data in Table 47 indicates that in the case of the Labour voters there is no relationship between economic satisfaction and middle-class identification. Whatever the reasons may be for this negative finding, the problem is extraneous to the present analysis. For one thing only 12 per cent of the Labour voters identify as middle class, compared to 35 per cent of the Conservatives. But more important, the Labour group can now be disregarded because the object of the exercise is to understand how economic satisfaction and middle-class identification are specifically related to Conservative voting.

We have found correlations between all three variables, but this does not tell us by which path the three are interconnected. The two most plausible possibilities are set out diagrammatically in Figure 1.

TABLE 47
Economic satisfaction and class identification

| | Tories | | | Labour | | |
	Satisfied	So-so	Unsatisfied	Satisfied	So-so	Unsatisfied
Working class	58	81	82	87	93	86
Middle class	39	16	15	13	7	14
Other, DK	4	3	3	0	0	0
Total per cent	100	100	100	100	100	100
Total number	141	75	88	47	29	51

Figure I

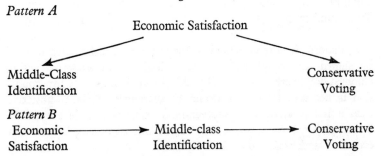

Pattern A

Economic Satisfaction

Middle-Class Identification

Conservative Voting

Pattern B

Economic Satisfaction ⟶ Middle-class Identification ⟶ Conservative Voting

In Pattern A economic satisfaction results in middle-class identification presumably because these manual workers think of middle-class people as being economically secure and contented, and since they share this perceived middle-class attribute they are led to envision themselves in just such terms. The other half of the hypothesis depicted in Pattern A—economic satisfaction resulting in a Conservative vote—is presumably due to the workers' belief that Conservative leaders and policies are best suited for the realization of their economic expectations. In Pattern B the same relationship between economic satisfaction and middle-class identification as in Pattern A is posited. However, here Tory voting is not independently affected by economic contentment as it is in Pattern A. Rather, economic satisfaction is a condition of Conservative voting in so far as it *first* results in middle-class identification, which then results in Conservative voting independently of the economic variable. This latter relationship is probably structured by the middle-class subjectives' belief that Conservative voting is in the economic interests of 'middle-class' people like themselves—a belief bolstered by the objective middle-class' solid support for the Tory Party.

TABLE 48

Economic satisfaction and voting behaviour with class identification controlled for[1]

| | Working Class | | | Middle Class | | |
	Satisfied	So-so	Unsatisfied	Satisfied	So-so	Unsatisfied
Conservative	28	31	25	66	57	26
Labour	72	69	75	34	43	74
Total per cent	100	100	100	100	100	100
Total number	127	89	116	65	15	19

If Pattern A correctly depicts the inter-relationship then it must be shown that economic satisfaction leads to Conservative voting amongst both working-class and middle-class identifiers. If this condition is not met Pattern A would be disconfirmed since subjective class is not posited as an intervening variable as it is in Pattern B. Table 48 has been constructed to settle this matter. It is seen that economic satisfaction does lead to Conservative voting amongst the *middle-class* identifiers, 66 per cent of these workers who are also economically contented voting Tory, with the proportion dropping to 57 per cent and 26 per cent amongst the partly satisfied and dissatisfied middle-class identifiers respectively. In contrast, there is no relationship between economic satisfaction and voting behaviour amongst the working-class identifiers. Since economic satisfaction is not associated with the voting behaviour of the working-class identifiers, the conclusion emerges that there is not a direct relationship between economic satisfaction and Tory voting. Pattern A is thereby invalidated and the strong suggestion emerges that Pattern B with class identification as the intervening variable, correctly posits the three variables' inter-relationship.

In fact, the validity of Pattern B has already been established, and

[1] The weighting index, according to which the number of Labour respondents has been multiplied by five, is used here.

it is just left to bring the strands of two previous arguments together. It has already been shown that economic satisfaction results in middle-class identification, although this applies solely to the Conservative supporters, the 'middle-class' Labour supporters tending to view themselves as such because of a high income level. And the second inter-relationship in Pattern B is the one which we set out to explain at the outset—namely, the tendency for those workers who conceive of themselves as middle-class to vote Conservative. To state the conclusion in a sentence, a sense of economic well-being frequently leads to middle-class identification because the workers define middle-class people as economically secure and comfortable and see themselves as such; and in turn, middle-class identification often results in Tory voting due to the dual belief that this is the 'proper' way for middle-class people to behave and that Tory measures are most likely to maintain their economic well-being.[1]

II. THE CLASS CONFLICT

Beliefs about the class conflict have literally inundated working-class politics in France and Italy. In provoking deep fissures in their political systems—both on a cultural and structural level—these beliefs have contributed to their political instability and non-democratic experiments. What is curious about the English working class is that the belief in the class conflict's importance is very much in evidence among both Conservative and Labour voters. But at the same time these attitudes have not had any debilitating effects upon the political system; unlike France and Italy, beliefs in the class conflicts' importance have not inflamed the issues separating the parties nor have they resulted in the fracturing of political groupings and the placing of heavy demands on the governmental institutions. The explanation which immediately suggests itself is that the English workers' beliefs about the class conflict are not held as intensely as are the French and Italian workers', thereby intruding themselves less frequently and less forcefully into the political system. Indeed, this is the broad answer to the problem, but in analysing the respondents' attitudes we

---

[1] This conclusion ought not to be taken to mean that economic satisfaction is the single factor patterning class identification. Region, neighbourhood and the class position of one's parents are also relevant. See Runciman, op. cit., pp. 165–167.

also want to know why they are held less intensely, concomitantly specifying the meaning which these beliefs have for the workers who hold them. And in doing so, it will be possible to elucidate the inter-relations between beliefs about the class conflict and the operation of the political system.

'Some people say that various social classes want different things and therefore come into conflict with each other. Do you think that the class conflict in England is very important, fairly important, or not important?' It is the responses to this question as they are set out in Table 49 which serve as the focal point for the ensuing discussion. It is seen that 60 per cent of the Tories, compared to 52 per cent of the Labour voters, replied that the class conflict is 'very important' or 'fairly important'. Contrary to previous expectations, the Tories actually attribute somewhat greater importance to the class conflict than do the Labour supporters even though they are voting for a party whose appeal is largely based on its claim to be a non-class, national party, and which is continually rebutting the Labour Party's inter-pretation of domestic politics in terms of the class conflict.

TABLE 49

Beliefs about the importance of the class conflict in England

	Tories	Defs.	Prags.	Labs.
Important	60	63	58	52
Not important	38	37	39	45
Depends, DK	2	0	3	3
Total per cent	100	100	100	100
Total number	320	90	230	127

It may be that the Conservatives believe the roots of the class con-flict to lie not with the 'higher' classes, but with the Labour Party's and the trade unions' continuous attempts to take a larger share of the national income for themselves and their supporters. If this were the case then it could be understood why the Tories attribute slightly greater importance to the class conflict than does Labour. Although seemingly plausible, the data do not lend the hypothesis any validity. If the Conservatives who attribute importance to the class conflict view the Left as the culprit in fomenting this situation, these Conservatives ought to be more partisan (in the *Gegnerschaft*) sense than those Tories who do not share their beliefs about the class conflict. Such a relationship would indicate a belief in the connection between class conflict and the Labour Party's and the trade unions' efforts. Yet when the Tory supporters are divided into those who believe the class conflict to be important and those who do not share this view, the former are not found to be more negatively oriented towards the Labour Party than the latter.

Another possible interpretation suggests that the deferentials and pragmatists, for different reasons, assign responsibility for the class conflict to the middle and upper classes. Favouring upper-class leaders who would presumably push forward the Disraeli-Macleod 'one-nation' idea with its emphasis upon the integration of society through class co-operation, the deferentials may well be especially disappointed in the structure of society. Desiring at least a diluted public (as opposed to a private) service society, the deferentials perceive the 'higher' classes to be acting in an outrageously self-interested manner. This interpretation is buttressed when it is recalled that the deferentials are the most anti-business oriented of the three groups, picturing business groups as having an inordinate amount of power which they use in their own self-interest. On the other hand, given their achievement values, the pragmatists possibly attribute particular importance to the class conflict because they do not see these values being implemented. Ascriptive qualities and social connections are perhaps seen as the main determinants of economic and political success, the middle and upper classes refusing to sanction the implementation of achievement criteria which might cost them their desired positions. For the pragmatists, the class conflict may then pit the traditional establishment types against a rising 'meritocracy'. Although these two arguments find some indirect support in other parts of the study and thus take on a measure of plausibility, the present data can neither confirm nor disconfirm them.

Since more than half the workers assign some importance to the class conflict, with nearly a quarter replying that it is 'very important', the question which ought to be asked of those respondents is whether or not they see the class conflict as significant on a general societal level or on a personal level. Do the workers believe the conflict to be important because it helps shape the society's broad economic and social contours, or because it is seen to have a direct personal meaning for the workers? All the available evidence points in the same direction. The conflict is thought to be important only on a general societal level, without personally affecting the workers (e.g. as an economic threat).

If the class conflict were viewed in personal terms those workers attributing importance to it ought to desire the reduction of class differences, thereby mitigating the conflict's personally undesirable effects. Yet when asked their reactions to the idea of reducing class differences[1] no positive correlation is found between a belief in the conflict's importance and a desire to have class differences reduced. A similar finding occurs when the respondents' preferences for a working-class solidarity[2] are correlated with their beliefs about the class conflict. If those workers replying that the conflict is important felt that it impinged upon them personally, they would opt for the security provided by a working-class togetherness more often than the workers who do not attribute any importance to the class conflict. However, only a slight correlation of this kind appears in the data. Thirdly, it can be presumed that if the class conflict did impinge upon the workers in personal terms, they would move into the protective arms of the Labour Party, described by G. D. H. Cole as 'a broad human movement on behalf of the bottom dog'. However, when the sample is divided up into three groups according to their beliefs about the class conflict's importance, the proportion of Labour voters to Tories does not increase as one moves from those workers believing the conflict to be unimportant, fairly important, and very important. Our conclusion thus appears to be eminently warranted: since the importance of the class conflict is not thought to be related to the individual workers' personal social and economic positions,

---

[1] This question reads as follows: 'Both the Labour and Conservative parties have adopted a number of policies which are intended to reduce class differences. Here is a list of possible reactions to this objective of the two parties. Which comes closest to how you feel about reducing class differences?' Since it was not deemed particularly useful to subject the responses to any extended analysis, they are simply reported here without comment. Amongst the Tories 74 per cent are either 'very much in favour' of reducing class differences or 'generally agree' with this goal. In comparison 81 per cent of the Labour supporters hold to one or the other of these views. Among the Conservatives 18 per cent generally disagree' with the idea of reducing class difference or are 'very much against it', with 12 per cent of the Labourites subscribing to one of these two views.

[2] See p. 180 below for the wording of this question.

its significance attaches to the structure of society and industry at a general level.[1]

Returning to the question raised at the outset, asking why it is that the manual workers' attribution of importance to the class conflict does not have a debilitating effect upon the political system, the answers can now be set out. In the first place, it is the Conservatives, voting for the party of the middle and upper classes who evidence the most frequent beliefs in the class conflict's significance and also attribute responsibility for the class conflict to the 'higher' classes. If the reverse were true, then the intensity of party conflict might have been heightened as a dual crystallization occurred within the working class: Left voting and assignment of responsibility for the class conflict to the 'higher' classes, combined with Right voting and the attribution of responsibility to the working class. But clearly of over-riding importance here is the fact that neither the Tory nor Labour supporters view the class conflict as something harmful or threatening to their personal social or economic positions.[2] Beliefs about the class conflict's importance on a general societal or industrial level does not motivate working people to seek political solutions to the class conflict, which would not be the case if the conflict impinged upon them personally. It is for this reason that even widespread beliefs about the class conflict do not detract from the political system's stability and effectiveness.

III. WORKING-CLASS SOLIDARITY

In a consensual two-party system where the stakes of power revolve around the electoral decisions of a small percentage of the population, the parties almost invariably attempt to outbid each other, promising

[1] There is a third possibility, namely, that a belief in the class conflict is simply an inoperative carry-over from an earlier period when the belief was behaviourally meaningful. However, the expected correlation between the holding of such beliefs and age is not borne out by the data. Moreover, if the hypotheses were valid, we should have found a far larger proportion of Labour supporters than Tories subscribing to this belief, the Labour Party having served as the chief propagator of this idea during the earlier period of a largely unmitigated capitalism, when it was much more applicable than it is today.

[2] It may even be, especially given the relatively realistic and sophisticated attitudes of some Conservative voters, that the class conflict is sometimes viewed as inevitable—as a necessary corollary of the class system and the division of labour. For a discussion of some other possible factors contributing to this personal unconcern for the class conflict, see Morris Rosenberg, 'Perceptual Obstacles to Class Consciousness', *Social Forces*, October 1965, pp. 22–27.

to provide more and 'better' material prosperity. The English are
no exception to this generalization. However, in terms of the means
by which the workers are to get ahead economically the two parties
project two decidedly different appeals. The Conservative Party
stresses the opportunities and advantages of individual economic
mobility in an affluent society. The appeal of a 'property-owning
democracy' is presumably beamed at those highly paid workers who
have the best opportunities for 'getting on' as individuals. In contrast,
the Labour Party ideology is largely based upon collective political
action and economic solidarity, and its appeal is more often than not
directed towards those workers who are least able to assert their economic demands as individuals.

In order to gauge the extent to which the workers think it best to
get ahead by individual or collective means, our informants were asked:
'Some people say that if working-class people want to get on they
have got to stick together, and stick up for each other. Other people
say that each person ought to try and get on, on his own. How do you
feel about this—should working-class people stick together in order
to get ahead, or should they try to get ahead on their own as individuals?'[1] The responses show that there is a significant overlap between
the parties' appeals and the related attitudes of their working-class
supporters (see Table 50). Twice as many Labour supporters (50 per
cent) as Tories (23 per cent) think that the workers ought to stick together in order to achieve their economic goals. From these figures it
might be surmised that the idea of collective economic and political
action continues to find a strong echo in the contemporary ethos
of the working class. Do not half the Labour voters and a quarter of
the Conservative supporters register their adherence to this appeal?
Notwithstanding these figures, the argument offered here interprets
this belief in class solidarity as an ideological hold-over from an earlier
period having little influence upon the workers' behaviour. The
conditions of working-class life have been so decisively altered as
to make the appeal of class solidarity largely irrelevant in the second
half of the twentieth century. The workers consequently invest this
idea with neither a political, social nor economic meaning.

[1] This item is taken from the interview schedule developed by R. T. McKenzie and Allan Silver for their study of working-class politics. I should like to
thank Professor McKenzie for allowing me to see his interview schedule while
the present one was being constructed.

Hoggart is undoubtedly right when he characterizes the ethos of some 'traditional' pre-1939 industrial workers in terms of the 'Them/ Us' dichotomy—a diffuse suspiciousness of all outsiders and a turning in upon one's own resources and those of relatives and close neighbours. Perhaps the single most powerful expression of this *Weltan-schauung* is the workers' belief in class solidarity, the idea that they ought to maintain a common front against the other classes in society. This class solidarity may be interpreted as the product of a largely unmodified capitalism operating under less than optimum economic conditions. The structure of industry made it obvious that (with some exceptions) any economic gains, and even the stabilization of current wages, could best be secured through collective trade union action, notwithstanding

TABLE 50

Beliefs about the desirability of working-class solidarity

	Tories	Defs.	Prags.	Labs.
Stick together	23	22	24	50
Individual efforts	71	69	71	48
Depends	1	0	2	2
DK	3	4	2	1
Other	2	4	1	0
Total per cent	100	100	100	100
Total number	320	90	230	127

the disappointments evinced in the wake of the 1926 General Strike. But even more important, working-class solidarity emerged out of a bitter sense of insecurity and helplessness in the face of the inequities and sufferings inflicted by impersonal economic forces—forces which could be partly countered by a banding together for mutual protection and assistance. This class solidarity found organizational expression in the flourishing of Friendly societies, mutual aid societies, co-operative schemes, trade unions, and as a last resort, in the urban burial societies.

What class solidarity there was thus emerged out of an economic insecurity. But what happened in recent years when economic insecurity largely disappeared? The point to be made is not that the belief in working-class solidarity also disappeared,[1] for the data in Table 50 indicate that these beliefs continue to be widespread throughout the working class. Rather, notwithstanding the holding of these beliefs, they have become irrelevant for the contemporary working class. Class solidarity was perhaps the only viable response for the traditional working class living under a harsh economic system, but when insecurity gave way to security its rationale became irrelevant— an irrelevance that was further heightened by a new-found prosperity that directed the workers' attention to further gains rather than greater security.[2] With the appearance of a full blown welfare state providing the workers with a basic measure of economic security, the disappearance of the haunting spectre of unemployment, the coming of a full employment economy, and the accretion of sufficient power to the trade unions so that they can now demand the satisfaction of the workers' interests—with the confluence of these factors in the postwar period the idea of a protective group solidarity no longer coincided with the economic conditions which called it into being.

Having become objectively irrelevant for the working class, the idea of class solidarity lost its political, social and economic meaning for the workers as individuals. The apparent widespread value still placed upon class solidarity is simply an instance of attitudes surviving the conditions which originally gave rise to them. If the idea of class solidarity has any political meaning for the workers who adhere to it they should manifest activist tendencies—in accordance with the dictates of collective political action—more often than those workers shunning this belief for individual efforts. Furthermore, amongst the Labour voters, a belief in class solidarity ought to predispose them in a particularly partisan direction *vis-à-vis* the Conservative Party; the Conservative Party's opposition to a working-class solidarity should be sufficient to lead these Labour supporters to take a dim view of its policies and motivations—at least if their attachment

[1] However, it is possible to substantiate this secondary point to some extent, for the data show that a belief in class solidarity progressively decreases with decreasing age, the older generations which have lived through the rigours of a harsh economic system placing a higher valuation upon this idea than the younger workers who have not shared these experiences.

[2] If this second hypothesis is successfully substantiated, then the first hypothesis—that class solidarity emerged out of a widespread sense of economic insecurity—will gain additional support. For if class solidarity is markedly weakened in a period of economic security, the implication is that it originally arose because of economic insecurities.

to the idea of class solidarity is politically meaningful to them. However, in both instances the data do not lend themselves to such a conclusion, there being only slight variations between those workers who adhere to collective action and those who believe in individual efforts.

Moreover, a belief in class solidarity has also lost its social meaning; for the workers no longer place a great value upon membership in the working class, although they have not developed aspirations for middle-class status. In the first part of this chapter mention was made of the question asking the respondents whether they would prefer a son of theirs to become friendly with a cabinet maker's son or the son of a bank clerk. For the sample as a whole only some 6 per cent preferred the cabinet maker's son, thereby indicating that the workers no longer maintain a strong social identification with their class. The vast majority of the respondents replied either that they 'don't care' which boy their sons are friendly with or that both are equally preferable.[1] And when the sample is divided into those who believe in class solidarity and those who prefer individual advancement, no difference appears between the two groups among the Tory voters, and only a 7 per cent difference within the Labour groups. Lastly, the idea of working-class solidarity does not appear to have any meaning for the workers in their economic roles. If the opposite were true we should surely find a relationship between this belief and the extent to which the workers take part in the affairs of their trade unions. However, when the two groups of workers are compared no such relationship emerges; those Tory and Labour workers who are trade union members and who believe in class solidarity are no more active in their unions' affairs than are their dissenting peers.

IV. SOCIAL RELATIONS WITHIN THE WORKING-CLASS COMMUNITY

What effect, if any, does the Conservatives' minority position within their neighbourhoods and work-places have upon the workers' social relations? Are the Tories integrated members of the working-class

[1] To which can be added Runciman's summary of the relevant sociological studies: 'the sense of community, and the frequent public, although not intimate, social contacts which characterize it, have given way to a greater reserve and home-centredness and an increasing awareness of distinctions of status within the working class itself.' Op. cit., p. 114.

community, or is there a social line of demarcation separating the two groups of voters because one group constitutes a minority which rejects the majority's partisan premises?

Workers join voluntary associations for relaxation, companionship, and entertainment—what Hoggart calls 'the friendly group tradition' with its emphasis upon sociableness. The frequency with which the Tory and Labour respondents join voluntary associations can then be taken as one indicator of the extent to which the Conservatives are socially integrated members of the community. When asked whether they belong to 'any organized group—social groups, sports clubs, religious organizations or any other type of organized group besides trade unions', 29 per cent of the Conservatives and 43 per cent of the Labour voters turned out to be members of at least one organization. These data appear to indicate that the Conservatives are not as well integrated into the working-class community as are the Labour voters. However, this is not necessarily the conclusion which follows from these figures. There are three possible interpretations which can be placed upon them. The lower rate of Tory group membership may be due to Labour hostility or coldness, making them feel undesired in associations largely made up of Labour supporters. It may also be that the Labour supporters do not direct any negative feelings towards the Conservatives, but that the latter simply feel uncomfortable in working-class associations in which they constitute a political minority. Or it may be that even though the Labour voters do not draw any social distinctions on the basis of political allegiances, the Tories as a group are simply less inclined towards the type of social intercourse offered by voluntary associations, conforming perhaps more closely to the picture of the 'home-centred society' drawn by Mark Abrams. Deciding between these three interpretations will serve as the focus of the ensuing discussion since it provides a convenient and important statement of the possible patterns of social inter-action between the two groups of voters.

The first and most important problem to be faced is one of deciding whether or not there is any hostility between the Tory and Labour voters. If there is any hostility then the first interpretation would appear to be the best one in accounting for the difference in group membership rates. The one writer who has discussed relations between Tory and Labour workers concluded that the Labour supporters 'despise and distrust' the Tories, especially if they are not trade union members.[1] Yet a 14 per cent difference in the two groups' organizational membership rates already leads to some scepticism about the applicability of this description to the urban working class.

In order to decide whether or not Stacey's conclusion is warranted the respondents were first asked if there are 'any groups in this neighbourhood or at your job that you would not become friendly with'. Approximately one-fifth of both groups of voters said that there are such undesirable groups with which they would have no social contact. These respondents were then asked to name the 'groups or people that you would not become friendly with'. Not a single one mentioned the supporters of the 'opposition' party. With the exception of four workers who referred to the Communists or Fascists, the responses were completely devoid of political content.[2] As a supplement to this free-answer question, the respondents were specifically asked about their feelings towards the manual workers who support the 'opposition' party: 'How do you feel about people of the same social class as yourself who support (the 'opposition' party)? Would you become friendly with these people?' Fully 95 per cent of the Tories and 93 per cent of the Labour voters replied that they would become friendly with such people. And when asked their reasons, practically all the workers replied in the following vein: 'Politics has no bearing on friendships'; 'They are all neighbours just the same'; 'We agree to differ—it's quite interesting'; 'There are good Tory men as well as Labour'; 'It never crops up and my best friend is Conservative'.

It is one thing to accept a friendship—a non-binding relationship—with an opposition party supporter. It is quite another to approve of one's son or daughter marrying such a person. Since most parents want to continue to have friendly if not close relations with their children after marriage, if there were any antagonism towards the supporters of the opposition party the parents would presumably not approve of such a marriage considering the strain it would place

---

[1] Margaret Stacey, *Tradition and Changes, A Study of Banbury*: 1960, p. 53. Martin Harrison cites an article in *The Journal* of the Amalgamated Engineering Union that calls the working-class Tory 'the Judas in our midst'. *Trade Unions and the Labour Party*: 1960, p. 47.

[2] To provide a flavour of the responses a handful of examples are included: 'People who think they are middle class but aren't'; 'The really tough types'; 'Work shy people'; 'Jehovah's witnesses'; 'The low groups of this unsavoury neighbourhood where there is sometimes violence'.

upon family cohesion. The question used to elicit the workers' reactions to this possibility reads: 'Suppose a son or daughter of yours
was getting married. How would you feel if he or she married a supporter of (the opposition party)? Would you be pleased, would you
be displeased, or would it make no difference?'[1] Only 5 per cent of
the Tory and Labour voters replied that they would be 'displeased'
with such a marriage.

The evidence that there is no hostility or even coldness between
the Tories and Labour supporters becomes even more persuasive
when we examine the workers' actual friendship patterns—which is
undoubtedly the crux of the matter. The informants were asked:
'Would you say that all of your friends support the same political
party as you do, most of them do, some of them do, or that none of
them prefer the same political party as you do?' From the data presented
in Table 51 it is seen that the Conservatives are hardly an isolated
group within their neighbourhoods and at their jobs. Among both
groups of voters friendship patterns cut across party lines. Only 4 per
cent of the Tories have friends who are exclusively Conservative supporters, while only another 13 per cent have friends who are practically all Tory voters like themselves. Or stated differently, more than
two-thirds of the Conservatives belong to friendship groups containing
many, if not a majority, of Labour supporters. Furthermore, the
data show that political discussion is not hampered within these
politically mixed friendship groups, thereby indicating that the expression of divergent viewpoints is not seen as a threat to the groups'
cohesion.

All the evidence then points in the same direction: contrary to
Stacey's conclusion regarding the manual workers in Banbury (a
town of 19,000), there appears to be no hostility whatsoever between
Tory and Labour supporters amongst urban manual workers.[2] In

---

[1] The wording of this question and the preceding point upon which its
interpretation is premised are taken from Almond and Verba, op. cit., p. 134.

[2] For this writer at least, the reason for the completely opposite conclusions
reached in the two studies remains inexplicable, except in so far as Stacey's
evidence may be inadequate. The only published evidence to support her
argument is an interview with a local trade union leader who would clearly be
more antagonistic towards the working-class Tories than a rank and file union
member. Although it ought to be recognized that in the 'closer' atmosphere of
a small town, marked political deviations are less likely to be sanctioned than in
the less confining atmosphere of urban life, it must not be forgotten that many
urban working-class neighbourhoods—with their well-marked social boundaries

TABLE 51

The proportion of the respondents' friends who support the same party
as they do[1]

	Tories	Labour
All	4	7
Most	13	27
Some	66	52
None	5	2
DK	11	12
Total per cent	100	100
Total number	315	127

attempting to decide between the three possible interpretations to
be placed upon the data relating to group membership, the first interpretation—that the Tories join voluntary organizations less frequently
than do the Labour voters because of the latter's hostility or coldness
—can be dismissed. It is left for us to decide between the remaining
two interpretations, but it should be noted that the disconfirmation
of the first interpretation is thought to be the most important conclusion regarding the workers' social relations.

In attempting to decide whether the Tories' lower rate of group
membership is due to their feeling uncomfortable in such groups
because they are a political minority or because they simply have less
interest in associational membership, we can ask what is probably a
more interesting question; namely, are the Tories seen as political
deviants by the Labour supporters? If they are seen as deviants, even
if this does not entail any outward coldness towards them, the Tories
may still feel uneasy in organizations that are dominated by Labour
supporters. However, if they are not viewed as political deviants,
even socially acceptable ones, this would suggest that their lower
rate of group membership is due to their own personal disinclinations
in that direction. Hoggart has underlined the conformity demanded
within the working-class community. According to him, the group

and social centralization at two or three local pubs—also have their distinctly
confining characteristics operating to penalize non-conformity.

[1] Those respondents who replied that they do not have any friends are not
included.

'imposes on its members an extensive and sometimes harsh pressure to conform. Those who become different, through education and one or two other ways, may often be allowed for, and I do not want to suggest a strong automatic hostility to any departure at all from the group or its attitudes. Indeed one of the marked qualities of working-class groups is a wide tolerance in some things; but it is a tolerance which works freely only *if the chief class assumptions are shared*.'[1] If Hoggart's statement is accepted as generally true for the contemporary working class, then it follows that the Tories are not seen as deviants; for if they were viewed as such they would be resented by the working-class majority—something which the foregoing data have shown not to be the case. The Tories may be seen as somehow 'different', yet their political differences apparently do not entail a rejection of the workers' 'chief class assumptions'. In short, there is nothing to indicate that the Tories are not fully accepted members of the working-class community. This conclusion accords with the one reached in the first section of this chapter, pointing out that the middle-class identification of some Tories is unrelated to any desire for increased social status. If the latter were the case, then these workers would be typed as deviants and treated accordingly, for the one attitude which the workers instinctively react against is a social snobbishness, acting 'above y'self' by 'putting on airs' and 'acting posh'.

Although the evidence is by no means conclusive, the fact that the Tories are not seen as deviants by the majority does suggest that their lower rate of group membership is not due to a feeling of uneasiness because of their minority position in working-class organizations. It would therefore appear that the Tories' somewhat weaker integration into the working-class community as measured by their rate of group membership is related to their personal disinclination to take up full membership, rather than by any negative reactions towards them on the part of the Labour majority. Yet it may be that their relative disinclination towards group membership is due to their *self*-defined minority position; feeling themselves to be 'different' they choose not to place themselves in a social situation where this difference may be highlighted.[2]

---

[1] Op. cit., p. 72 (Italics added).
[2] Some evidence for this point is found on pp. 208–209 below.

CHAPTER 8

Work-Place Relations

___

I. WORKER-EMPLOYER RELATIONS

SINCE Karl Marx, writers of the political Right and Left have argued that the workers' class consciousness is dissipated when they develop close personal relations with their employers. In what is probably the leading study of the work-place environment as it patterns political behaviour and attitudes, Lipset, Trow and Coleman approvingly cite Marx, and point out that attachments to trade unions and Left parties dedicated to improving the workers' economic position tend to be discarded by workers who know their bosses on a personal basis; these workers rely on their employers' beneficence for any economic gains and upon their personal relations for social and psychic satisfactions.[1] In her study of Banbury, Stacey makes the distinction between 'traditional' firms in which the owner takes a direct part in the business, and 'non-traditional' firms which are 'organized on a large scale with remote ownership'. Her survey data indicate that in the traditional firms nearly half of the manual workers are Conservatives or Liberals, whereas less than one-quarter of the workers in the non-traditional firms fall into this category. Stacey suggests a two-fold explanation for this pattern: in the traditional firms the long-standing 'gaffer to man' relationship continues to influence the workers to vote 'with' their bosses, and secondly, in these small enterprises there is little trade union organization which would both disrupt the close employer-employee relationship and lead to Labour voting.[2]

Notwithstanding the unanimity of Marx, Lipset, *et al.*, and Stacey, the position taken here is the reverse of theirs; personal relations between English workers and employers do *not* predispose the workers

___

[1] Seymour Martin Lipset, Martin Trow and James Coleman, *Union Democracy*: 1962, p. 172. The passage cited from Marx comes from 'Germany: Revolution and Counter Revolution', in V. Adoratsky, ed., *Selected Works of Karl Marx*: International Publisher, N.Y. (n.d.), Vol. II, p. 47.

[2] Stacey, op. cit., pp. 21, 46–47.

in a conservative political direction.[1] But before enlarging upon and attempting to substantiate this argument, it would be well to note the differences between the present data and that offered by the sociologists just cited. Marx may or may not have been correct in suggesting that the workers' political attitudes are shaped by their enjoyment of a personal relationship with their employers. Below it will be argued that he was most probably right, but largely for the wrong reason. The point here is that Marx's generalizations refers to the nineteenth-century working class, and it therefore cannot be simply transposed to the twentieth century with its drastically changed conditions of employment and fundamental alterations in the social structure. Then, too, the data Lipset, *et al.* present as evidence for the hypothesis that personal employer-employee relations lead to the attentuation of the workers' Leftist attachments are either questionable or do not directly bear upon the hypothesis. There is evidence to indicate that the workers in the small shops, where personal employer-employee relations are presumably encouraged, have 'a lower interest and involvement in union politics' and maintain different types of achievement aspirations (i.e. owning one's own print shop *v.* becoming a shop foreman in a large plant).[2] Yet it may be that the weakening of trade union activity as shop size decreases is a function of shop size rather than the workers' personal employer-employee relations, while the workers' differing occupational goals cannot be used as direct evidence for a hypothesis about political attitudes. In order to substantiate their hypothesis, Lipset, *et al.*, would have had to show that the workers enjoying closer employer relations more often vote Republican in national elections than do those workers who do not maintain such relations and that the former group more often appear on the Right end of a political liberalism-conservatism scale. Both of these measures were available for analysis, yet they were not utilized in this part of the study. However, in a secondary analysis of the same data by another sociologist, just the opposite pattern appeared than the one which would be necessary to substantiate the authors' argument; namely, that the workers in the smaller shops where there are presumably more frequent and more meaningful

---

[1] However, among the German workers, those who like to talk socially with their superiors, but not with their colleagues, vote for the Christian Democrats more frequently than do those workers who *prefer* to talk with their colleagues. Juan Linz, op. cit., p. 402.

[2] Op. cit., pp. 172–174.

employer contacts vote Democratic more often than do the workers in the larger shops.[1] If anything then, the *Union Democracy* data support the argument to be offered here.

Regarding Stacey's study, the focal point is a town of 19,000 people in rural Oxfordshire, whereas the present sample is restricted to urban workers. We cannot decide whether the opposite conclusions reached in the two studies are due to urban-rural differences or whether they are related to the different methods of collecting the data; for Stacey offers no evidence to support her contention that the higher rate of Conservative and Liberal voting in the 'traditional' firms is in large part due to the worker-employer relations found in these enterprises. All we have is a correlation between the workers' party attachments and the type of firm in which they are employed. It is therefore plausible to suggest that the extensive Conservative and Liberal voting in the 'traditional' firms is due to factors other than closer employer-employee relations—the physical size of the firm as it patterns social and thus political relationships among the men, and the extensiveness of trade union membership, are two alternative possibilities.

What evidence is there then to support the argument that the contemporary urban workers' politics are *not* conservatized by personal relations with their employers? In order to identify those workers who have face-to-face contact with their bosses, the respondents were asked: 'Do you ever come into contact with the head or owner of the firm? I mean, do you ever speak with him?' The data generated by this question show that the frequency of Tory voting among those workers having such contacts with the 'head' is no higher than that of the workers who do not know their employers on a personal basis.[2] Secondly, we would want to know whether personal contacts with employers have influenced the workers to adopt a deferential political outlook. Again, the finding is a negative one. The proportion of deferentials among the Tory voters who have personal contacts with their employers (25 per cent) is actually *lower* than the proportion of deferentials not enjoying such relations (33 per cent).[3] Turning to the Labour

[1] Gene N. Levine, *Workers Vote: The Political Behaviour of Men in the Printing Trade*: 1963, pp. 152, 155. The conservatism-liberalism scale is not related to shop size in this volume.
[2] A secondary analysis of the Almond and Verba data produced almost identical results.
[3] Although Stacey has written that the workers in the traditional firms 'recognize the right of those in the higher classes to lead', in part because

supporters, although contact with employers has obviously not led them to vote Tory, it may still be that such contacts have dampened their negative attitudes towards the Conservative Party. Yet, when the Labour voters are divided into those who do and do not come into personal contact with their employers, there are only 5 per cent fewer weak partisans amongst the former than the latter. All the available evidence thus points in the same direction: face-to-face contacts with one's employer do not predispose the workers to the Right politically.[1]

Now it could reasonably be objected that the question asked of the respondents about their employer relations was framed too loosely. Under the heading of personal contact are included both those workers who simply exchange a few formalized pleasantries with their employers and those who might actually have a relatively close personal relationship with their bosses. Amongst workers in large factories, 38 per cent claim to have face-to-face contact with the 'head', but it is doubtful that more than a small number have personally meaningful relations with their employers. On the other hand, in the medium and small-sized firms where 67 per cent and 81 per cent of the workers respectively, report personal contacts, many of these workers presumably have a close relationship with their bosses.[2] Thus it may be that after factory size is controlled for, and a comparison is made between workers experiencing personal employer contacts with those not having such experiences, it will turn out that in smaller plants where these contacts are more often of a close and meaningful variety, the workers coming into contact with their bosses will be more conservative than those not having such personal contacts. Although this line of criticism is well taken, the data found in Tables 52 and 53 indicate that it is inapplicable.

In the small and medium firms, the workers coming into personal contact with the 'head' continue to vote Tory less frequently than do the workers in those plants having personal employer contacts, and in

---

of the personal employer-employee relations in these firms, no evidence is offered in support of this generalization. Op. cit., p. 47.

[1] Further evidence is found when the workers' attitudes towards the idea of working-class solidarity are used as the dependent variable, there being no difference in the frequency with which the two groups of workers espouse this doctrine. However, it ought to be recalled that the workers do not attach very much meaning to the idea of class solidarity.

[2] Small firms are those with 1 to 300 employees, medium-sized firms are those with 301 to 1,000 employees, and large firms have more than 1,000 workers.

TABLE 52

Personal contacts with employers and voting behaviour when plant size is controlled for[1]

| | Small Plants | | Medium Plants | | Large Plants | |
| | | No | | No | | No |
	Contact	Contact	Contact	Contact	Contact	Contact
Conservative	41	44	29	51	29	23
Labour	59	57	71	49	71	77
Total per cent	100	100	100	100	100	100
Total number	98	24	81	58	67	93

this case it can be assumed that these contacts are in many instances more than a mere exchange of pleasantries. It is, in fact, in the large firms where face-to-face contacts with the boss are rarely personally meaningful that workers maintaining employer contacts vote Conservative slightly more often than do those workers not enjoying such relations. Moreover, from Table 53 it is seen that the proportion of deferentials amongst the Conservative voters having employer contacts is smaller in those firms of less than 1,000 workers (22 per cent) than the same group in firms with more than 1,000 workers (31 per cent). And it is actually in the small firms that the greatest difference is found in the proportion of deferentials having no personal contacts (42 per cent) and those with personal employer relations (22 per cent). The same analysis ought also to be carried out in order to measure the effects of employer contacts upon the Labour voters' partisan attitudes. Unfortunately, the number of Labour respondents is too small to allow them to be broken up into six groups so that plant size can be controlled for.

The data thus abundantly support the argument that knowing one's employer on a personal basis does *not* induce the workers to follow in his political footsteps.[2] The data then go on to suggest that knowing

---

[1] The weighting index, according to which the number of Labour respondents has been multiplied by five, is used here.

[2] Another type of evidence for this negative proposition is found in the fact that the first unions in England (and America) emerged not in the larger factories with their impersonal employer-employee relations, but in those industries characterized by small-scale production and close employer-employee relations. See Mancur Olson, Jr., *The Logic of Collective Action*: 1965, p. 66.

7

TABLE 53

Personal contacts with employers and deferential attitudes when plant
size is controlled for among the Conservatives

	Small Plants		Medium Plants		Large Plants	
		No		No		No
	Contact	Contact	Contact	Contact	Contact	Contact
Deferential	22	42	22	30	31	36
Pragmatist	78	58	78	70	69	64
Total per cent	100	100	100	100	100	100
Total number	76	19	54	47	45	56

one's boss on a closer personal basis actually predisposes the workers
somewhat Leftwards politically. For it is in those smaller plants
where employer-employee relations are closer and where there is
greater opportunity for the workers to observe the employers' behaviour,
that the workers having personal contacts are more Left inclined
compared to those not having such relations. Only in the large plants
where employer-employee relations take on a diluted form and where
there is little chance for the workers to see their employers 'in action',
are the workers with employer contact slightly more Conservative
than those workers not experiencing personal employer relations.
A similar pattern occurs when deferential attitudes are used as the
dependent variable. In the small plants, the proportion of deferentials
among those Tories having personal contacts is 20 per cent less than
the proportion not enjoying face-to-face employer relations, the difference dropping to 8 and 5 per cent in the medium and small-sized
plants respectively. And it should be stressed that this Leftward pattern
as one moves towards the smaller plants is strong enough to be able to
run counter to the influences of both 'unionization' and factory size.

To offer the maxim that 'familiarity breeds contempt' as an explanation would be a gross overstatement. Yet the data do intimate that the
closer the workers' relations with the boss the less likely they are to
attribute desirable qualities to their employers; for the degree to which
the workers 'look up to' their bosses, as indicated by their willingness
to pattern their own political attitudes in accordance with those of
their employers, is inversely related to the extent of contact between
the two and the opportunity the workers have to observe their bosses'

behaviour. As a somewhat more sophisticated explanation for these data, we might utilize what sociologists have called the 'halo effect'. It would appear to be generally true that the less contact a person has with those holding higher positions in the same hierarchy, the greater will be his idealization of those persons. This tendency would then account for the data in Tables 52 and 53. Whether it actually does, however, must remain a moot point until further evidence becomes available.

We can now ask why it is that knowing one's boss on a personal basis does not induce the workers to follow in his political footsteps. Of the three most plausible explanations, one has already been invalidated. The data in Tables 52 and 53 indicate that the employers' lack of political influence is not due to the absence of close and personally meaningful worker-employer relations in an age of large and impersonal firms. Secondly, it may be that personal employer contacts are necessary but not sufficient to move the workers to the Right politically; besides personal contacts with the boss, it may also be necessary that the workers believe that their interests are respected by the employers. If there are personal employer contacts without a belief in the employers' positive attitude towards the workers' interests, there would be little reason for the workers to succumb to their employers' politics. In order to substantiate this hypothesis, the data would have to indicate that the workers in the larger plants more often believe their employers to be men who are concerned with the interests and welfare of their workers, since it is in the larger plants that the workers with personal employer relations take on conservative political attitudes. However, as will be seen below, there is no relationship between plant size and the workers' beliefs about their employers' attitudes.

Turning to the third hypothesis, it would seem plausible to argue that the explanation lies with the absence of any economic dependence of the workers upon their employers. The workers no longer experience the economic insecurities of their nineteenth- and early twentieth-century predecessors which forced them into a posture of economic dependence *vis-à-vis* their employers, leaving them open to the latter's political tutelage. Clearly the contemporary situation is qualitatively different from that prevailing during Marx's time when the workers had neither unions to advance their interests, a full employment economy to give high value to their labour, nor a welfare state to secure their basic needs in periods of unemployment, sickness, and old age. In Chapter 5 it was seen that nearly 90 per cent of the workers replied that they felt free to complain to their superiors if a decision were made which they didn't care for. This is as good an indication as any that the contemporary working class does not feel dependent upon their employers for a job.

The economic strength and security felt by the workers repeatedly appear in the second-wave interviews, and the respondents are well aware that their economic independence is a result of fundamental structural changes. When asked what he thought of 'the way that workers are generally treated by their employers', a deferential Tory working as a plumber in Fulham replied: 'Nowadays quite good. But not so years ago. I think in a way it's because there's much less unemployment and employers seem to be a lot more tolerant, more approachable than they used to be'. The retired Royal Navy engineer living in Epsom replied to a similar question in the same fashion: 'I think the workers are treated fairly by their employers. There's so much scope for the worker if he feels he's being underpaid. He can always move. Plenty of jobs. If you get a good man, the employer pays him over the top to keep him . . . the workers know as much about the rules of the game as the boss, so the boss can't take advantage even if he wanted to. In most cases, the workman is having the best deal now. He's independent now, due to full employment.' According to the long-distance lorry driver from Manchester, it is the unions which give the workers their strength: 'Big firms are in no position to take advantage of the workers. But in little firms the men are not represented—they have no union, no works committee. If they've a grievance they've no comeback. Either you do the job as the guv'nor says or you get out of those small firms.' It is this independence and the related absence of economic insecurities that have obviated the workers' necessary reliance upon any one employer, and with the disappearance of the workers' dependence upon their bosses, the latter lost their political influence.

Returning to the problem posed at the outset of this chapter, it is entirely probable that Marx was correct in saying that personal worker-employer relations led to the weakening of the workers' political loyalties to their class. However, it must be added that the employers' political influence was not due to the personal nature of their employee relations alone, for it was only in a context of economic insecurity that the workers responded to their employers' political tutelage. Applying this conclusion to the present data, it would seem that the inability of the employers to influence their workers politically, even through the medium of personal relations between the two groups, is attributable to the workers' economically secure and independent position.

Up to this point in the present chapter, we have only examined one aspect of worker-employer relations. A second variable which could have a conservatizing effect upon the workers' politics is the belief that their interests and needs are given consideration by the employers. Those workers who maintain this belief would presumably develop a great respect for their employers, which in turn could either unconsciously increase their susceptibility to their employers' political views, or induce them to take up a less critical attitude towards the Conservative Party. In order to tap the workers' beliefs about their bosses' actions towards them, they were asked: 'The way things are, do you think that those who run the place where you work take your interests and needs into account when they make decisions affecting you, or do you ignore your interests?'

The effects which these beliefs have in reinforcing political allegiances can be gauged from Table 54. The rate of Tory voting increases from 24 per cent amongst those workers who say that their interests are ignored, to 31 per cent of those who replied that their interests are sometimes considered, to 38 per cent of those believing their employers to be concerned about their interests. It could be argued that the causal interpretation placed upon these data is unwarranted; that it is just as likely that party allegiances influence the workers' beliefs about their employers as vice versa. Perhaps; but when other data are introduced, this criticism loses its force. Another set of correlations suggest that deferential attitudes are strengthened by the workers' beliefs in the good intentions of their employers; amongst those Tories who hold this belief there is a higher proportion of deferentials than amongst those Tories who do not share it. Unlike the data in Table 54, these figures cannot easily be interpreted to indicate that the deferentials see their employers in a better light than do the pragmatists *because* of their differing political attitudes. For as was shown in another chapter, the deferentials express negative beliefs about the business community more frequently than do the pragmatists. It might be added that the politically conservatizing effects of positive beliefs about one's employer also operate among the Labour sympathizers. Those Labour voters who view their bosses in this light, are led to express less intensely partisan beliefs than those Labour voters holding negative beliefs about their employers, 28 per cent of the former compared to 8 per cent of the latter being grouped together as weak partisans.

TABLE 54

Beliefs about the employers' interest in their workers and voting behaviour[1]

	Employers Take the Workers' Interests into Account		
	Yes	Sometimes	No
Conservative	38	31	24
Labour	62	69	76
	—	—	—
Total per cent	100	100	100
Total number	235	109	66

II. TRADE UNION MEMBERSHIP

The statement that trade union members vote Labour more often than do manual workers who are not trade unionists is probably the second most frequently recurring generalization about English voting behaviour. Indeed, 73 per cent of the union members in our sample vote Labour, compared to 50 per cent of the non-members.[2] And when it is noted that 72 per cent of the workers are union members, the political relevance of such membership is strongly underscored. Although this point is often made, it is just as often left undeveloped. It is assumed that trade union membership helps pattern voting behaviour; since the unions are integrally and influentially connected with the Labour Party, the members tend to vote Labour because of their unions' political influence over them.[3] This is obviously a patently

[1] The weighting index, according to which the number of Labour respondents is multiplied by five, is used here.

[2] There are three groups which are included here as non-members: non-members in firms which have a trade union, non-members in firms without a union, and self-employed workers (e.g. window washers and painters). In each case the percentage of Labour voters does not vary by more than one point from the 50 per cent figure.

[3] In contrast, the Conservative Trade Unionists' Organization plays an almost insignificant role within the Conservative Party. Not only is their influence

valid point. Yet it would seem to be equally valid to hypothesize that the two variables are also inter-related in reverse fashion: Labour supporters are originally led to join trade unions (while the Conservatives tend to prefer non-membership) because of the ideological affinities, common aims, and organizational inter-connections between the Labour Party and the trade union movement; for party identifications are usually formed prior to the age at which a decision is made whether or not to join a trade union.

In order to test this hypothesis in a rigorous manner, it would be necessary to know the party allegiances of the workers during their adolescent years (i.e. before a decision regarding membership had to be made). The workers would then be grouped according to their party identification in order to compare the frequency with which they joined unions as adults.

Unfortunately, the available data do not contain a direct indicator of the respondents' party identification at the time of late adolescence or early adulthood. It is therefore necessary to utilize a substitute, or indirect indicator, which turns out to be the party identification and the extent of political interest shown by the respondents' fathers. Given the universally high correlation between the party identification of father and son, especially when the father is interested in politics and the son is only in his politically formative years, it is safe to assume that our indirect measure of the respondents' early party identification is a fairly reliable one. The Tories were split into three groups: those whose fathers had been Conservatives or Liberals and who were 'very much interested' in politics, those who had simply been Conservative or Liberal supporters without taking a great deal of interest in politics, and those who had other or no political preferences. As can be seen in Table 55, the Labour voters were grouped in a similar fashion according to the strength with which their fathers did or did

___

almost non-existent, as pointed out in the introductory chapter, they sometimes suffer the added injury of being exhibited as manikins to show the working class that there are such entities as Tory trade unionists. Conservative manual workers in any position of responsibility within the Party are so scarce that one serious-minded Tory manual worker was motivated to stand as an Independent Conservative in the 1964 General Election. He was reconciled to the loss of his £150 deposit, believing it to be money well spent if he could 'punch some sense into the Conservative Party and get them to adopt more trade unionists as (parliamentary) candidates'. He considers it grossly unfair and unwise that 3,500,000 Conservative trade unionists should not have a proper representation on the Party's benches in the Commons. *The Times* (London), October 14, 1964.

not support the Labour Party.[1] Among the Tories, the proportion of trade unionists decreases as their presumed adolescent identifications with the Conservative Party increases, the latter leading them to shun membership in an organization affiliated with the Labour Party. Among Labour, the proportion of members increases as their presumed pre-adult attachments to the Labour Party increases. The small differences of 9 and 12 per cent found in the two parts of Table 55 are not unexpected. The indicator used to get at the workers' early adult political loyalties is too crude to permit accurate measurement, while many workers will have only decided to join or not to join a union in their later adult years when their political allegiances may be different from what we assumed them to be during early adulthood. Then, too, many workers have undoubtedly been pressured into union membership due to economic circumstances, industrial conditions, and the 'closed shop',[2] whereas others were unable to join a union because their plants did not contain one. But notwithstanding the crudeness of our measuring device and this set of intervening factors, what evidence there is does support the hypothesis that party identification influences the decision to become or not to become a union member; for although the percentage differences are small, they 'run' in the right direction for both Tories and Labour and they do so in a linear fashion.

Having seen that trade union membership is inter-related with party identification in a two-fold manner, what else can be said about the Tories' and Labour's attitudes towards the unions? From the open-ended interviews it seems that the Tories almost invariably have criticisms to make of the unions, though never going so far as to suggest that the country would be better off without them, the emphasis being reversed among the Labour group. This point is illustrated by a handful of second-wave interviews, while from the first-wave data it will be seen that for the Tories union membership is something of a

---

[1] The respondents were asked: 'Did your father have any particular preference for one of the parties when you were young?' (If Yes) 'Which party was that?' Considering that in the past the Liberals were almost as hostile to the unions as were the Conservatives, fathers who supported either party are grouped together. In order to measure their fathers' interest in politics, the respondents were asked: 'Do you remember whether your father was very much interested in politics, somewhat interested, or didn't he pay much attention to it?'

[2] For a discussion of compulsory unionism, see W. E. J. McCarthy, op. cit.

negative experience, whereas the Labour voters place a positive valuation upon it.

Those Tories who do praise the work of the trade unions refer either to the past when the unions were needed in order to protect the workers or to the conception of worker 'unity' in theory; but these positive comments are then always followed by oftentimes deeply felt criti-

TABLE 55

Fathers' politics as an indicator of the workers' adolescent political attachments and trade union membership

| | Tories | | |
	Father Cons. or Lib. and very interested in politics	Father Cons. or Lib.	Father neither Cons. nor Lib.
TU member	51	57	63
Non-member	49	43	37
Total per cent	100	100	100
Total number	53	132	134

| | Labour | | |
	Father Lab. and very interested in politics	Father Lab.	Father not Lab.
TU member	86	82	77
Non-member	14	18	23
Total per cent	100	100	100
Total number	21	44	62

cisms. These criticisms are summarized in two interviews. The first man is a pragmatist working as a Treasury messenger in charge of eight men. Although a union member himself, when asked what he thinks of the trade unions he curtly replied that he hasn't 'got much use for them'. He began by criticizing their 'restrictive practices which I'm against in all trade unions. They will keep a man back who is ambitious or progressive. And they are all politicians when you come down to it. They do the most sinful things possible in this country—the political levy is the curse of the working man. Whether Conservative, Liberal or Labour, you have to pay to conform by contributing to the party you oppose. That goes against my grain'. When asked what effect the unions have on their members this pragmatist responded with the statement that 'if it weren't for their jobs they wouldn't belong . . . In most cases they've got to belong; it's coercive and restrictive even in the social side of life'.

The young deferential who is an electronics engineer elected not to join a union even though there is one in the plant where he works. For the unions 'seem to have a very powerful effect on the members politically. They tell them which way to vote. I suppose they wouldn't have joined the union if they weren't Labour Party members. There seem to be a lot of men who are trying to get rich positions in the union without regard for their members, but just for themselves.' The unions have now also 'got too powerful. The concept at the start was a good one, but it has got out of hand at this moment. The way they strike over ridiculous things they abuse the power that they have been given. They seem to strike only to get their own way; striking seems to be their only weapon whereas it should be talk. I should hate to think where the working class would be without the trade unions, not having anyone to speak up for them and to fight for them. But the business of who does what is taken to extremes . . . The trade union leaders should rein in and remember just what they were for, and not make their members strike over small unimportant things.'

Turning to the Labour supporters we find a greater appreciation of the unions' efforts on behalf of the workers, yet here too, criticism is not absent. When asked to evaluate the trade unions, a post office sorter from Epsom quickly said that they are a 'very good thing. I can't say any other. I happen to be the collector for my branch. With our union they take care of us. The welfare side supply lawyers free of charge to fight a case for you. Our branch secretary will take up any case where they think you're justified in making a claim. Our Secretary, Mr Ron Smith, he fights for us; he understands. He was a postman once himself (and) worked himself up to that position. He knows what he's talking about when he claims for better conditions.' Referring to the role of the unions in more general terms, this Labour voter went on to say that they 'definitely give the men strength. If the men follow their trade union as they should as a body not as an individual, they can win most cases if they're in the right. You get a lot of men who take no interest in their union and complain when they have to pay the dues, but they're the first ones in line when there's an improvement in pay.'

Another Labour voter, while valuing the work of the unions, remains critical of some of their methods. 'As for myself personally,' this machinery inspector for the National Coal Board replied, 'I've never had any disputes and I've been a member for many years. I have my doubts as to the methods they adopt like restricting people with initiative and the will to do the job. I don't agree with this. They hold people back. In the workshops the rule is as in the Army: you march by the slowest man. The same applies to the union. If you can work harder and make more money you're held back all the time. I'm not against unions at all. They do a good job and I'd hate to think what it would be like without them.'

Having used the open-ended interviews to illustrate the argument that the Conservatives are negatively oriented towards the unions compared to the Labour voters, what evidence can be supplied to support it? The trade unionists in the sample were asked whether they 'are active in union affairs, occasionally active, or inactive'. Although the workers hold somewhat inflated estimates of their own union activities, the data indicate that the Tory members are less interested in their unions than are their Labour counterparts; 58 per cent of the Tories are inactive compared to 48 per cent of the Labour supporters (see Table 56). Not only are the Tories less concerned with their unions, union membership actually leads them to take a dimmer view of the Labour Party with which they are usually affiliated through the Trade Union Congress. When the Tories are divided into members and non-members, the members turn out to have stronger partisan (i.e. negative) beliefs about the Labour Party than do the non-members; 27 per cent of the former are strong partisans compared to 15 per cent of the latter.[1] There is thus something about union membership which leads the Conservatives to view the Labour Party in more of a critical light. Whether it be their required contribution to the Labour

[1] Among the Labour voters, union membership has the expected opposite effect. The members are more partisan *vis-à-vis* the Conservative Party than are the non-members, 21 per cent of the former compared to 12 per cent of the latter being classified as strong partisans.

Party coffers or their having been economically pressured into joining an organization whose political affiliations they oppose, must remain unanswered.

TABLE 56

The trade union activity of union members

	Tories	Labour
Active	19	25
Occasionally active	23	27
Inactive	58	48
Total per cent	100	100
Total number	189	102

Furthermore, if union membership has any positive meaning for the workers, their predispositions towards political activism ought to be reinforced; the union would serve as a practical and psychological resource under stress conditions, thereby increasing the probability that the members would attempt to influence a governmental decision. Among the Labour supporters, 40 per cent of the non-members are potential activists, with the proportion jumping to 76 per cent amongst the members. However, within the Conservative group there is no difference in the proportion of potential activists amongst the members and non-members. This would indicate that the Tories' identification with their unions is minimal since it does not induce them to think of their unions as an organizational or psychological resource.

III. PLANT SIZE[1]

One of the most consistent findings which political sociologists have turned up is the correlation between factory size and Left voting.[2] From Table 57 it is seen that this relationship is also applicable to the English working class. In the smallest plants having one to ten employees, 62 per cent of the workers vote Tory, with the proportion decreasing in a linear fashion until it reaches 25 per cent in the large

---

[1] In this section the handful of self-employed workers is omitted.

[2] See the Italian and German data reported in Seymour M. Lipset, *Political Man*: 1960, p. 250; also Hamilton, op. cit., for the French data.

plants with 1,000 or more workers. Is this pronounced pattern due
only to the differing types of employer-employee relationships and the
varying rates of 'unionization' found in the small and large firms?
Or is there also something about the factory environment of different
sized plants which patterns voting behaviour?

TABLE 57
Plant size and voting behaviour[1]

	1–10	11–50	51–300	301–1,000	1,000+
Conservative	62	38	37	34	25
Labour	38	62	63	66	75
Total per cent	100	100	100	100	100
Total number	37	61	82	81	160

We have already seen that workers in small plants tend to have more
frequent and closer contacts with their bosses than do manual workers
in larger plants. Yet it has also been shown that such personal employer
relations do not have any conservatizing effect upon the workers'
voting behaviour. We have also seen that those workers who believe
that their interests are given consideration by their employers tend to
vote Conservative more often than do those workers replying that their
interests are ignored. Yet here it turns out that the workers in small,
medium and large firms do not manifest any differences in the extent
to which they believe their interests are given consideration by the
employers, indicating that plant size is not related to this aspect of
employer-employee relations. Employer-employee relations can therefore be dismissed as an explanation for the covariation of Tory voting
and plant size.

Plant size has been thought to be related to voting behaviour to the
extent that trade unions are more often found in the larger factories;
and since trade union membership helps shape party preferences in
a Leftward mould, this would partly account for the higher rate of
Labour voting in the larger plants. When asked whether their firm
contains a trade union, the proportion replying that it does increases
linearly from 33 per cent amongst those working in the smallest firms

[1] The weighting index, according to which the number of Labour respondents is multiplied by five is used here.

to 97 per cent among those in the largest. The higher rate of Labour voting in the larger plants can consequently be accounted for by the high rate of 'unionization' entailing increased membership rates, with the members taking on Leftist political preferences. But the structurally determined pattern of 'unionization' does not account for all the differences in voting behaviour found in the various sized firms. The data clearly indicate that factory size has an independent effect both on the frequency with which the workers join trade unions when the presence or absence of such an organization in the plant is controlled for, and upon voting behaviour after union membership is controlled for.

The proportion of workers who have taken out union membership in those firms in which a union is to be found increases from 73 per cent to 93 per cent as one moves from the smallest to the largest firms (see Table 58). There is something intrinsic to factory size that predisposes workers to join or not to join a union, and in doing so, indirectly influences the workers' voting behaviour. There are three factors which might lead the workers in the larger factories to join unions more frequently.

TABLE 58

Plant size and trade union membership (in those plants were a union is present)[1]

Trade union	1–10	11–50	51–300	301–1,000	1,000+
member	73	83	94	90	93
Non-member	27	17	6	10	7
Total per cent	100	100	100	100	100
Total number	13	37	62	73	152

Given the concentration of large numbers of workers in the bigger plants it is to be expected that the unions in these plants would engage in more strenuous recruitment efforts—both intensively and extensively—than their counterparts in the smaller plants. The upshot is

[1] The weighting index, according to which the number of Labour respondents is multiplied by five is used here.

a higher percentage of trade unionists in the larger plants.[1] Secondly, it may be that in the larger firms the workers experience more frequent and forceful social pressures to join a trade union. It would seem plausible to argue that such pressures towards social conformity increase inversely with the size of the minority group, in this instance the non-members. When the latter is relatively large, as in the smaller plants, the pressures are probably not as intense or frequent compared to a situation, as in the larger plants, in which the minority is relatively small.[2] The third explanation offered here is based on the supposition that whatever the size of the plant, the workers want to be able to express their interests and grievances in an effective manner by having them taken to a sufficiently high authority, perhaps the 'head' himself. In the smaller factories this is no problem, but in the larger factories it becomes increasingly difficult given the bureaucratic chain of command which must be surmounted before the proper authority can be reached. It is therefore probable that the workers in the smaller factories do not feel that same need to join a trade union in order to establish access to those in authority, whereas in the larger plants it would presumably be necessary to become a trade unionist to gain an effective communications channel for the expression of one's grievances.

These three factors most probably go a long way in accounting for the increased rate at which the workers join trade unions as factory size increases, and once having taken out membership, they are guided 'Leftwards' politically. But plant size also has a direct effect upon voting behaviour *after* trade union membership is controlled for. In the smallest plants 63 per cent of the trade unionists vote Labour, increasing steadily until it reaches 77 per cent in the largest firms (see Table 59). A similar pattern is found among the non-unionists although here it is not a linear one. Two hypotheses present themselves as possible explanations here.

---

[1] To say that the unions' recruitment efforts in the larger plants is more intense, and thereby produces a higher proportion of members, is not to say that after joining a union the workers in the larger plants are more interested in union affairs than are the trade unionists in the smaller plants. In fact, the data indicate that there is no relationship between the members' concern with union affairs and size of plant.

[2] Although it was argued in the preceding chapter that the Tories are not perceived as political deviants and do not experience social pressures to conform, this does not remove the possibility suggested here—that trade union strength is thought to be sufficiently important to the workers to cause them to pressure the minority into taking out membership.

TABLE 59

Plant size and voting behaviour amongst trade union members[1]

	1–10	11–50	51–300	301–1,000	1,000+
Conservative	38	33	32	28	23
Labour	63	67	68	72	77
Total per cent	100	100	100	100	100
Total number	8	31	53	59	140

The concentration of large numbers of trade unionists and Labour voters in the larger plants might lead the Labour Party (and the trade unions as Labour Party affiliates) to pay particular attention to these larger firms in their vote-getting activities. Being more frequently exposed to Labour Party workers and propaganda, the men in these larger plants would consequently vote Labour more frequently than in the smaller plants. As plausible as this argument may sound, the data do not bear it out.[2] For if the Labour Party made special efforts in the larger plants, and if these efforts were at least partially successful, then it should be found that the Labour voters in the larger plants are more politically active and more partisan than the Labour voters in the smaller plants. Yet the former are no more politically active as measured by the frequency with which they discuss politics with their friends and their scores on the political awareness scale, nor do they manifest stronger partisan beliefs about the Conservative Party.[3]

Having previously noted the amicable social relations existing between Conservative and Labour supporters, it is unlikely that any direct pressures are exerted upon the Tories to vote Labour in the larger plants where they are in a distinct minority. But it may be that

[1] The weighting index, according to which the number of Labour respondents is multiplied by five is used here.

[2] Rather, it may be that Labour Party propaganda is concentrated upon the marginal constituencies—and these do not usually contain large industrial establishments.

[3] This finding also applies when union membership is controlled for. It might also be noted that these data rule out a hypothesis suggested by Juan Linz to account for the increase in Left voting with increasing plant size which he found in his West German data. According to Linz, 'There is evidence that the larger plants offer greater opportunities for social contacts among workers, a factor that in itself contributes to raising the level of political information, interest, understanding and awareness of class interests.' Op. cit., p. 400.

in the larger plants, the Conservatives' minority position is more apparent to *themselves*, compared to the smaller firms where it becomes increasingly difficult to talk about a minority given the roughly equal proportions of Tory and Labour voters. And wishing not to appear 'different' to themselves or others, and as a minority, finding it difficult to justify their party allegiances to themselves and others, some of the Conservative inclined workers in the larger firms gradually move to the Left. Although suggested in a highly tentative manner, this interpretation does accord with the one offered at the end of the preceding chapter; namely, that the Tories' lower rate of group membership is partly due to their *self*-identification as politically 'different', and not wanting to expose their differences, they are less inclined to take out associational membership.

CHAPTER 9

A Theory of Stable Democracy

ONE OF the 'great'—if not the most crucial problem—confronting contemporary political science is the construction of a theory of stable and effective democracy. The last few years have witnessed a burgeoning literature on this subject, as both political scientists and sociologists have attempted to set out the conditions that are conducive for the stable operation of democratic systems. Yet notwithstanding the spate of hypotheses that have been suggested to account for the operational contours of democratic systems, few attempts have been made to offer a coherent theory, integrating a number of hypotheses and specifying those conditions that are necessary for the maintenance of stable democracy. The goal of this chapter is to outline just such a theory, attempting to demonstrate how a single variable might serve as a sufficient explanation for stable democracy, in part, because this single variable is intimately connected with a number of others that have been thought necessary for stable democracy.

The explanatory variable in this theory is the same as the study's primary focus: attitudes towards political authority. The final justification for the selection of this independent variable will, of course, rest with the validity of the theory itself. Yet it may be noted that the findings of this study implicitly point to the importance of the non-elite's attitudes towards political authority as an explanation for the operation of democratic systems. It was suggested that the characteristic dimension of the English working-class political culture is the diffusion of acquiescent attitudes towards authority. At the same time, English democracy must be accorded the highest ranking in terms of its stability, authenticity and decisional efficiency. At a minimum, the confluence of these two phenomenon suggests that there may be a crucial inter-connection between them. Furthermore, our examination of another political system points to the same conclusion. In the case of France, we find a confluence of a political culture characterized by attitudes towards political authority that are almost the exact opposite to those found within the English working class, and a democratic system that must be ranked at the other end of the scale from the British in terms of its operating features. In this concluding chapter an attempt will be made to develop a theoretical statement about the operation of democratic systems, and then to apply this theory to England and France with their widely differing measures of success as stable democratic systems and their sharply diverging orientations towards political authority.

Before proceeding with the delineation of this theory it would be well to specify exactly what it is that we are trying to explain. What is meant by the term stable democracy? In the first place, following Schumpeter's definition, a democratic system is one in which there is a regular competition for control of the government, with the electorate choosing from among the competitors.[1] These competitors may be individuals, different elite groupings, or political parties. After having identified democratic systems in terms of this definition, they may then be differentiated according to the extent that they are stable, effective and authentic. In short, we are trying to account for the widely differing operational characteristics found among democratic systems.[2]

Stability refers to viability—to the persistence of constitutions and governments over time. Is a democratic system able to operate according to the procedural rules set out in the constitution, or does it become necessary to substitute another constitution during times of crisis? Is the life of governments calculated in terms of months or years? Effectiveness is taken to mean the ability of the government to take decisions as they are called for by pressing conditions and events.

[1] By giving great emphasis to the need for leadership in his analysis, Giovanni Sartori arrives at an almost identical definition, which lends the choice of the above definition something less of an arbitrary flavour. See *Democratic Theory*: 1961, esp. p. 126.

[2] See Eckstein, *A Theory of Stable Democracy*, op. cit., pp. 1–3. These characteristics of stable democracy are spelled out in greater detail and given operational meaning in Harry Eckstein, ' "Measuring" the Effectiveness of Democracies', 1962, mimeo. This paper is a particularly important contribution because without operational indicators of stable and unstable democracies it would be impossible to test out any theory of stable democracy. Moreover, Eckstein's indicators are of a refined enough variety to allow the employment of the method of concomitant variation. Since democracies are neither completely stable nor unstable, it is necessary to be able to measure the *extent* to which they are stable or unstable; a theory must be able to account for both those systems found at the two extremes of the stability-instability spectrum and those that occupy the centre positions on the spectrum.

An effective government is able to govern, taking decisive decisions when these are thought to be called for; an ineffective government is hampered as a decision-making organization by structural, constitutional or cultural impediments. Authenticity (or the *degree* to which the system is democratic) refers both to the translation of electoral outcomes into the party make-up of governments, changes of opinion among the voters being reflected in a restructuring of the government's political complexion, and the exercise of decision-making responsibilities by those institutions that are constitutionally accountable—decisions being made by the executive and the legislature rather than by the civil service, the army or particularly powerful interest groups. Thus when we speak of stable democracy it is not just the persistence of constitutions and governments that is being referred to. Rather, it is a shorthand term for democratic systems that are stable, effective and authentic; all three factors must be considered when 'measuring' their success or failure.[1]

I. THE DUALISTIC ORIENTATION TOWARDS
POLITICAL AUTHORITY

The crucial characteristic of government is its possession of authority, which has been defined by Weber and by most social scientists since him, as the ability to engender an extensive level of voluntary submission.[2] As the repository for this authority, democratic governments are charged with two responsibilities: to govern and to represent the citizens. As a government, it must be able to lead; as a democratic government, it must respond to the wishes of the electorate. All governments need a sufficiently wide scope of authority if they are to govern in an independent fashion when conditions and events demand it. Governments must maintain a broad enough plain of authority in order to be able to make decisions without first having to consider

[1] As a working hypothesis it might be worthwhile exploring the extent to which these three variables are interdependent. With the exception of the French Third Republic, whose persistence over time was not matched by its authenticity and decisional effectiveness, it might turn out that democracies will have similar scores on all three dimensions. For the argument that representativeness increases the likelihood of both effectiveness and stability, see Eric A. Nordlinger, 'Representation and Democratic Stability', in J. Roland Pennock, ed., *Political Representation*: 1967.

[2] Max Weber, *The Theory of Social and Economic Organization*: 1947, p. 324. Cf. Blau, op. cit.

public opinion polls, and even to take actions that are distinctly un-popular among the voters. Without this leeway there is a high proba-bility that the government's effectiveness will be impaired, in turn leading to governmental instability. At the same time, a democratic government must be attuned to public opinion, remaining responsive to the wishes of the non-elite. Otherwise the democratic system would be no more than a façade. Even though a democratic government may have some difficulty in concurrently leading and mirroring public opinion, it must nevertheless incorporate these frequently incom-patible activities into its behavioural equation. If the two are not balanced, there will either be governmental ineffectiveness and insta-bility, or inauthentic democracy in which the political elite is able to disregard the non-elite's demands.[1]

The problem is now posed somewhat more clearly. Instead of asking under what conditions democratic governments are stable, we can start by logically inferring the conditions under which these two imperative activities of democratic systems are fulfilled. The position taken here is that these conditions are to be found primarily within the non-elite rather than the political elite; that when the non-elite acts in a certain manner, the political elite will respond in such a fashion so as to produce a stable democratic system—at least with respect to the developed 'western' democracies. Specifically, stable democracy is thought to require a non-elite political culture characterized by a dualistic orientation towards political authority. The political culture must contain a mixture of different sets of attitudes towards political authority: an acquiescent set accepting political authority, recognizing that it is the function of government to govern, and thereby leading to the acceptance of independent governmental authority; and secondly, a set of directive attitudes towards political authority based upon the normative belief that it is the function of higher authorities to be attuned to the self-interested claims and views of reality put forward

---

[1] Eckstein has placed the appropriate label of 'balanced disparities' upon these two necessary activities of democratic governments. See *A Theory of Stable Democracy*, op. cit., p. 29. A similar point is made in Bernard Berelson, *et al.*, *Voting*: 1954, Chapter XIV. The point that contradictory demands are placed upon a democratic government—the balance between 'power and re-sponsiveness' as Almond and Verba call it—also serves as the starting point of these two writers' theory of stable democracy. Op. cit., pp. 476–479. By impli-cation, Aristotle makes a closely related argument in Books IV, V and VI of *The Politics*.

by the non-elite, thereby setting up powerful incentives and penalties for keeping the political elite responsive to the electorate.[1]

It is also necessary to specify how these acquiescent and directive attitudes are to be patterned within the non-elite. What form is a mixture of the two to take? Ideally, the conditions for stable democracy would be maximized if the vast majority of individuals maintained a dualistic orientation towards political authority, i.e. that both directive and acquiescent attitudes be found *within* a majority of individuals. This is not to argue that these individuals must maintain a static position on the centre of the authority spectrum, nor that it is even desirable that they do so. We are speaking of attitudes as predispositions towards a certain type of behaviour, not as automatic response sets in which the nature of the behavioural stimuli does not influence the particular behaviour. Given the kaleidoscope of political stimuli to which the non-elite react, it would be implausible to expect a particular response to reoccur continually within the same individuals. Rather, it is expected and desired, that their political responses fluctuate around the centre position on the authority spectrum. For if the 'governors' are to be legitimately allowed to increase their sphere of authority in order to meet the demands of critical events and to disregard the views of the non-elite when these are thought to be inappropriate, while being kept responsive during less critical times, it is necessary that non-elite individuals adapt their responses to the particular demands of the situation. To posit the existence of a mixture of the two sets of attitudes within a large majority of individuals is to say that the non-elite political culture (at least in this respect) is strikingly uniform—a condition which is unlikely to be found in more than a handful of countries. For this first condition postulates a common orientation towards political authority despite possible social, economic, cultural and geographic divisions.

There is, however, a second pattern according to which the two sets of attitudes can be mixed so that they support stable democratic systems. Whereas the first condition postulated a mixture of acquiescent and directive attitudes within individuals, this second condition requires a mixture within certain elements of society. Although given individuals primarily subscribe to one or the other of these two attitudes, they must be found on both (or all) sides of the main cleavage(s)

---

[1] See p. 227 below for a specification of the objects and relationships constituting 'political authority'.

around which political competition takes place. There must be a mixture of these two attitudes within the primary political conflict groups. Thus in a society whose main line of political cleavage runs between the working class and the middle class, both classes have to contain some individuals who are primarily acquiescent and some who are primarily directive in their predispositions towards political authority. The relevance of this condition for a theory of stable democracy will perhaps become more evident if the point is stated in a negative fashion. It is necessary that there should not be a congruence between a society's fundamental lines of political conflict and the two opposing attitudes, for such a balance could easily entail a dysfunctional segmentalization in which opposing attitudes towards governmental authority, and thus conflicting procedural norms, are superimposed upon substantive, ideological and cultural divisions. Not only would political conflicts then be particularly difficult to settle without agreement upon conflict-resolving procedures, they would possibly escalate until even the constitutional framework was called into question.

At the present stage of the theory's development we are not prepared to inquire into the conditions that lead to the formation of the dualistic orientation or into the frequency with which it may appear in different societies. Yet this second form that the dualistic orientation may take raises the question of the likelihood that a political grouping based upon substantive (i.e. policy) or ideological divisions will contain both acquiescent and directive attitudes. Perhaps the pattern is empirically non-existent. It is undoubtedly true that the possibilities for finding both types of attitudes within the same political groupings are decidedly limited. Even particular policy positions sometimes imply a fixed attitude towards political authority, and where the divergence between attitudes towards authority and substantive issues become too great, the resulting psychological strain would probably force a choice between the two. On the other hand, there is reason to think that differing attitudes towards authority might be found on both (or all) sides of a society's major political divide; that procedural style does not always dictate the holding of a corresponding set of substantive policy preferences, and vice versa. Since procedural and substantive predispositions refer to different types of political objects and relationships, when the two diverge, psychological strain or problems of cognitive dissonance may not be involved.

Although there is a good deal of controversy about the inter-relationships amongst personality type, social class and political attitudes, there is a school of thought whose conclusions suggest that it is possible to find opposing attitudes towards political authority within the same political conflict groupings. According to Alex Inkeles, 'The formal or explicit "content" of one's political orientations—left or right, conservative or radical, pro- or anti-labour—may be determined mainly by more "extrinsic" characteristics such as education and social class; but the form or style of political expression—favouring force or persuasion, compromise or arbitrary dictation, being tolerant or narrowly prejudiced, flexible in policy or rigidly dogmatic—is apparently determined by personality. At least this seems clear with respect to the political extremes.'[1] Applying this argument to the present discussion, if education and social class shape one's substantive preferences and personality influences one's political style, and assuming that differing personality types are found within the various class and educational strata, it would appear that individuals with opposing attitudes towards authority may be found on the same side of a society's main substantive or ideological cleavages. At present, this is no more than a highly tentative hypothesis which might help to account for this second pattern of the dualistic orientation where (and if) it were found to exist.

II. ATTITUDES TOWARDS POLITICAL AUTHORITY AS THEY ARE RELATED TO PARTICIPATION, CONSENSUS, EMOTIONALISM AND SOCIAL TRUST

To recapitulate, it has been claimed that if a democratic government is to be stable, effective and authentic, it must carry out two frequently conflicting activities: it must both govern and represent the citizens. From this it closely follows that if a government is to incorporate these two disparate activities into its behavioural equation, the non-elite must at once ensure the government's responsiveness and allow it the scope to act in an independent fashion. At the same time, the non-elites' acquiescent and directive attitudes must be patterned in such a way so as not to exacerbate the society's political cleavages.

Instead of further developing the present theory independently of the work of other writers, it would be advantageous to rely upon

[1] 'National Character and Modern Political Systems', in Francis L. K. Hsu, ed., *Psychological Anthropology*: 1961, p. 193. A related point is made by David Riesman, 'Psychological Types and National Character', *American Quarterly*, 1953, p. 33.

the theory of stable democracy set out by Almond and Verba in the concluding chapter of *The Civic Culture*. These two political scientists have set out an analytically attractive and empirically complete theory which must be accorded a high degree of plausibility. However, it is thought that a number of points may be improved upon, and that it is possible to encompass Almond and Verba's four necessary conditions of stable democracy within the present theory relying upon a single explanatory variable. By subsuming these four variables under one encompassing variable—or to put it differently, by indicating how Almond and Verba's four conditions are functionally equivalent to the dualistic orientation—the resulting theory is thought to constitute a theory in the strict sense of the term, being made up of an interlocking set of hypotheses flowing from a central explanatory variable. At least this is the goal of the following pages.

Also relying heavily upon the point made by Eckstein and others that a stable democratic system demands a set of 'balanced disparities' between governmental power and responsiveness, in setting out their first condition of stable democracy Almond and Verba arrive at a conclusion similar to the one stated here; namely, the necessity of 'balanced inconsistencies between (political) activity and passivity'.[1] Their use of the term political activity or participation is very similar to the way in which the directive attitude is employed here, both referring to a predisposition to view government in instrumental terms and to act in such a way so as to influence governmental decisions. But political passivity, or non-participation, is not always the same as the assumption of an acquiescent stance towards governmental authority, necessarily entailing a respect for that authority. Quiescence is not the same as acquiescence. Furthermore, non-participation may be found together with a thorough-going political cynicism, political alientation or a refusal to accord the governmental system legitimacy. And as Kornhauser has noted, mass apathy may be highly unstable, transforming itself into extremist attacks against the political system during crisis periods.[2] Thus notwithstanding the correctness of the

---

[1] Op. cit., p. 484. The most frequently used questions in this exceptional five-nation survey study are designed to elucidate the extent to which non-elite attitudes conform to this balance. The respondents were asked whether or not they could influence their local and national governments, and the likelihood that they would actually make the attempt to do so under stress conditions.

[2] Op. cit., p. 46.

assertion that non-participation is necessary to provide the government a wide sphere of authority within which to exercise its leadership prerogatives, the set of attitudes which are sometimes associated with political passivity may actually be dysfunctional for the system's stability and authenticity. A balance between participation and passivity as postulated by Almond and Verba could, therefore, result in a measure of governmental instability when passivity is the outer coating for an underlying disaffection from the political system which may erupt in a mass movement politics—something which cannot be said of a political passivity founded upon an acquiescent attitude towards political authority.

According to Almond and Verba a balance between participation and passivity is only one of four necessary conditions for stable democracy. 'Not only must involvement and activity be balanced by a measure of their opposites, but the *type* of political involvement and activity must itself be balanced. In particular, there appears to be a need for a balanced affective orientation towards politics . . . Politics must not be so instrumental and pragmatic that participants lose all emotional involvement in it. On the other hand, the level of affective orientation towards politics ought not to become too intense.'[1] If there is only a modicum of 'system affect' the attachments to the political system will not be lasting ones, especially during times of adversity and crisis, while such a purely pragmatic politics without meaningful emotional attachments may also lead to a dysfunctional cynicism. In contrast, there are the dysfunctional consequences following from an overabundance of emotional attachments: it endangers the balance between participation and passivity; it would 'raise the stakes' of politics and lead to the formation of mass movements; such intense attachments to subgroups can lead to fragmentation of the political system; and excessive emotional loyalty towards the elite would lead its members to become less responsive to the non-elites given the latter's unquestioning attachments.[2]

Each of these arguments relating to the necessity for a balance between emotional and affectively neutral attachments is indeed convincing. The question then arises whether or not it is possible to subsume Almond and Verba's second condition for stable democracy under the single variable theory. It would appear that when the

[1] Op. cit., pp. 487–488. (Italics in the original.)
[2] Ibid., p. 488.

dualistic orientation is present, the emotional balance that Almond and Verba call for logically (and presumably empirically) follows from it. Given the presence of this orientation towards political authority, it is difficult to see how there can be either an overabundance of emotional attachments or affective neutrality. Acquiescent attitudes towards governmental authority are explicitly founded upon a respect for and an emotional attachment to the government. Acquiescent attitudes are then psychologically dissonant with a purely instrumental attitude towards the government; for a person who is willing to accept the government's wide-ranging authority is sure to have some affective-attachments to that government. At the same time, directive attitudes towards authority are unlikely to be held in conjunction with overly pervasive, intensive, and unquestioning attachments to the political system and the elite. How is it possible for an individual holding to the normative belief that he ought to be able to direct the manner in which the government's authority is exercised—that the government ought to be even minimally responsive to his demands—simultaneously offer the government and its incumbents his unquestioning loyalty, irrespective of whether or not they are responsive to his interests? It therefore seems warranted to suggest that if the dualistic orientation is present, the balance between emotional and purely instrumental or pragmatic attachments will also be present, for the presence of acquiescent attitudes eliminates the possibility of purely instrumental attitudes while the presence of directive attitudes obviates the possibility of an excessive emotionalism.[1]

Before going on to Almond and Verba's third condition, two further remarks about the present theory ought to be made. It was just argued that an acquiescent set of attitudes towards governmental authority would obviate the possibility of an inordinate affective neutrality. However, if the key variables employed were that of Almond and Verba's participation-passivity balance rather than the dualistic orientation towards political authority, this argument would not be valid. It is perfectly possible for political passivity (as opposed to acquiescence towards authority) to be found in conjunction with an extreme affective neutrality, thereby adding a second reason for thinking that the authority variable is preferable to the participatory variable. It should

---

[1] The proposition cannot, however, be stated in the reverse manner; the dualistic orientation is not necessarily present when the affective neutrality balance is present.

also be noted that the connection between attitudes towards authority and the extensiveness of emotional attachments would not necessarily hold true were there merely a balance (as Almond and Verba conceive of it) rather than a mixture between the two sets of attitudes towards authority. There could then be a segmentalization of the two emotional attitudes, with one section of the population adhering to a submissive orientation towards authority and an extremely affect-laden politics, while the other section of the population subscribed to a directive attitude towards authority and a non-affective (or purely pragmatic) attachment to the regime. In such a situation it is not difficult to imagine the probable deleterious consequences for the political system, thereby suggesting another reason for positing the necessity of a mixture rather than a balance between the directive and submissive attitudes towards authority.

Almond and Verba's third condition for stable democracy is a balance between consensus and cleavage. Cleavage serves as the basis for the political competition which is a defining characteristic of democratic systems. If there were not any cleavage, politics would lack any meaning for the non-elite leading to a disaffection from the system, with the elite consequently becoming unresponsive to the non-elite. Yet, if there were excessive cleavage—if there were little or no concensus —the polity would be pulled asunder by the intensity of political, social and economic conflict; and without a procedural consensus there would not be any conflict-resolving norms to which political differences could be referred and settled. In short, a necessary condition for stable democracy is what Talcott Parsons once called a 'limited polarization' of society.

Notwithstanding the argument's plausibility, half of it is thought to be irrelevant for a theory of stable democracy while the other half can be subsumed under the present theory. It is empirically impossible (at least for this writer) to locate a society with a differentiated political system in which there is an excessive amount of consensus, where there is an absence of meaningful issues which serve as the basis for political competition. Surely Almond and Verba would not want to limit their definition of significant cleavages to those centring about ideologies, the legitimacy of the régime, or a society's fundamental values (e.g. the place of religion). And if this is accepted, it would certainly be a challenge to locate an open society with a differentiated political system in which there are no conflicts over the distribution of wealth or the contours of the social structure, to name only two common dissensual foci. On the other hand, the assertion that there cannot be too much cleavage if the political system is to be stable can easily be subsumed under the present univariable theory. What Almond and Verba fear in this connection is that with the existence of deep cleavages the over-arching consensus necessary for the orderly settling of disputes will not exist, and that even if the conflicts are only of a substantive, as opposed to a procedural type, governmental stability would be adversely affected. However, it is highly improbable that we would be able to locate a political system that is rendered asunder by such deep cleavages when the non-elite's attitudes towards political authority conform to the postulates of the dualistic orientation. If there is a mixture of acquiescent and directive attitudes, this in itself is evidence of a procedural consensus. In particular, acquiescence towards political authority, combining the belief that the government is there to govern and that it is the government's responsibility to settle outstanding conflicts, is as good an indication as any that there is a procedural consensus. Moreover, this particular type of consensus is especially functional for the orderly resolution of conflicts. The belief that it is the government's responsibility to govern will temper even the deepest substantive cleavages and thereby facilitate their resolution.

This last point suggests a further modification of the Almond and Verba statement. Although political scientists are convinced of the need for a wide consensus as a necessary condition for stable democracy, they have not usually specified the nature of this consensus except to say that a procedural consensus is more important than a substantive one. But is it not possible to have a procedural consensus that *reduces* the chances for democratic stability? Surely not every procedural style, no matter how diffused it is throughout the society, strengthens the stability and efficiency of democratic systems. For example, neither an excessive legalism of the German variety nor a tenacious refusal to accord political leaders authority, as is the case in France, contribute to the stability of these two democratic systems. Moreover, consensus as such cannot be employed as an explanatory variable because it does not have an empirical referent—consensus about what? In and of itself consensus is therefore inadequate as an explanatory variable in a theory of stable democracy. The nature of that consensus which is necessary for stable democracy must also be specified. In the present theory, it is found in the dualistic orientation towards political authority.

The fourth variable analysed by Almond and Verba is the need for a diffuse social trustfulness, and this for three reasons. 'Social trust facilitates political co-operation among the citizens . . . and without it democratic politics is impossible.' Secondly, the sense of trust in which the political elite is held by the non-elite is rooted in diffuse attitudes of social trustfulness; if the non-elite is to turn over power to the elite, the former must trust in the basically good intentions of the latter. 'Furthermore, these general social attitudes temper the extent to which emotional commitment to a particular subgroup leads to political fragmentation. This general set of social attitudes, this sense of community over and above political differences, keeps the affective attachments to political groups from challenging the stability of the system.'[1] Each of these three hypotheses relating attitudes of social trust to the stability of democratic systems will be discussed separately, starting with the third one.

Almond and Verba are probably quite correct in asserting that a sense of social co-operation and trust will place a damper upon those centrifugal forces flowing from overly strong emotional attachments to political subgroups, such exclusive attachments not being found in cultures characterized by a strong strain of social trust. However, as was already suggested in another connection, the same effect also follows when acquiescent attitudes towards political authority are present. Acquiescent attitudes not only presuppose a primary emotional attachment to the political system rather than to any of its subgroups, they are also intrinsically connected with the belief that it is the function of government to govern, thereby mitigating any exclusive subgroup attachments which threaten to cripple the political system. The second point, that attitudes of social trust are needed if the non-elite is to allow itself to be governed by the elite makes eminent sense, for a

---

[1] Ibid., p. 490. Almond and Verba suggest a fourth relationship between attitudes of social trust and a democratic system; namely, that these attitudes both reduce the 'availability' of the non-elite for mobilization in mass movements and lead the individual to maintain a certain degree of political independence. However, at this point Almond and Verba are no longer thinking in terms of attitudes of social trust, but of another set of attitudes referring to the independence of social life from politics. This fourth point is, therefore, not part of the argument delineated by Almond and Verba regarding a diffuse social trustfulness, but ought actually to be found under their first condition—the balance between participation and non-participation.

country's political culture is solidly embedded in the broader social culture. In terms of the present theory, this point states that attitudes of social trust are the underpinning for acquiescent attitudes towards political authority, which is to say that the former affect the stability of democratic systems indirectly, their impact being significant in so far as they first shape acquiescent attitudes towards political authority. Thus when the occasion arises for inquiring into the sources and conditions for the formation and maintenance of the dualistic orientation, Almond and Verba's point will take on a great deal of relevance. But since the present theory only attempts to outline the *direct* 'causes' or conditions of stable democracy rather than its indirect 'causes' or pre-conditions, Almond and Verba's hypothesis refers to a different explanatory level than the one at which the theory resides at this stage of its development.

Thirdly, it is suggested that 'social trust facilitates political co-operation among the citizens . . . and without it democratic politics is impossible'. Since they say nothing more about it, it is difficult to know exactly how Almond and Verba view this inter-connection between co-operation among non-elite individuals and the operation of democratic systems. Most probably they mean to suggest that without such co-operation the non-elite's efforts to hold the elite responsive will not be effective. Organization (or co-operation) breeds strength. And attitudes of social trust are in turn necessary if non-elite individuals are to be able to co-operate in attempting to influence the political elite. Almond and Verba are thus perhaps separately setting out a fifth condition of stable democracy, namely, the necessity of an active associational life, which is itself predicated upon a diffuse social trustfulness.

In order to evaluate this hypothesis it is necessary to make the significant but sometimes fuzzy distinction between voluntary associations that meet for social, cultural and civic purposes, and pressure groups which are primarily organized around the goal of seeing their interests translated into legislation or administrative regulations. After this differentiation is made, it is seen that the absence of attitudes of social trust act to inhibit the frequency with which individuals interests translated into legislation or administrative regulations. After this differentiation is made, it is seen that the absence of attitudes of social trust act to inhibit the frequency with which individuals join social and cultural associations (as in Italy), and the degree to which these associational members meaningfully participate (as in France and Weimar Germany), and to that extent it might be reasonable to argue that non-elite individuals are in a somewhat weaker position *vis-à-vis* the political elite. However, the absence of attitudes of social trust do not appear to hinder the formation of pressure groups nor the active pursuance of their interests, as seen in the Italian and French political systems, where the non-elite keeps the elite attuned and responsive to their interests largely through pressure group activities. This would suggest that half of the Almond and Verba argument referring to the presence of social, cultural and civic associations is not necessary for keeping the elite responsive, at least when there are numerous and effective pressure groups around to serve this purpose. The other half of the argument, referring to pressure groups, does not hold up because such organizations can and do flourish despite the absence of attitudes of social trust. Consequently, attitudes of social trust as they 'facilitate co-operation among the citizens' do not have to be included in a theory of stable democracy. All that is necessary in this connection is that there be numerous and active pressure groups, and this condition is already met by the present theory. For when the non-elite is imbued with directive attitudes towards political authority, they will surely form pressure groups in order to press their interests upon the parties and governmental institutions—and this despite the absence of a diffuse social trustfulness, because as in Italy and France, this disability can be overcome when sufficient value is placed upon one's interests and a directive attitude is present.

To summarize at this point, it is thought that the Almond and Verba theory is intimately related to the present one in that the latter single-variable statement is functionally equivalent to the four conditions of stable democracy posited by Almond and Verba. The balance between political participation and passivity is related to the operation of the political system in a similar fashion as is the dualistic orientation. Yet the latter formulation takes into account the dysfunctional possibilities of political disaffection (which are sometimes found in conjunction with political passivity, but not with acquiescence towards political authority), and the possibilities for a conflict between two political traditions (something that is possible when there is a balance, but not when there is a mixture, of acquiescent and directive attitudes). Morover, when the dualistic orientation is present, there is good reason to expect there also to be a balance between emotionalism and affective neutrality. It has also been suggested that the problem of political cleavage (or conflict) is empirically irrelevant for a theory of stable democracy since it is found in all societies with differentiated political systems, while the need for consensus is accounted for by the presence of acquiescent and directive attitudes towards authority. And lastly, it was suggested that attitudes of social trust are not a necessary condition (although they are probably a necessary pre-condition) of stable democracy when both acquiescent and directive attitudes towards authority are present, the latter leading to an active pressure group politics and the former preventing the emergence of overly powerful emotional allegiances to politically divisive subgroups.

The broad outlines of the theory may now be brought together in the form of four broadly stated hypotheses, each of which has previously been set out in a greater detail.

Hypothesis 1. The mixture of acquiescent and directive attitudes towards political authority, either within individuals or within a society's major conflict groups, is a necessary (or sufficient) condition for stable democracy.

Hypothesis 2. The four conditions posited by Almond and Verba are necessary conditions for stable democracy.

Hypothesis 3. The mixture of acquiescent and directive attitudes is functionally equivalent to each of Almond and Verba's four conditions, the former being able to subsume the latter within a theory of stable democracy.

Hypothesis 4. When the mixture of acquiescent and directive attitudes are present then the first three, but not necessarily the fourth condition, set out by Almond and Verba will also be present.[1]

From these four hypotheses it appears that the present theory is a theory in the literal sense because it is made up of an inter-related group of hypotheses centring about a single variable. From hypothesis 3, it follows that whatever validity attaches to the Almond and Verba formulation, and there is good reason for believing that it is eminently valid, also attaches to the present theory because it is able to

---

[1] It should be noted that this hypothesis cannot be reversed, to the effect that the mixture of acquiescent and directive attitudes will be present when Almond and Verba's first three conditions are fulfilled.

encompass the former. To be sure, this last claim by no means asserts that the present theory is a valid one. The claim is a conditional one in two respects; only if the Almond and Verba formulation is valid, and if the two theories are empirically and logically inter-related, does it follow that the theory delineated here is valid. At this point, the most that can be said for the theory is that it is a plausible one given the explanatory power—the ability to subsume a number of seemingly disparate variables—of the dualistic orientation towards political authority. To which may be added the argument regarding the dualistic orientation that was originally deduced from the two sometimes conflicting demands that have to be met if a system is to be a democratically stable one.

III. DEMOCRATIC STABILITY AND INSTABILITY: ENGLAND AND FRANCE

The operationalization and testing of the present theory would demand its own full-scale study. But if we cannot attempt to validate the theory at this time it is still worthwhile applying it to two democratic systems. Such an analysis should provide an illustration of the theory's analytical applicability in accounting for the operation of a stable and an unstable democratic system. In analysing the English and French political systems in terms of the theory, an attempt will be made both to relate the presence and absence of the dualistic orientation to the operation of these two political systems directly, and to illustrate the applicability of the theory's set of secondary hypotheses derived from the Almond and Verba formulation. And if this objective is accomplished successfully —if the theory is substantiated by the English and French cases— then a significant step will have been taken towards the theory's confirmation, thereby increasing the plausibility which attaches to it.

England is an exceptionally stable democracy according to each of the three criteria of stability. In terms of viability, less than half a dozen twentieth-century governments have been forced to go to the country before the expiration of their constitutionally prescribed four-to five-year term of office. In those few instances in which governments were restructured without the calling of a General Election— when, for example, a Lloyd George replaced a Herbert Asquith or a Harold Macmillan supplanted an Anthony Eden—the changes were carried out quickly with imperceptible disruptions to the Government's activities. The constitutional framework has only suffered from two frontal attacks, revolving around the powers of the House of Lords and the position of Ireland, and although they occurred almost simultaneously, even this additional difficulty did not cause any lasting damage to the constitution. For the most part, constitutional changes have occurred in an orderly and piecemeal fashion, without detracting from the extensive legitimacy accorded the constitution. The government's decisional efficiency—its ability to take decisive and independent action when it believes such action to be called for—has not been impaired by a fragmentation of the party system, structural impediments, or constitutional roadblocks. In terms of authenticity, electoral majorities have with but one exception been automatically translated into governmental majorities, while the decisive decision-making power has remained in the hands of cabinet ministers rather than civil servants.[1] It is this exceptional stability of the system that has to be accounted for by the non-elite's orientation towards political authority.

In the previous discussion of the political culture approach, it was stated that attitudes could be differentiated according to the types of political objects and relationships towards which the actors are orienting their behaviour.[2] The cultural dimension which we have conceptualized as attitudes towards political authority can then be broken down and operationalized according to the four types of political objects and relationships which have been employed in this study: the sphere of independent action allowed the government; the acceptance or rejection of the party leaders' definition of the 'correct' position on substantive policy issues; the non-elite's normatively proper influence upon governmental decisions; and the role of the individual as a political activist. By drawing together the relevant strands of Chapters 3, 4 and 5, it will be seen that the English working-class manifests the postulated mixture of acquiescent and directive attitudes towards each of these political objects and relationships.

The scope of independent action allowed the Government is closely bound up with the hypothesized requirement for stable democracy; without such leeway governments would not be able to act quickly or

---

[1] Herbert Spiro has written of the constitution's stability, the absence of violence, and the efficiency and 'resoluteness' of British Governments. Op. cit., pp. 123–125.

[2] See Chapter 2 above.

effectively since it would first be necessary to secure the electorate's consent—and that consent may not be forthcoming despite the Government's firm conviction that a decision must be taken. The workers' attitudes towards the Government's procedural authority were operationally defined by placing them in a hypothetical situation in which a Government staffed by the party to which the respondent is opposed believes one policy to be called for, whereas a majority in the electorate prefers another. It was found that approximately half of the workers interviewed (44 per cent of the Tories and 51 per cent of the Labour voters) would allow an 'opposition' Government the independent authority to act as it sees fit despite the unpopularity of its policy. On the other hand, slightly less than half the workers (49 per cent of the Conservative and 40 per cent of the Labour voters) would disapprove of the Government acting contrary to the wishes of the majority.[1] In this respect there thus appears to be a nearly equal balance between acquiescent and directive attitudes towards independent government action.

When we examine the workers' beliefs regarding the influence of the non-elite upon governmental decisions, it is eminently clear that the workers perceive the political system as hierarchically structured, in which their role is an 'essentially passive' one. Only slightly more than 10 per cent of the workers believe the non-elite to have 'a good deal' of influence upon governmental decisions. The vast majority believe the non-elite either to have 'a little' influence upon governmental decisions or 'none at all'. More significant than the workers' perceptions are their normative reactions to their largely passive role, in which the Government initiates and makes policy while the non-elite is only able to hold them responsible in a tenuous fashion. In order to elicit their representational norms, the workers were asked whether the political system 'ought' to be structured hierarchically. Among those respondents who perceive the non-elite to have 'a little influence' upon government approximately two-thirds (79 per cent of the Conservative and 60 per cent of the Labour voters) replied that the non-elite ought only to have this modicum of political influence. In contrast, about one-third of these workers who believe themselves to have only 'a little influence' upon government are dissatisfied with the situation as they perceive it. Amongst those workers believing

<hr />

[1] See p. 83 above.

themselves to have no influence whatsoever, slightly less than a third are normatively content with their political impotence, with some 60 per cent recording their dissatisfaction.[1] Taking these data together, there appears to be an approximate balance between those workers with directive attitudes towards political authority who are dissatisfied with their modicum of influence upon governmental decisions, believing that they should have a larger role in directing the government, and those workers with acquiescent attitudes towards authority whose representational norms dictate a satisfaction with their minimal political role.

Not only do the workers manifest a dualistic orientation towards the Government's sphere of independent authority and the extent to which the non-elite is to be an integral part of the governmental decision-making process, this orientation is also directed towards the leaders of the political parties. Party leaders have been included here even though they are not always the incumbents of governmental positions of authority. For at a minimum they are potential occupants of executive and legislative positions. As such, it is necessary that they are both independent of and dependent upon the non-elite in their role of party leader, for many of the decisions made in that capacity are implemented in their executive and legislative roles. The workers were asked about their probable reactions to a situation in which their own views on a particular policy matter were in conflict with those of their party leaders. It then turns out that slightly more than half of both the Conservative and Labour supporters replied that they would alter their own positions in conformity with those of their party leaders. The reasons given by this group for their acquiescent predispositions did not always refer to the confidence that they have in the abilities of the party leadership. But leaving aside the different evaluational and normative bases of acquiescence towards political authority—a vast subject that would require a separate study—the relevant point regarding the relationship between the operation of the political system and the non-elite's attitudes is that these workers are apparently willing to forgo their own views when these do not accord with those of their party leaders. They are ready and willing to accept political leadership. In contrast to this group of workers making up somewhat more than half the sample, there are those workers making up one-third of the sample who replied that they would maintain their own

[1] See pp. 98–102 above.

views in the face of their party's position.[1] These workers cannot be said to be taking up a directive stance *vis-à-vis* their party leaders since they are not replying that they would attempt to influence the leaders' positions. All that can be said about them is that they are unwilling to adopt an acquiescent posture.

The fourth dimension of political authority treated here is the conception of the self as a political activist or inactivist, what has sometimes been termed participation or non-participation. Although not conceived as such in other studies, participation and non-participation may be interpreted as one type of attitude towards political authority. Almond and Verba's use of the term political participation is very similar to the way in which the directive attitude is employed here, both referring to a predisposition to view government in instrumental terms and to act in such a way so as to influence governmental decisions. In fact, the question used in the present study to get at potential activism is taken almost directly from *The Civic Culture*. But as was already noted, political passivity, or non-participation, is not always equivalent to the assumption of an acquiescent stance towards governmental authority, necessarily entailing a respect for that authority. For non-participation may be found together with a thoroughgoing political cynicism, political alienation or a refusal to accord the governmental system legitimacy. Yet in the case of the English manual workers, it is possible to interpret non-participatory attitudes as nearly equivalent to acquiescent ones given the minimal extent to which the workers are politically alienated and the widespread (if not complete) acceptance of the régime's legitimacy. When we then examine the data on political participation and non-participation, the former being taken as an indicator of a directive and the latter as an indicator of an acquiescent attitude towards political authority, we find the English working class conforming to another dimension of the dualistic orientation. On the basis of their responses to the question asking them how likely it is that they would make an attempt to influence the Government if it were considering a regulation that they thought was 'very unjust or harmful', the respondents were classified as potential activists or inactivists. It then turns out that over half the workers (61 per cent among the Tories and 56 per cent amongst the Labour voters) are potential activists; they are predisposed towards

[1] See pp. 91–92 above.

participation in the decision-making process under stress conditions, although it is realized that not all of these workers would actually make the effort were such a situation to arise. In comparison, somewhat more than a third of the workers (34 per cent and 43 per cent of the Conservative and Labour voters respectively) replied that they would not bestir themselves in an effort to influence the Government; that they would, in effect, acquiesce in the exercise of authority by the Government even when it is thought that the Government is not acting in their best interests.[1]

Up to this point it has only been shown that directive and acquiescent attitudes are both present in the working-class political culture. But according to the theory they must not only be present or balanced one against the other, they must also be distributed according to a certain pattern. There can either be a mixture of acquiescent and directive attitudes within individuals or within the major groupings around which the political conflict centres. From the preceding data, it is clear that the two sets of attitudes are distributed in such a way as to satisfy the second condition. One of this study's most significant conclusions is that acquiescent attitudes are found almost as frequently amongst the working-class Labour voters as amongst the Tories, and this despite the Labour Party's 'democratic' and egalitarian ideology. Thus at least with respect to the working class, acquiescent and directive attitudes are found on both sides of the country's main line of political cleavage. We have here not a case in which the two attitudes are only balanced within the working class, with the Tories primarily subscribing to an acquiescent set of attitudes and the Labour voters mainly adhering to a directive set, but in which the two attitudes are found mixed together in both political camps.

It can also be shown that the first pattern by which the two sets of attitudes can be mixed is also fulfilled by our working-class respondents; that acquiescent and directive attitudes are found mixed together within individuals. For example, among those Tories who are potential activists and who perceive the non-elite to have little or no influence upon governmental decisions, only 41 per cent are normatively dissatisfied with this situation. That is to say, amongst those workers with directive predispositions on the activist dimension of attitudes towards political authority, only 41 per cent maintain representational

[1] See p. 117 above.

norms that are also of a directive nature, while another 54 per cent of the Tory group manifests a mixture of acquiescent and directive attitudes on these two dimensions. Similarly, amongst those Conservatives whose representational norms are not satisfied (who thereby manifest a directive attitude towards political authority), 33 per cent take up an acquiescent position on another dimension by allowing a Government constituted by the party which they oppose to act contrary to the wishes of the majority. In both instances the data indicate that many individual workers do not adhere solely to either a directive or acquiescent attitude, but that a directive attitude with respect to one dimension of political authority is commonly found together with an acquiescent predisposition on another dimension. Although only two examples have been offered, the statement is true of both Conservative and Labour voters with regard to every set of inter-relations between the four dimensions of attitudes towards political authority that were used in this study.[1]

*

Having shown how the English working class conforms to the requirements of the dualistic orientation, we now run up against a major problem in attempting to apply the theory of democratic stability to England. The theory utilizes the attitudes towards authority of a country's entire non-elite as the explanatory variable, not just the attitudes of the working class. Yet the present study's concentration upon the working class unfortunately leaves it denuded of any data regarding middle-class attitudes towards authority. There is no satisfactory way to get around this difficulty, and in reading the balance of this section this *caveat* ought to be kept in mind.

However, notwithstanding this gap in the study, there is reason to think that the middle class' attitudes towards political authority do not significantly differ from those of the working class. In the first place, no writer has suggested that such a difference exists; that the middle class is more prone to question and limit governmental authority, for

[1] See pp. 117–118 for another instance of a mixture of attitudes towards political authority within individual workers; potential activism is related to attitudes towards the Government's sphere of independent action.

example. If there were such a difference, it is reasonable to assume that at least one or two students of English politics would have recognized it. In fact, those writers who have analysed the English political culture —Bagehot, Beer, Eckstein, and Rose—have all pointed to the procedural concensus found throughout the society; and the consensus that they have in mind is very much the one that is characteristic of the workers' attitudes that have been spelled out in the present study. And in concluding an historical survey of authority and paternalism in Britain, A. P. Thornton wrote that contemporary Britain does 'not distrust the presence of strong central government, since the entire evolution of the country—its laws, its liberties, and its assumptions about both—was dependent on that government's efficiency at any given time. It was still habituated to authority, and still—despite the satire from the flanks of the middle-class—inclined to that deference to it that Bagehot had commented on a century before, although more perceptive as to its nature.'[1] While this historian remains aware of the many class differences—one could easily say 'two cultures'—found throughout British history, for present purposes it is significant that he does not point to a conflict between working- and middle-class attitudes towards governmental authority. Secondly, looking at the political behaviour of working-class and middle-class people there does not appear to be any significant difference in their political style. For example, in comparing working-class and middle-class dominated pressure groups it is difficult to detect any differences in the degree to which they make unacceptable demands upon the Government. Thirdly, given the fact that the great majority of middle-class voters are Conservative supporters, and considering that it is the Tories' hierarchical traditions that form the core of the country's political culture, it is reasonable to presume that these middle-class Conservatives are securely wedded to an acquiescent set of attitudes towards political authority, while Tory notions of constitutionalism and consent would suggest the presence of directive attitudes.

Thus in attempting to suggest that the middle class' attitudes towards authority do not significantly differ from the working class', it can at least be said that no writer has noted such a difference, and that this 'negative' conclusion is supported by a few impressions and inferences. But to repeat, this by no means ought to be taken to imply that the point has been established.

[1] A. P. Thornton, *The Habit of Authority: Paternalism in British History*: 1966, p. 386.

*

Before turning to French attitudes towards political authority, it is first necessary to spell out, at least on a partially impressionistic basis, the political system's operational characteristics—the dependent variables as it were. The French political system's outstanding characteristic is its historical instability. Beginning with the early nineteenth-century period of mass suffrage, we see a constitutional monarchy being overthrown by a revolution, replaced by a republic, which in turn quickly evolved into a dictatorship, and when it too was dismissed by an armed uprising, the interminable squabbles amongst the monarchist factions allowed another republic to come into existence—by default. But for an 'accident' of history, this republic too would have given way to a dictatorship through the bloodless medium of the *coup d'etat*. While the republic tottered on in the interwar period the life-span of its governments was calculated in terms of months rather than years, and with its 'collapse' under the *coup de grâce* of military defeat, a new dictatorship immediately sprang up to take its place, to be succeeded by another republic lasting for twelve years amid constantly recurring cabinet crises, then falling in the wake of an eminently successful revolution, out of which emerged the present republic. Here we have what the sociologists might label the 'institutionalization of instability'—a phrase which summarizes French democracy's lack of both constitutional and governmental viability.

In terms of its decisional effectiveness the system fared slightly better —but only slightly—for the *immobilisme* of the Third and Fourth Republics which produced a decisional paralysis does not allow us to assign it a high score on this measure. The responsibility cannot be simply placed upon the system's structural and constitutional difficulties, themselves very largely the products of French attitudes towards political authority. It might also be warranted to say that in the Fourth Republic the parliamentarians had suffered a loss of nerve, in part, due to the non-elite's tenacious devotion to directive attitudes towards governmental authority. The two crucial decisions that had to be taken during the lifetime of the Fourth Republic revolved around Indo-China and Algeria, but to quote Duverger:

As early as 1951—that is, three years before the armistice in Indo-
China—it was recognized in all political quarters that peace would
have to be made there. Everyone was of the opinion that a treaty
would have to be signed, that we had to get out of this affair . . .
But no politican would dare to say so officially, for this would have
exposed him to attacks from all sides. The political system was not
equipped to make important decisions. This was also true about
Algeria. Ever since 1956, everybody was convinced that there would
have to be negotiations with the FLN, and that the result would be
either independence in co-operation with France or semi-autonomy.
Again and again, one would hear in confidential conversation with
ministers and politicians: 'Of course we must negotiate with the
FLN.' But they did not say so in the National Assembly and they
did not say so to the people, for they knew that in this case they
would have to force a political decision upon the French people
and that they would have to fight.[1]

Nor is it possible to assign the French political system a high score
in terms of its democratic authenticity. The organizational demands
of any national political system already dictate that the legislature
be once removed from the electorate. However, in the French case,
this situation was doubly compounded, parliamentary politicians being
especially far removed from the electoral arena. In the Third and
Fourth Republics the system was unrepresentative to the extent that
governments were formed and re-formed largely irrespective of movements of opinion within the electorate. Major ministerial changes
occurred between elections when the voters obviously took no part.
Moreover, a relatively small party (the Radicals) sitting in the strategic centre position in the Assembly's hemicycle, managed to occupy
the office of Prime Minister far out of proportion to the numbers of
their *piétaille* (backbenchers). And given the high death rate of French
governments combined with an immobilized legislature, is it no
wonder that except in periods of crisis when the government was
finally able to act, effective decision-making power usually resided
with an unaccountable civil service.

Alongside of this particularly unstable democratic system, we find
a clear-cut cultural divergence from the postulated requirements of a

[1] Maurice Duverger, 'The Development of Democracy in France', in Henry
W. Ehrmann, ed., *Democracy in a Changing Society*: 1964, p. 80.

dualistic orientation towards political authority. The *malaise* of French politics has commonly been interpreted as a product of a deep-seated conflict between the 'two Frances'. Whether these two political sub-cultures are viewed as the parties of *mouvement* and of *l'ordre etabli*,[1] the 'administrative and representative traditions',[2] or as the France of the Left and the France of the Right, for our purposes the upshot is the same. There is a fundamental divergence between the two Frances' attitudes towards political authority. Traditional France, favouring order at the expense of liberty, the Catholic Church at the expense of the republics, following and pushing forward the 'caesars' of France in the face of democratically constituted authority, can most succinctly (for our purposes) be subsumed under the phrase 'the France of hierarchical order'. In contrast, there is the France of the Left, with its clarion call for liberty and equality, for decades working towards a levelling state socialism, believing in the camaraderie of the working class, which can most aptly be characterized as 'the France of idealistic egalitarianism'. Here there is a strongly felt directive predis-position—a predisposition that is forcefully underlined in Alain's Radical doctrine in which the non-elite's control over the elite trans-forms a democratic system of representation into a system of control by the electorate.[3] We are a long way from Burke's theory of repre-sentation in which the legislator is the representative of the electors, yet at the same time, he is independent of them, choosing to rely upon his own judgement rather than theirs when the two diverge.

According to this interpretation of the two Frances, the French political culture does not feature a dualistic orientation towards authority. Although both acquiescent and directive attitudes are present, they do not form a mixture as postulated here. Rather, there is a dysfunctional balance between the two. The disparate political attitudes dividing the France of hierarchical order from the France of idealistic egali-tarianism are (or were) of fundamental importance in accounting for the system's constitutional and governmental instability and ineffec-tiveness. The two conflicting conceptions of political authority con-tinually called into question the legitimate form of the state as pre-scribed by the constitution, and their near balance of strength placed

---

[1] François Goguel, *La Politique des partis sous la troisième Republique*: 1946.
[2] Nicholas Wahl, 'The French Political System', in Beer and Ulam, op. cit.
[3] In fact, according to Alain, 'Il n'y a point de bon roi'. *Propos de Politique*: 1934, p. 71.

a heavy burden upon cabinet government. Yet what made the mutual antagonism exceptionally intense and pervasive is the solid congruence of these two conceptions of political authority with their accompanying attitudes towards religion, the family, social equality, and the distribution of the country's economic wealth, resulting in two remarkably resilient cultural edifices supporting the two conflicting attitudes towards political authority. It is just this structural rigidity—this congruence of political and non-political attitudes—that severely militated against the two political sub-cultures becoming inclusive rather than exclusive towards each other. Or to put it differently, this congruence prevented the transformation of the balance between these two conflicting attitudes towards political authority into a mixture either within individuals or competing political groups.

Notwithstanding the extensive validity and explanatory power attaching to this interpretation of the French political system as a conflict between two political sub-cultures, there are three reasons for thinking it inadequate; first, the dichotomous picture is too simplistic,[1] particularly as modernization and industrialization have erased the acute distinctiveness of the two cultures, leaving only vastly depleted political troops as representatives of the traditional France of hierarchical order;[2] secondly, the argument is difficult to apply to the actual workings of the *governmental* system—a system founded on excessively pragmatic bargaining techniques rather than the clash of ideologies and differing conceptions of political authority,[3] and thirdly, with the recent publication of Michel Crozier's *The Bureaucratic Phenomenon*,[4] a more powerful and contemporaneously valid inter-

[1] In fact, in at least one important respect, the argument breaks down completely. According to this interpretation the parties of the Left should be markedly less centralized and disciplined than the parties of the Right given the latter's hierarchical political and social values. Yet just the reverse is true; during the Fourth Republic it was the parties of the Left that managed to effect a greater measure of centralization and internal control. For a detailed and comprehensive analysis of internal party structures, see Duncan MacRae, Jr., *French Politics and Society: An Analysis of the Decline of the Fourth Republic*: forthcoming.

[2] The royalists, bonapartists, the politically militant catholics, the Action Française, and the semi-fascists have almost entirely disappeared, and to the extent that they do exist, their influence is negligible.

[3] See Constantin Melnick and Nathan Leites, *The House Without Windows*: 1958. Cf. MacRae, ibid.

[4] *The Bureaucratic Phenomenon: An Examination of Bureaucracy in Modern Organizations and Its Cultural Setting in France*: 1964, translated by Michel Crozier.

pretation of the French political system is available. This is not to suggest that the argument of the two Frances is invalid; it is most useful as an explanation of French political instability, and it certainly helps to substantiate the theory of stable democracy offered here. But especially with regard to French politics since about 1955, Crozier's interpretation seems to have greater applicability.

At the core of Crozier's interpretation of the French political culture is found the statement that the French have a hardy distaste for entering into authority relations, especially when such relations entail personal interactions with one's superior, what Crozier aptly terms *l'horreur du face à face*. 'Authority is therefore converted, as much as possible, into impersonal rules. The whole structure (of French institutions) is so devised that whatever authority cannot be eliminated is allocated so that it is at a safe distance from the people who are affected.'[1] This pattern of authority stems from two contradictory goals: the extremely high value placed upon personal independence— or in reverse fashion, the abhorrence of personal dependence relations —and the recognized need for a directing authority if any co-operative activity is to succeed.

In order to create for themselves a solid sphere of independence the French insist upon a strict equality between the members of the same strata. Protection is afforded the individuals belonging to a particular strata by the imposition of this equality, preventing interference from higher authorities through a defensive banding together whenever a superior authority attempts to exercise his formal authority. Jesse R. Pitts comes to much the same conclusion when he describes both formal and informal French associations as 'delinquent communities'. These are characterized by 'a conspiracy of silence against superior authority'. They do not deny authority, however. Indeed, they are incapable of taking initiatives except in interpreting the directives of superior authority and accommodating themselves to those interpretations. 'In an effort to create for each member a zone of autonomy, of caprice, of creativity, these peer groups thrive on the unrealism of the authority's directives.'[2] French associational activities thus exhibit a negative or protective solidarity—a solidarity *against* authority. A rabid egalitarianism prevents the emergence of peer-group leader-

---

[1] Op. cit., p. 222.
[2] 'Continuity and Change in Bourgeois France', in Stanley Hoffmann, *et al.*, *In Search of France*: 1963, p. 259.

ship, or even acceptance of the authority of formal superiors, to whom it might be easier to accord this prerogative since peer-group jealousies would not be at stake. In short, because of the French fear of face-to-face authority relations any attempt on the part of superior authority to act according to its formal prerogatives meets with a negative solidarity, while any attempt of a peer-group member to act as an informal leader in order to encourage initiative, is disposed of with the epithet of 'bossism'.

However, under certain extreme conditions even the French recognize the need for authority. An attempt is then made to reconcile their desire for independence and the need for leadership by allowing for a centralized authority, while at the same time insisting upon impersonal, protective relationships, i.e. the isolation of strata in order to prevent interference from above. This reconciliation may be satisfactory for the individual, but it is dysfunctional for the efficient operation of formal and informal systems of action. For what the French are doing is balancing (rather than integrating or mixing) two absolutist conceptions of authority. Central authority is formally invested with an abundance of power, yet the people subject to that authority refuse to give up even a modicum of their independence so that its directives can be carried out. Both superiors and subordinates claim for themselves an absolute right that cannot be shared or compromised.

Such a system of action cannot handle moderate and steady change. It produces a cyclical alternation between periods of unrelenting, inefficient and stubborn routine, and periods of crisis when change finally becomes inevitable. Crozier believes this pattern of action to be 'a distinctly French feature, inasmuch as it relies on the complex model of individual isolation, lack of communications between strata, and avoidance of face-to-face dependence relationships.'[1] Since authority cannot be shared or diffused, while dependence relationships are not easily accepted, impersonal rules and centralization offer the only escape. Consequently, power tends to be pushed further and further upward until, even if the subordinates were to permit interference by their leaders, the leaders could not act effectively because of the distance separating the order from its execution. Thus continuous leadership is impossible.[2] The system cannot adapt to change;

---

[1] Op. cit., pp. 224–225.

[2] This situation finds its reflection in the French language. Up until quite recently there has been no common equivalent for the term 'leader'. The

when change does come it must be in the form of a crisis. Although the people at the top 'are all powerful because they are at the apex of the whole centralized system, they are made so weak by the pattern of resistance of the different isolated strata that they can use their power only in truly exceptional circumstances.'[1]

Given the French pattern of interpersonal and intergroup relations based upon a hardy aversion to authority, the instability of the political system is hardly surprising. Neither parliaments nor the governments which they produce have regularly enjoyed that measure of authority which would allow them sufficient scope to act as leaders rather than solely as representatives of their constituents. In Duverger's words, the French view democracy 'first and foremost as a system in which the citizen is free, in the sense that he has the possibility to resist the pressure of authority—i.e. the state—to the greatest possible extent'. The freedoms that the French are most closely wedded to—the freedom of association, of assembly, and of free speech—are just those freedoms that can be used to *oppose* governmental authority.[2] The upshot is that French governments do not govern; they simply occupy power. Since the legislature and the government are unable to find or impose solutions upon the problems gripping the society, except when the issue has taken on critical proportions, conflicts have had to be resolved outside the governmental system, as in 1958.

The stability, authenticity and decisional efficiency of the democratic system have thus been further damaged through an institutionalized resort to violence, what Crozier calls 'the revolutionary grievance-settling subsystem'. Referring to the Fifth Republic, Stanley Hoffman could write that 'never before has resort to violence been so widespread and treated so casually. The ungodly spectacle of party squabbles and cabinet crises had been eliminated, only to be replaced by an even ungodlier one. If the institutions of yesterday were too close to a shaky ground, those of today are too far removed, and dissent tends to express itself through direct action—strikes, plots, bombs and coups.'[3]

---

closest alternative is the term *élite*. Moreover, as suggested by one of the earliest students of 'national character', 'while leaders implies leading, and therefore movement, *élites* conveys more than an idea of position: it is static'. Salvador de Madariaga, *Englishmen, Frenchmen, Spaniards*: 1929, p. 145.

[1] Crozier, op. cit., p. 225.

[2] Op. cit., pp. 69–70.

[3] 'Paradoxes of the French Political Community', in Hoffmann, *et al.*, op. cit., p. 94.

Nor is this political style confined to a particular time period or to a particular social class. When other avenues have failed to provide complete satisfaction, resort to direct action has been a common French reaction. Since the end of the nineteenth century, workers, farmers, civil servants, shopkeepers, students, and *colons* have all resorted to this style of decision-making; and its acceptance by the French is perhaps best illustrated by the leniency with which the courts treated the perpetrators of terrorism and rebellion under the Fifth Republic.

Hence the instability of the French political system is directly related to the absence of a dualistic orientation towards political authority. The excessive and one-sided adherence to directive attitudes has spelled the ineffectiveness, instability and inauthenticity of French democracy. The placing of excessive representational demands upon the governmental system is largely responsible for its failure to offer leadership and for its inability to resolve the conflicts plaguing the society. In turn, decisional ineffectiveness has produced further governmental and constitutional instability, leaving the field open to those groups that have little compunction about resorting to the politics of the street when the orderly politics of the voting booth leaves them dissatisfied. And finally, instability has led to democratic inauthenticity as the civil service has stepped into the parliamentary breach.

⋆   ⋆   ⋆

It was just argued that Britain is an eminently stable democratic system and that its political culture meets the requirements of a dualistic orientation towards political authority. In contrast, France's political system is best characterized by an almost endemic instability, while its political culture does not feature a mixture of acquiescent and directive attitudes, the latter completely overshadowing the former both extensively and intensively. It is now left to show that the dualistic orientation is directly related not only to the operation of democratic systems, but that it is closely associated with the three other attitudinal variables in England and France which have been thought necessary for stable democracy. A mixture of acquiescent and directive attitudes is thought to be linked with an emotional balance, a procedural consensus and attitudes of social trust.[1]

For a whole host of reasons Almond and Verba pointed out that

---

[1] The dualistic orientation will not be specifically related to the balance between participation and passivity. Given the large overlap between these two

stable democratic government requires 'a balanced affective orientation towards politics'. In the case of the English non-elite, its dualistic orientation towards political authority ensures the presence of this behaviour. Acquiescent attitudes are intimately associated with an emotional commitment to the system's procedural and symbolic elements, while the directive attitudes guarantee the absence of an excessively emotion-laden politics, concomitantly introducing a set of pragmatic attachments to individual political leaders and substantive issues. Eckstein's generalizations about the British political culture emphasize the presence of a balanced affective orientation: 'the British invest with very high effect the procedural aspects of their government and with very low effect its substantive aspects; they behave like ideologists with regard to rules and like pragmatists in regard to policies'.[1] Elsewhere, Eckstein has arrived at a similar statement by a different path. According to him, the British have a 'profound emotional attachment to persons and institutions that are, from a superficial practical standpoint, mere glitter and gloss . . . (and) although they probably have as much need for emotional behaviour as any other people, (they) can act with sober pragmatism in parliamentary politics because their political passions are channelled towards and satisfied by other aspects of the political system: their ceremonial institutions—above all, of course, the monarchy.'[2] Here then is an emotional balance, and a highly functional one at that: affective pre-dispositions are directed towards the systems's symbols of legitimacy and its procedural rules, whereas affectively neutral attitudes are manifested towards substantive issues and political sub-groups, the one ensuring acquiescence towards governmental authority even under adverse conditions, the other allowing for the settlement of conflicts at a low emotional plateau.

Emotional orientations towards politics are particularly difficult to isolate in a survey study. However, at least one aspect of our data directly indicates the presence of an emotional balance amongst the manual workers. The measured affective content of partisan attitudes is seen in the limited extent to which both Tory and Labour voters

---

concepts, the foregoing discussion also serves to characterize English and French patterns of political participation.

[1] *A Theory of Stable Democracy*, op. cit., pp. 30–31.

[2] Harry Eckstein, 'The British Political System', in Beer and Ulam, op. cit., p. 71.

adhere to a set of negative beliefs about the party which they oppose. Negative attitudes towards the 'opposition' party are not transformed into excessively hostile ones based upon strong emotional dislikes. For the data show that negative attitudes towards the 'opposition' party are tempered by a respect for these party leaders and a partial agreement with their policies.[1]

Turning to the French political system, we find a close relationship between an exaggerated directive attitude towards political authority and an emotion-charged politics. Neither the emotional adherence to the demands made upon the political system nor the actions designed to achieve these demands are mitigated by the presence of acquiescent attitudes. Given the non-elite's absolutist conception of authority as something that they alone possess and which cannot be shared, it is only a small further step towards an emotionally uninhibited activism in an attempt to achieve one's political objectives. The resort to an emotion-charged violence and obstructive mass demonstrations is an inheritance from France's nineteenth-century politics, while an affect-laden ideologism and the related rise of mass movements were superimposed upon the easy resort to violence in the twentieth century. Although there is some debate whether the Third Republic 'collapsed' or whether its demise was simply due to military defeat, in either case the proliferation of mass movements in the 1930's made its signal contribution. Two rapidly growing parties on the Left—the Communists and Socialists—were able to mobilize a mass following, while the nationalist and semi-Fascist Right was spewing out a host of mass movements, at the head of which stood the Croix de Feu. And after 1945 the Fourth Republic had to contend with a massive Communist movement and an ugly Poujadism, to be succeeded in time by a successful Gaullist revolution which only narrowly succeeded in averting civil war. Thus by closely embracing a directive attitude towards political authority, the French are led to express their political allegiances and attachments in an emotionally unattenuated style.

Almond and Verba made the point that a balance between consensus and cleavage is another necessary condition of stable democracy. The position taken here is that cleavage is always present so that it need not be included in the theory, and that there will necessarily be a sufficient procedural consensus when the dualistic orientation is

[1] Also see pp. 107–108, 147–148 below, which provide data that obliquely indicate the presence of an emotional balance.

present. Moreover, it is not every type of consensus that is functional for stable democracy, some types having debilitating effects upon the system. What happens when these last two points are applied to England and France? One of the characteristic features of English political culture is the practically unchallenged consensus regarding procedural values. And this consensus revolves around just those attitudes that have been labelled the dualistic orientation towards political authority—a type of consensus that clearly strengthens the democratic system. Then, too, the diffusion of acquiescent attitudes, with their emphasis upon the Government's leadership as opposed to its representational activities, means that those substantive cleavages which do exist will be mitigated by the expectation that it is the Government's responsibility to resolve them quickly and efficiently.

Whichever interpretation of French politics is accepted—the one relying upon the two Frances or Crozier's analysis of the French fear to face-to-face authority relations—the outcome in this respect is the same: neither fulfil the conditions of a functional procedural consensus. In almost all the explanations offered for the ineffectiveness and instability of French democracy, the factor that figures most importantly is the intense procedural and substantive conflict between what was here called the France of hierarchical order and the France of idealistic egalitarianism. The absence of a procedural consensus is most poignantly seen in the strikingly different way in which Marianne, the supposed legitimizing symbol of the Third and Fourth Republics, was treated by the two Frances: for the France of the Left she represented Liberty; the France of the Right depicted her as a whore. There is a fervent devotion on the part of both the Left and the Right to *la patrie*, to France. But what exactly is this nebulous nationalistic entity? And how significant can its unifying appeal be if during a national war with its ensuing foreign occupation the nation found itself divided against itself? Thus the conflict between the two Frances— the balancing rather than the mixing of the two sets of attitudes towards political authority—spelled the absence of a procedural consensus. Largely because of the absence of such a consensus substantive conflicts could not be resolved by the electorate, the parliament, or the government; conflicts escalated in an upward spiral partly because there was no agreement on the procedures for their settlement. Conflicts were therefore resolved either through extreme measures—the toppling of governments, the rewriting of constitutions, or a resort to mass action and violence—or through inauthentic democracy in which decisions were made by an unaccountable civil service or an inordinately powerful parliamentary autocrat.

Thus if the *malaise* of French politics is interpreted as a product of a deep-seated conflict between the two Frances with their differing conceptions of authority it is, in effect, the absence of a procedural consensus that places such an exceptionally heavy burden upon cabinet government. On the other hand, if Crozier's interpretation is accepted, in which he argues (to alter his language) that the French almost vehemently embrace a directive attitude towards political authority, this would entail the presence of a procedural consensus— but as we have already noted, it is a consensus that is primarily responsible for the system's instability. The argument can now be restated in a different fashion in order to emphasize the presence, and at the same time the debilitating effects, of the French procedural consensus as shaped by the desire to be free of almost any type of political authority.

Two attitudinal corollaries of the French fear of entering into authority relations with others are their well-known *incivisme* and an absolutist conception of authority—both of which are found throughout French society. In the non-political sense *incivisme* refers to a mixture of a diffuse social negativism, a refusal to co-operate with others or to accept responsibility, and a fierce clinging to individual independence—a string of attitudes that might fall under the rubric of 'privatization'. Part of the reason for the tenuous and disorderly two-way flow of communication between the governed and the governors can be traced back to this cultural trait to the extent that it prevents the formation of an active and personally meaningful associational life.[1] On a political plane, *incivisme* refers to a singular distrust of politicians and a pervasive suspiciousness of most governmental activities. In the popular Radical doctrine of Alain, democracy becomes nothing more than the control of the governors by the governed— a system of surveillance rather than one of leadership and representation. Since practically every student of French politics has noted the

---

[1] See Nordlinger, op. cit., pp. 145–149, where it is argued that the French join voluntary organizations nearly as frequently as do the English and Germans, but that the quality of their membership in terms of participation leaves much to be desired; and that the extent to which the members participate is as important as the number of people who join voluntary associations in accounting for the rise of mass movements. A similar point is made by Almond and Verba, op. cit., pp. 318–319.

broad diffusion of these attitudes of *incivisme*, we can conclude that a procedural consensus is indeed present, but it is clearly not the type of consensus conducive for stable democracy.

The second attitudinal corollary of the French fear of authority is the maintenance of an absolutist conception of authority—authority becomes something that the individual citizen alone possesses and which cannot be shared with others. The only two groups who do not conform to this generalization are the Communists and the traditional France of hierarchical order. Both are willing to accord authority to political leaders, so long as these leaders are of their own political stripe, and in the case of the traditional Right, there is the additional proviso that the leader exercise his authority in the Caesaristic tradition. But since the Communists have not been able to staff either the presidency or the office of prime minister, and since the France of hierarchical order has been almost reduced to the proportions of a pressure group, there would appear to be a wide-ranging consensus regarding the absolutist conception of authority. All manner of disabling political effects can be traced back to this attitude towards authority: it goes a long way in explaining why French governments have not been accorded that measure of authority sufficient for their survival and effectiveness, at the same time accounting for the temporary resort to an inordinately powerful executive after a long period of governmental instability in which crisis conditions have continued to spiral, finally necessitating their resolution by a powerful leader; this absolutist conception of authority also has a direct bearing upon the easy resort to mass action and violence since the individuals involved are able to legitimate their actions by thinking of themselves as the sole and supreme possessors of political authority; and it helps to account for the coarse style of interest articulation and the weak processes of interest aggregation characterizing the system, as the citizens and their interest groups state their desires not as requests but as demands upon the government—and exaggerated demands at that—which, if they are not completely fulfilled, are considered to be unfulfilled.

The last condition set out by Almond and Verba making for stable democracy is the need for a diffuse social trustfulness. Of the three reasons given to account for the inter-connection between attitudes of social trust and the operation of a democratic political system, two of them were said to be already accounted for when the dualistic orientation is present. The third hypothesis—that if the non-elite is to allow itself to be governed by the elite it must adhere to a social trustfulness—is an important one. It suggests that if the non-elite is to maintain acquiescent attitudes towards political authority these attitudes must be rooted in a diffuse sense of social trust which is transferable to the political sphere; if the non-elite does not believe in the basically good intentions of other non-elite individuals, it is highly unlikely that it will believe in the good intentions of the political elite, and therefore improbable that it will maintain an acquiescent posture. Although the present theory has not yet been developed to the extent that it can offer a systematic account of the historical, social and cultural conditions that are necessary for the development and maintenance of acquiescent attitudes, it can be shown that in the case of England and France, attitudes of social trust are found together with an acquiescent attitude, and vice versa.

In order to get at these attitudes of social trust, Almond and Verba employed the set of five questions constituting a 'faith in people' scale as developed by Morris Rosenberg.[1] In order to place Almond and Verba's British data in a perspective comparable to the type of responses we would *expect* to find in France, it would be useful to utilize the responses provided by their national sample of Italians as an *approximate* substitute for the unavailable French data. When the respondents were asked whether or not 'most people can be trusted', an especially striking difference comes to light; whereas 49 per cent of the British respondents said that 'most people can be trusted', only 7 per cent of the Italians replied in the affirmative. Or to take another question indicating relatively frequent attitudes of social trust amongst the British—one which asks the respondents whether they agree with the statement that 'most people are more inclined to help others than to think of themselves first'—it was found that 28 per cent of the British sample believed others to be altruistic compared to 5 per cent of the Italian sample.[2] Thus if it is accepted that Italian society approximates French society in terms of the frequency with which we find attitudes of social trust,[3] then the Almond and Verba data

[1] 'Misanthropy and Political Ideology', *American Sociological Review*, Vol. XXI, pp. 690–695.
[2] Almond and Verba, op. cit., p. 267.
[3] For a striking picture of the Italian peasants' distrustful attitudes, see Banfield, op. cit. Also see Joseph La Palombara, in Pye and Verba, op. cit., and the studies cited there.

indicate the British to be more strongly attached to such attitudes than are the French.

Turning directly to the French case, what evidence is there to support the statement that the French do not manifest a social trustfulness, and that the absence of such attitudes helps to account for their adherence to strictly directive attitudes towards political authority? We can begin by citing André Siegfried's study of French 'national character' in which he describes them as 'incurably suspicious'.[1] This early study is complemented by Wylie's more recent intensive study of a single village where he found such attitudes of mutual suspiciousness solidly embedded in the villagers' social relations. The families continually give vent to their feelings of resentment towards each other, even resorting to outright lies in their attempts to dishonour the reputations of families with whom they are *brouillé*. Although there is only the most negligible amount of stealing in the village, it is not uncommon for families to accuse each other of such dishonesty.[2] It is also possible to get at the French attitudes of social distrustfulness in an indirect manner. A rough measure of the trustfulness found in inter-personal relations is the frequency with which individuals engage in social (or outgoing) activities. If people are suspicious of their neighbours they are much less likely to socialize with them than if a mutual trust existed between them. In a national survey carried out by *Sondages*, the respondents were asked to list the ways in which they spend their leisure time. Only 12 per cent replied that they participated in any social activities (*jeux de societé*).[3] When this figure is compared to comparable ones gathered by Almond and Verba for the United States (40 per cent) and England (30 per cent)—two societies characterized by attitudes of social trust—it is found to rank quite low.[4] It is not suggested that these differences are due solely to the suspiciousness with which the French regard each other, but it is certainly reasonable to assume that this is one factor which helps account for the relatively low rate of social activity in France outside the family.

It would seem reasonable to assume that the distrust manifested

[1] *France: A Study in Nationality*: 1952, p. 26.
[2] Laurence Wylie, *Village in the Vaucluse*: 1957, pp. 194–197.
[3] *Sondages*, 1954, No. 2, p. 20.
[4] Op. cit., p. 263. The question asked of the American and English respondents read: 'Now aside from your work and your family, what are the activities that interest you most that you spend your free time on?'

in French inter-personal relations is transferred to, or affects, relations between the non-elite and the political elite. For if one's neighbours are seen in a suspicious light, how much more so would we expect politicians to be eyed in this fashion, residing at a marked social and geographic distance from their constituents who are thus encouraged to place highly uncomplimentary interpretations upon their actions. Wylie has noted that the villagers whom he studied are generally distrustful and sceptical of the political news provided by the radio and newspapers; for the citizens of Peyrane are extremely sensitive to attempts by the outside *ils* to control them, whether these be politicians or newspaper editors. Except for the MRP voters, everyone in the village expresses contempt for their political leaders. To the extent that the people respect the authority of their party leaders, this is not due to their being seen as more trustworthy or able than the average citizen, but because they are more powerful than the latter and more violent in their opposition to the government.[1]

Wylie's generalizations about a single village find striking confirmation on a national scale. In 1952 a national sample of Frenchmen was asked: 'Do you think that the present government is made up of a majority of honest men, of a minority of honest men, or of men who are all dishonest?' Only about one-quarter of the respondents thought a majority of the ministers to be honest.[2] It is just this questioning of the motives and good intentions of the political elite that has presumably led to the popular acceptance of Alain's Radical doctrine in which he warns the citizenry to be continually on the alert for signs of autocratic rule, for government is thought to be inherently self-interested and oppressive.[3] In the words of one sociologist, 'Rank or office does not receive implicit recognition—either because of a lack of confidence

[1] Wylie, op. cit., pp. 207, 214, 221.
[2] The poll was carried out by the Institut Français d'Opinion Publique in February 1952. At that time the government of René Pleven had just recently been replaced by one headed by Edgar Faure; both governments were made up of a coalition of Radicals, MRP and Conservatives.
[3] However, it ought to be noted that the distrust in which French politicians are held, even though it has solid roots in the 'incurable suspiciousness' of the French, is also maintained by the actions of the politicians themselves. Contrary to the interpretation of French politics as a pervasive ideological conflict, this is not true of the politicians in their dealings amongst themselves. Parliamentary activity largely revolves around non-ideological squabbles in which pork-barrel legislation, private gain, personal vendettas, and political advantage for the individual deputy and his party take pride of place. See Melnick and Leites, op. cit.

in the values represented by the hierarchy of which it is a party, or even because of a sceptical attitude towards any established hierarchy. In a society in which power is held to corrupt, the possession of power may inspire a variety of feelings, ranging from mere distrust to envy, or fear, it can hardly be conducive to respect.'[1] It is just this sharp separation of power and respect—the inability to transform naked power into political authority—that goes a long way in accounting for the instability of French democracy.

IV. THE APPLICABILITY OF THE THEORY

In the preceding pages a beginning has been made in the development of a theory relating a set of non-elite attitudes to the operation of democratic systems, illustrating its applicability (rather than testing its validity) in the case of a highly stable democratic system and a particularly unstable one. Clearly, much further work needs to be done before the theory can be adequately tested, particularly in the further specification, operationalization and development of attitudinal indices that are comparable across national boundaries. It will be necessary, for example, to specify in exactly what proportions acquiescent and directive attitudes are to be found so that they maximally support stable democracy. Also to be taken into account are the intensities with which these two types of attitudes are held, for it may very well turn out that their intensity is equally as important as their frequency and distribution. These and other tasks presently remain unfulfilled.

However, at this point it is necessary to specify the range within which the theory is thought to be applicable. For it is not a theory pertaining to every type of political system, but only to those that can be classified as democratic. We can lead up to this point by first considering an equally important question, namely, whether the dualistic orientation is to be taken as a necessary or sufficient condition of stable democracy? There are two reasons for viewing the theory as a sufficient statement of the conditions of stable democracy. In the first place, if it is accepted that the authority variable is intimately associated with the four other attitudinal variables that Almond and Verba think necessary for stable democracy, then it would seem

[1] Michalina Clifford-Vaughan, 'Some French Concepts of Elite', *British Journal of Sociology*, December 1960, p. 320.

warranted to view the theory as a *possible* sufficient explanation of stable democracy. For although single variable theories are thought to be highly suspect by social scientists, in this instance the central explanatory variable is closely related to four others. If each of the five factors is thought to be a necessary but not sufficient condition when taken alone, if four of them are intimately related to the fifth it would seem reasonable to view the presence of the fifth variable as a possible sufficient explanation.

There is a second reason, in this case a strategic one, for conceiving of the theory as a sufficient explanation for stable democracy. Given the plausibility attaching to the theory, even if it turns out not to be a sufficient explanation, the authority variable undoubtedly holds an important place in any equation leading to stable democracy. The question then becomes: just *how* important is it? In order to be able to gauge the explanatory power of the authority variable it would be best to state the theory as a sufficient one for explaining the operation of democratic systems. After applying the theory in this fashion, it will be possible to judge just what proportion of cases the single variable is able to account for. If this strategy were not followed, and the authority variable were viewed as one necessary condition amongst others, it would not be possible to gauge the relative explanatory powers of these variables, deciding whether or not the authority variable is a better explanatory variable than the others. In this connection, a second strategic reason can be suggested for using the authority variable as a sufficient condition for stable democracy. If this is done and it is found that the theory does not hold in a handful of countries, the next step in theory construction is already made easier. For it may be that this small group of 'deviant' cases all have a particular characteristic in common, which, if taken into account by modifying the present theory, or if another variable is added to the present one, the resulting theory could then account for the operation of all democratic systems.

Having suggested two reasons for applying the present theory as a sufficient one for explaining democratic stability and instability—the first reason being based on the assumption that the theory might be successfully applied in these terms, the second presuming that it will only be partly successful—we run up against a limitation of major proportions if the theory is to be interpreted in this manner. The present theory was developed in the course of an analysis of the French political system, and later refined in the present analysis of English politics. Thus the theory has been developed only with respect to the politically developed countries. It would therefore not be at all surprising to find that the authority variable alone is unable to account for democratic stability and instability in the politically under-developed states—states that have not yet achieved the *pre*-conditions of democratic systems such as structures of political competition and channels of communication between the elite and the non-elite. Or to make the point differently, the theory is only thought to be applicable to systems which can already be characterized as democratic, and it will then presumably be able to account for the operation of those democratic systems: the extent to which they are stable, decisionally effective and democratically authentic.

Yet if the theory is a good one for explaining the operation of democratic systems once they have been established, it ought also to have some relevance to those systems that may be moving towards democracy. There ought, in other words, to be some overlap between a theory of stable democracy and a theory of democratic political development. And given our limited knowledge of the political systems of Asia, Latin America, Africa and the Middle East, it might be useful at least to make the attempt to transfer some hypotheses generated through a study of European political systems to the former. Thus it may be that after suitable adaptations have been made the present theory will have something to contribute to a theory of democratic political development. It is highly improbable that such a theory can be constructed which relies upon a single variable, for it is necessary to take into account such non-political pre-conditions as literacy rates and communications networks over and above those conditions that are necessary for the development of viable governmental institutions and structures of political competition. Regarding the latter two, however, the concept of the dualistic orientation might very well find some relevance.

Interview Schedule
FIRST WAVE

1. First, I would like to ask you a few questions about your education. Can you tell me how old you were when you left school?

2. What were the teachers like? How strict were they—*very* strict, *moderately* strict, or *lenient*?

3. (a) If you felt that you had been treated unfairly in some way, or disagreed with something the teacher said, did you feel *free* to talk to the teacher about it; did you feel a bit *uneasy* about talking to the teacher; or was it *better not to* talk to the teacher?

   (b) Would speaking to the teacher have made any difference? A lot, some, or none?

   (c) Do you remember ever doing this—do you remember doing it often, occasionally, or never?

4. Did your teachers treat everyone fairly or were some treated better than others?

5. Let me ask you two somewhat different types of questions. Some people say that most people can be trusted. Others say that you can't be too careful in your dealings with people. How do you feel about it?

6. Would you say that most people are more inclined to help others, or more inclined to look out for themselves?

7. Now I would like to ask you some questions about your party

preferences. If there were a General Election tomorrow, which party would you vote for?

8. (a) Which party did you vote for in the last election in 1959?

(b) Which party do you think will generally be the best one for governing the country—Conservative or Labour?

9. (a) When people talk about politics, some say that political parties try to get laws passed just to get votes, while others say that political parties have the best interests of the country at heart. Do you think that a Labour Government usually has laws passed just to get votes, or for the good of the country?

(b) Do you think that a Conservative Government usually has laws passed in order to get votes, or for the good of the country?

10. (a) You have stated that you tend to support the ....
(INSERT ANSWER TO Q. 7) Party. Now suppose that on the issue of the size of old-age pensions, for example, you favoured a position contrary to the one later adopted by the ....Party. In such a case, would you then still be in favour of your own position or would you take up the .... Party's position?

(b) Why do you say this?

11. (a) As you know, under the present system of government, the Queen has little to do with the actual running of the country. Government affairs are conducted by the Prime Minister, the Cabinet and Parliament. Some people say that there is really no need for the Monarchy. What do you think? Is the Monarchy needed or not?

IF RESPONDENT SAYS MONARCHY IS NEEDED, ASK:
(b) (SHOW LIST I) Here is a list of reasons which people have given as to why the Monarchy is needed. Which of these do you think is the most important?

(c) Which reason is next in importance?

A nation needs someone to symbolize it to foreign countries

People get real pleasure out of following the activities of the Queen

A nation, like a family, needs a respected figure at its head

The Queen is needed to appoint the Prime Minister and to open Parliament

A nation needs someone at its head who stands above political conflict

12. (a) In the last few years there has been some talk about the usefulness of the House of Lords. Do you think that the House of Lords serves any useful purposes in the life of the country?

IF 'YES' (b) What are these useful purposes?

13. (a) Do you think that people like yourself have any say in how the country is run? Do people like you have a good deal of say, a little, or none at all?

(b) Do you think that this is the way things ought to be?

14. Thinking of the important national and international issues facing the country—how well do you think you understand these issues, very well, moderately well, or not at all?

15. (a) Suppose there were some question that you had to take to a government office—for example, a tax question or a housing regulation. Do you think you would be given equal treatment— I mean, would you be treated as well as anyone else?

(b) If you explained your point of view to the officials, what effect do you think it would have? Would they give your point of view serious consideration, would they pay only a little attention, or would they ignore what you had to say?

16. (a) One sometimes hears that some people or groups have so much influence on the way government is run that the interests of the majority are ignored. Do you agree or disagree that there are such groups?

IF RESPONDENT AGREES, ASK:
(b) Which people or groups have such influence?

17. (a) Now I would like to ask you some questions about your job. Are you at present employed, or self-employed?

(b) What did (do) you do for a living?

(c) Could you tell me how big the firm is (was) that you work(ed) for? I mean, how many people are employed at the place where you work?

IF 'SELF-EMPLOYED', SKIP TO QUESTION 25.

18. Do you ever come into contact with the head or owner of the firm? I mean, do you ever speak with him?

19. I would like to find out how decisions are made on your job. When decisions are made affecting your own work, do those in charge ever consult you about them? Do they *usually* consult you, do they *sometimes* consult you, or are you *never* consulted?

20. (a) If a decision were made affecting your own work that you disagreed with strongly, what would you do—would you feel *free* to complain, would you feel *uneasy* about complaining, or would it be better to accept these decisions and *not* complain?

(b) If you actually did complain, would it do any good?

(c) Have you ever actually complained about such a decision? Have you done it *often*, *a few times*, or *never*?

21. What is the authority of your immediate supervisor like? Would you consider him to be *very* strict, *moderately* strict, or *somewhat easygoing*?

22. The way things are, do you think that those who run the place where you work take your interests and needs into account when

they make decisions affecting you, or do they ignore your interests?

23. Think of the man who supervises your work. Would you be willing to take over his job if it were offered to you?

24. (a) Is there a trade union in your firm?

IF 'YES'
   (b) Are you a member?

IF A MEMBER, ASK:
   (c) Would you say you are *active* in union affairs, *occasionally active*, or *inactive*?

25. Thinking about the economic situation of your family in general—the money you earn, the chances for advancement, etc.—do you think it is satisfactory or not?

26. (a) Now I would like to ask you a few more questions about public affairs and politics. Could you tell me what you particularly like and dislike about the Conservative Party? First, what are the things you *like* about the Conservatives?

(b) What do you *dislike* about the Conservatives?

(c) Now could you tell me what you particularly like and dislike about the Labour Party? First, what are the things you *like* about the Labour Party?

(d) What do you *dislike* about the Labour Party?

27. (a) Let us say that a certain issue arose, like raising taxes, on which a Labour Government had one opinion and the majority of the people had another opinion. The Labour Government thought that it was doing the best thing for the country, even though most people did not think so. If this were to happen, do you feel that the Labour Government should go ahead with its policies?

(b) Why do you say this?

9

(c) And how do you feel were a similar situation to arise under a Conservative Government? Should the Conservative Government go ahead with its policies which it believes to be for the good of the country even though the majority of the people do not agree with them?

(d) Why do you say this?

28. Most of the people who support a political party do so mainly for one of two reasons: either because they believe in the party's policies or because they have confidence in the abilities of the party leaders. Could you tell me which of these two reasons is the *more* important one for you in your decision to support the .... (INSERT) Party, its policies or its leaders?

29. (a) Do you feel that a Conservative Government does more to better the lot of workers than it does for other people?

(b) Do you feel that a Labour Government does more to better the lot of the workers than it does for other people?

30. (a) In the next set of questions, I shall be asking you to choose between two candidates. In doing so, completely forget about the parties of the candidates—their party connections should not influence your choice at all. Suppose there was an election which would decide which of two candidates would become the next Prime Minister. They are both equally good men, making it very difficult to choose between them either on the basis of experience or ability. Both of them seem to be excellent candidates. Yet the father of one of them was a member of the House of Lords, while the other's father was a file-clerk in one of the ministries. Do you think that the peer's son or the clerk's son would make a better Prime Minister?

(b) Why do you say this?

(c) Suppose now that there are two other men, one of them went to an excellent grammar school while the other went to Eton. Which of the two men would make a better Prime Minister, the man who went to the very good grammar school or the man who went to Eton?

(d) Why do you say this?

(e) Now let us take two more men and suppose that one was an officer in the Guards while the other entered the army as a private in one of the regular regiments and was promoted to officer rank. Which of these two men do you think would make a better Prime Minister, the Guards officer or the man who was promoted to officer rank in one of the regular regiments?

(f) Why do you say this?

31. We're also interested in how well known the national leaders of the various parties are in this country.

(a) Could you name three leaders of the Conservative Party?

(b) Could you name three leaders of the Labour Party?

(c) And could you name a leader of the Liberal Party?

32. (a) Suppose a regulation was being considered either by Parliament or the local council which you considered very unjust or harmful, what do you think you could do about it?

(b) If you made such an effort to change this regulation, how likely is it that you would succeed?

(c) If such a case arose, how likely is it that you would actually do something about it?

(d) Have you ever actually tried to influence a decision of Parliament or the local council? Have you made the attempt a few times, once, or never?

33. When a new Prime Minister comes into office, one of the first things he must do is appoint people to cabinet positions and

ministries. Could you tell me what some of these cabinet positions are?

34. Considering the policies of the Labour and Conservative Parties, would you say that there is *a good deal* of difference between their policies, *some* difference, or *very little* difference?

35. Speaking generally, do you think that most of the people at the top in this country deserve to be there?

36. Suppose a son or daughter of yours was getting married. How would you feel if he or she married a supporter of the .... (INSERT OPPOSITION PARTY) Party? Would you be *pleased*, would you be *displeased*, or would it *make no difference*?

37. (a) Are you a member of any organized group—social groups, sports clubs, religious organizations or any other type of organized group *besides* trade unions?

IF 'YES' (b) How many of such groups do you belong to?

38. How long have you lived in this neighbourhood?

39. (a) Do you have *many* friends in this neighbourhood and at your job, *some* friends, *one* friend, or *none* at all?

(b) (UNLESS RESPONDENT HAS NO FRIENDS AT ALL, ASK) Do you discuss politics with your friends *often*, *sometimes* or *hardly at all*?

(c) (UNLESS RESPONDENT HAS NO FRIENDS AT ALL, ASK) Would you say that *all* of your friends support the same political party as you do, *most of them* do, *some of them* do, or that *none of them* prefer the same political party as you do?

40. (a) Are there any groups of people in this neighbourhood or at the job that you would not become friendly with?

IF 'YES' (b) What groups of people are they that you would not become friendly with?

(c) How do you feel about people of the same social class as yourself who support the .... (INSERT OPPOSITION PARTY) Party? Would you become friendly with these people?

(d) Why do you say this?

41. All of us have ideas about what people should be like. Here is a list of characteristics you might find in people. (LIST 2) Could you select the quality you admire most? Which one would be next?

LIST 2

Does his job well
Ambitious, wants to get ahead
Generous, considerate of others
Keeps himself to himself
Respectful, doesn't overstep his place

42. Let us say that you have a son at a grammar school. Would you prefer that he became friendly with the son of a cabinet maker or the son of a bank clerk?

43. (a) If you had your life to live over again, would you have tried to stay on in school longer than you actually did?

IF 'YES' (b) Why do you say this?

44. Would you agree or disagree with the idea that if you don't watch out for yourself, people will take advantage of you?

45. Would you agree or disagree with the statement that no one is going to care much what happens to you, when you get right down to it?

46. (a) What is your religion?

(b) Do you consider yourself a religious person?

47. People usually agree that there are such things called social classes. Now if a friend of yours from Australia were to ask you to describe the different social classes in this country, how would you do it? You would want to tell him how *many* social classes there are, and what *kind of people* are in each class.

48. Some people say that various social classes want different things and therefore come into conflict with each other. Do you think that the class conflict in England is *very* important, *fairly* important, or *not* important?

49. Both the Labour and Conservative Parties have adopted a number of policies which are intended to *reduce* class differences. Here is a list (SHOW LIST 3) of possible reactions to this objective of the two parties. Which comes closest to how you feel about reducing class differences?

LIST 3

VERY MUCH IN FAVOUR
GENERALLY AGREE
GENERALLY DISAGREE
VERY MUCH AGAINST

50. Here is one type of list of various social classes found in this country (SHOW LIST 4). People are sometimes placed in these classes. Which one would you say you belonged to?

LIST 4

LABOURING WORKING CLASS
SKILLED WORKING CLASS
LOWER MIDDLE CLASS
MIDDLE CLASS
UPPER MIDDLE CLASS

51. Some people feel that they have a lot in common with other people in their own social class, but others don't feel this so much.

How about you? Would you say that you feel pretty close to people of your own class, or that you don't feel closer to them than you do towards people in other classes?

52. Some people say that if working-class people want to get on, they have got to stick together and stick up for each other. Other people say that each person ought to try and get on on his own. How do you feel about this—should working-class people stick together in order to get ahead, or should they try to get ahead on their own as individuals?

53. Could you tell me whether you agree or disagree with the statement that human nature is fundamentally co-operative?

54. (a) I would like to ask you some questions about the way that decisions were made in your family when you were a youngster, let us say at the time you were thirteen years old. Here is a list of different ways that decisions can be made (SHOW LIST 5). In general, which of these ways best describes the way decisions were made in your family?

LIST 5

By and large, *father* made the decision
By and large, *mother* made the decision
Both parents acted *together*
Both parents acted *individually*

(b) What about decisions on the punishment of children for misbehaving? How did your parents make those decisions? (SHOW LIST 5 AGAIN)

(c) Are you now married, or have you ever been married?

IF 'YES', ASK:

(d) Here is a list of the different ways a husband and wife can make decisions. (SHOW LIST 6) In general, which of these ways best describes the way decisions are (were) made in your own family?

LIST 6

By and large, *husband* makes the decisions
By and large, *wife* makes the decisions
Both act *together*
Each acts *individually*

55. (a) How did your father generally treat you when you were about thirteen years old? Was he *very* strict, *fairly* strict, or *rather easy*?

(b) How did your mother generally treat you when you were about thirteen years old? Was she *very* strict, *fairly* strict, or *rather easy*?

56. When your parents made decisions affecting you, how well *did* you think they understood your needs? Did they understand them *very well*, *fairly well*, or *not at all*?

57. (a) As you were growing up, let us say at about thirteen, how much influence do you remember having in family decisions affecting yourself? Did you have *much* influence, *some* influence, or *none at all*?

(b) Were you satisfied or dissatisfied with this amount of influence?

58. (a) At around the same time, if a decision were made which you didn't like did you feel *free* to complain, did you feel *a little uneasy* about complaining, or was it better *not to complain*?

(b) At that time—when you were about thirteen—do you remember actually complaining? Do you remember doing this *often*, *once in a while*, or *never*?

(c) (UNLESS RESPONDENT SAYS HE NEVER COMPLAINED, ASK) When you did complain, did it make any difference in your parents' decisions? Did it make *a lot* of difference, *some* difference, or *none at all*?

59. In general, how much voice do you think youngsters of thirteen *ought* to have in family decisions—a good deal, some, or none at all?

60. There is a saying that the man ought to be master in his own house. How do you feel about this?

61. (a) Do you remember whether your father was *very much* interested in politics, *somewhat* interested, or *didn't pay much attention* to it?

(b) Did your father have any particular preference for one of the parties when you were young?

IF 'YES' (c) Which party was that?

(d) How about your mother; did she have any particular preference for one of the parties?

IF 'YES' (e) Which party was that?

62. Could you tell me what sort of place your parents were living in when you were born? Was it a farm, a village, a town or a city?

63. Could you tell me how old you are?

64. If you do not think it too personal a question, would you tell me how much money you usually earn per week, after deductions?

65. Finally, I wonder if you would be good enough to read over the statements on this sheet, and tick either 'agree' or 'disagree', depending on how you feel about each statement.[1]

(a) The artist and the professor are probably more important to society than the businessman and the manufacturer.

(b) The findings of science may some day show that many of our most deeply-held beliefs are wrong.

[1] These items represent a revised F-scale and a set of questions designed to get at the dominance-submission dimension of personality.

(c) I must admit I try to see what others think before I take a stand.

(d) Human nature being what it is, there must always be war and conflict.

(e) People ought to pay more attention to new ideas, even if they seem to go against the English way of life.

(f) I have to stop and think before I act, even in small matters.

(g) What young people need most of all is strict discipline by their parents.

(h) It is highly unlikely that astrology will ever be able to explain anything.

(i) I would rather not have very much responsibility for other people.

(j) There are times when I act like a coward.

(k) Sex criminals deserve more than prison; they should be whipped in public or worse.

(l) I like to give orders and get things moving.

(m) Bosses should say just what is to be done and exactly how to do it if they expect us to do a good job.

(n) I do many things which I regret afterwards.

Interview Schedule
SECOND WAVE

1. We're interested in how people are getting along these days—work and housing and so on. Tell me something about your job—how you came to be in it and so on.

2. So if you were starting your working life again, would you go in for the same work or something a bit different?

3. I'd like you to imagine you've been asked to give advice to a fairly bright boy of fifteen about his future. What would you suggest he should do as far as education is concerned? And what sort of jobs might you suggest to him, assuming he hasn't much idea what he wants to do?

4. (a) Thinking now about trade unions, what do you think of them?

    (b) So what sort of effect do they have on the trade union members?

    (c) and the general public?

5. (a) What do you think of the way that workers are treated by their employers, generally?

    (b) Some people think that working people are treated fairly by their employers, others say that employers sometimes try to take advantage of the workers. How do you feel about this?

6. (a) How do you happen to be living here? Tell me about the district from your point of view.

(b) People have different ideas about living in a mixed district. How would/do you feel about living in an area that had a fairly high proportion of immigrants, you know—including Irish and coloured people?

(c) How about the extent to which these immigrants mix socially with British people—what do you feel about this?

7. I'd like you now to tell me something about the people you get on best with, say two or three of your closest friends—what sorts of things do you have in common?

(a) Where do you usually meet?

(b) What do you find yourselves talking about usually?

(c) Do you ever discuss politics at all?

(d) So which political party do they support?

8. Thinking of yourself, do you take any interest in politics or things to do with the government?

9. (a) Do you read any of the morning or evening papers? Which?

FOR EACH PAPER MENTIONED
(i) How often do you read ....?

(ii) Is there anything you particularly like about the ....?

(iii) Do you think that the .... favours any political party particularly? (IF YES) Which?

(b) What kinds of news interest you most?

10. So which are the three politicians or government leaders that you admire most? It doesn't matter if they're living or not.

11. (a) Thinking first about the Labour members of Parliament, what made them go into politics, do you think?

(b) And the Conservative MP's?

(c) So which would you say had the best reasons? Why is that?

12. Still thinking about the government, and about the decisions they have to make, how much say, does the Queen have, when political decisions are made, would you think? How do you feel about that? Would this apply equally to the House of Lords, House of Commons and Prime Minister or not?

13. Some people say that for a man to be made a Minister of, say, Aviation in the government, he should have had a career in the aircraft industry. Other people say he is better equipped for the job if he has had more general experience in different types of business. What do you think about this, assuming of course that the two men are equally intelligent?

14. How do you feel about public school education and the type of men who have been to a public school?

15. (a) So how do you think politicians who have been to a public school compare with those who have been to, say, a good grammar school?

(b) Which do you feel *should* hold the higher positions of leadership in politics?

(c) And which, on the whole, do you think actually *do* hold these higher positions? Why do you think this is so?

16. Thinking now of the different backgrounds the politicians come from, how do you feel a man from an aristocratic, very upper-class background compares with a man from a more usual working-class background when it comes to taking positions of leadership in the government?

17. Some people have said they think that what is good for big business is good for the country as a whole. What do you feel about this?

18. Do you feel that men in big business are closer to either the Labour or the Conservative Parties?

    IF YES: How do you feel about this?

    Would you think that this has any effect on the ....
    Party?

19. (a) As you know, people talk about different social classes. How would you describe the different social classes there are in this country today?

    (b) So where would you say you fit in?

20. What do you think of this system of putting people in these classes?

21. (a) How do you feel about people moving from one class to another?

    (b) So what sort of things make this move possible? How do you feel about it?

Note: Page numbers of Tables in italics